Buyer's Handbook for Cooperatives and Condominiums

Buyer's Handbook for Cooperatives and Condominiums

Steven James Lee, Esq.

VNR VAN NOSTRAND REINHOLD COMPANY
NEW YORK   CINCINNATI   ATLANTA   DALLAS   SAN FRANCISCO
LONDON   TORONTO   MELBOURNE

Van Nostrand Reinhold Company Regional Offices:
New York Cincinnati Atlanta Dallas San Francisco

Van Nostrand Reinhold Company International Offices:
London Toronto Melbourne

Library of Congress Catalog Card Number: 78-1508
ISBN: 0-442-23284-5
    0-442-2385-3 pbk.

Manufactured in the United States of America

Published by Van Nostrand Reinhold Company
135 West 50th Street, New York, N.Y. 10020

Published simultaneously in Canada by Van Nostrand Reinhold Ltd.

15 14 13 12 11 10 9 8 7 6 5 4 3 2 1

Library of Congress Cataloging in Publication Data

Lee, Steven James.
   Buyer's handbook for cooperatives and condominiums.

   Includes index.
   1. Condominium (Housing) 2. Apartment houses,
Cooperative. 3. House buying. I. Title.
HD7287.7.A3L43   643   78-1508
ISBN 0-442-23284-5
ISBN 0-442-23285-3 pbk.

PREFACE

Making a real-estate investment will probably be the most important financial decision you will ever undertake. Until now, however, there has been no systematic instruction designed to allow the layman to uncover basic pitfalls of cooperative and condominium ownership. Therefore, this handbook has been designed to be a layman's guide to buying a cooperative or condominium. To get maximum benefit, it is suggested that you read the entire text before attempting the calculations contained in the worksheets. If you use this handbook properly, there is an excellent chance that the home you purchase will provide both physical comfort and financial security for you and your family.

STEVEN J. LEE, Esq.

The author wishes to express his personal appreciation for the time and efforts of Edward Rogers, Eugene Falken, Alberta Gordon, and Patricia Mansfield. Without these people, the technical problems of producing this book might have caused serious ulcers.

My grateful thanks also go to:

Jim Ruth for his ingenious drawings,

Ted Birnbaum for his smashing tennis serve, and

My wife, Karen, for her patience.

CONTENTS

8

1

SINGLE-FAMILY HOUSE OR COMMON PROPERTY?

The price of a single-family house in the United States has exploded in the past 10 years. The MIT-Harvard Joint Center for Urban Studies reports that between 1970 and 1976, the median price of existing housing shot up 65% and new-house prices rose 89%, while median income rose only 47%. Aside from the initial cost of such shelter, carrying costs such as local real-estate taxes and school taxes have also risen sharply. The same study concludes that between 1970 and 1976, the cost of owning a single-family home rose 73.4% for older houses and 102.3% for new ones. For most people, this has made it difficult to accumulate a down payment or to meet the monthly carrying costs. In such cases, people often have to settle for a house that really does not fulfill their needs or desires.

On the whole, cooperatives and condominiums can deliver more luxury and value than a single-family house priced at the same level. For instance, they put facilities such as pools, tennis courts, and clubhouses within the life-style of medium-income families. The sharing of costs to build and maintain recreation facilities among numerous common owners dramatically cuts the cost for the individual owner. Acquiring and maintaining such items in addition to meeting the normal upkeep expenses of a single-family house, are beyond the average homeowner's income.

Single-family houses, when financed through a bank, normally require a down payment of from 15% to 30% of the purchase price. Individual builders sometimes provide their own financing to reduce down payments and certain government programs give some relief, but the average down payment for a single-family home is about 20% of the purchase price. The standard interest charges on a mortgage vary throughout the country but generally range from 8% to 9.5%.

Ten years ago, it was often possible to convince a seller to extend private mortgage financing to the purchaser of his or her home. This financing was

called a *purchase-money mortgage*, and no financial institution was involved in the transaction. Today, it is rare that a seller is willing or able to extend a purchase-money mortgage to the buyer on favorable terms. The seller generally needs all of the proceeds of the sale to purchase another shelter. In contrast, developers of a cooperative or condominium often arrange for very favorable long-term financing and minimum down payments for the purchaser.

In a cooperative or condominium, you are offered essentially the same tax and equity advantages of a single-family house. What you don't have is the responsibility for shoveling snow, lawn mowing, roof repair, painting, and the thousand other odd jobs required by a single-family house. If you are not handy, this is important to keep in mind.

WHAT IS A COOPERATIVE?

Cooperatives are predominately high-rise buildings that get maximum use from expensive real estate, whereas the other major form of common ownership, the *condominium*, is usually most successful where land costs are relatively low.

From 1945 through 1961, cooperative housing corporations were the most popular type of community housing in the United States. In major cities such as New York, Chicago, San Francisco, and Miami, a large amount of the available housing funds were invested in cooperative housing. Shortages of desirable apartments in central, high-rise locations spurred the trend toward conversion of existing rental buildings to cooperative ownership. Currently, more condominiums than cooperatives are under construction. However, most experts believe that in dense urban areas, the cooperative will maintain its dominance.

The cooperative form of ownership provides the purchaser with shares of stock in a *Building Corporation*, which owns the multiple-unit property. In addition, the purchaser receives a *Proprietary Lease*, which contains the rights and obligations of the owner-tenant to a particular unit in the building. The price of each apartment as well as monthly common charges assigned to it depend on the number of shares of stock allocated to the individual unit. Factors such as location within the property, number of bathrooms, layout of rooms, and comparable rental in the marketplace are weighed initially when shares are allocated for the entire cooperative.

The Proprietary Lease given to the purchaser should be legally inseparable from the cooperative stock. This will ensure that the party who owns the shares is also the tenant living in the apartment. Along with the Proprietary Lease, there is a set of *Bylaws*, which specify the government rules of the corporation, and *House Rules*, which supervise the activities of occupants. All of the tenant stockholders should be subject to substantially the same form of the Proprietary Lease so that there is no friction among residents. Oftentimes, the lease specifies certain related individuals who may also occupy the apartment. Generally, subletting, boarders, or permanent guests are prohibited without the express written permission of the *Board of Directors*.

A commercial-type mortgage is widely available to the purchasers of cooperatives. Although the stock certificates and a Proprietary Lease are not considered real estate in a strict legal sense, most lending institutions will accept them as security for a cooperative mortgage loan. As a rule, a larger-percentage cash down payment (approximately 25%) is required for the purchase of a cooperative than for a condominium (approximately 20%) or a single-family home (approximately 20%). This is probably because lenders feel less secure with the stock and lease collateral they hold on a cooperative mortgage than with the bond and mortgage required in other real-estate purchases. Sponsor-sellers often finance their own cooperative projects with low down payments and very reasonable interest charges so that potential purchasers do not encounter these financing problems.

A cooperative is run by a Board of Directors, which functions in the same basic capacity as does the Board of Managers in a condominium. The cooperative organization usually requires the board to obtain insurance against hazards and liability on cooperative property and also to render annual financial reports that include tax-deduction information. In general, a cooperative offers the owner the same tax advantages as a condominium or single-family home. These are: the deduction of mortgage interest, real-estate taxes, and a *pro rata* portion of interest on the blanket mortgage from federal and most state tax returns.

WHAT IS A CONDOMINIUM?

In the 1960s, when it became necessary to explore different concepts in housing construction to insure meeting residential housing demands for all Americans, attention was focused on common ownership. Builders' development plans in many regions of the country began to use common recreation areas and facilities. All 50 states passed laws permitting the special arrangements needed for condominium dwelling. The trend was accelerated when construction costs began to skyrocket and the amount of desirable property on which residential housing could be placed began to shrink. Thus, the condominium form evolved into a very significant portion of our residential housing stock in just 15 years. The U.S. Department of Housing and Urban Development expects half the population to live in some form of common-ownership housing within the next 20 years. Presently, it is estimated that about 4 million Americans live in 1.25 million condominium units.

The term *condominium* refers to a form of real-estate ownership in which an owner has a recordable deed to his or her own sole homestead in a multiple-unit property, together with an undivided portion of ownership in areas and facilities that are shared with his or her co-owners. The facilities, jointly held and undivided, are a specific portion of the complete bundle of property rights. This form of packaging, a combination of shared and undivided property rights, has come to be known as condominium ownership.

Condominiums are not limited to a specific type of physical shelter. Condominium ownership may be used in high-rise apartments, attached townhouses, groups of townhouses, detached one-family homes, garden-type apartments, and other real-estate forms. The basic element that defines and creates the condominium is the *Master Deed*, which is a declaration of the separate ownership of individual units and an affirmation of the shared obligation for commonly used areas.

Banks, savings-and-loan institutions, and insurance companies are all permitted to lend to condominiums. The ordinary concepts of appraisal of real estate for mortgage purposes, title insurance policies, and recorded deeds have been retained for condominiums; this permits long-term mortgage financing similar to that which is available for single-family homes. Also, under the National Housing Act, federal government programs make alternate financing available to certain qualified individuals. Individual states and localities have established their own controls, however, so it is wise to check with a local lender to find out specific lending policies in the geographic area in which you wish to buy.

Condominiums are run by a *Board of Managers*, which is usually elected by the residents. The Board of Managers supervises services and repairs, directs the budget of expenses, and passes on all rules and regulations. They also supervise the insurance of all aspects of the property, whether separate or jointly owned.

Each deed-owner of an individual unit is required to carry adequate protection for the normal risks of fire, liability, and other hazards. There is an

CONDOMINIUMS ARE RUN
BY A BOARD OF MANAGERS
USUALLY ELECTED BY
THE RESIDENTS.

additional package-insurance policy on the common elements of the condominium. Maintenance expenses are proportionately divided among the individual units after adoption of the budget by the Board of Managers.

The Board of Managers also approves unit transfers when units are sold. Thus, the rest of the condominium owners are assured that new buyers are aware of the rules applicable to the particular condominium project and agree to abide by them. It also provides a control on the creditworthiness of potential buyers to ensure that they can meet their common obligations.

The owners of units in a condominium may deduct mortgage interest and real-estate property taxes paid on their units from their personal federal tax return. *Pro rata* payment of interest on an overall leasehold mortgage and the real property taxes contained in monthly maintenance are also usually deductible. The Board of Managers is required to render to all unit owners annual financial reports that include tax-deduction information. These tax advantages are similar to those enjoyed by owners of a single-family home or a cooperative, and you will learn to calculate them in Worksheet 3.

VACATION COOPERATIVES OR CONDOMINIUMS

Although most cooperatives and condominiums are purchased as principal places of residence, there is nevertheless a growing demand for recreation shelter. Desirable land near beaches and ski resorts is being developed for vacationers who don't want to have to search for space each crowded tourist season. When properly purchased, a vacation cooperative or condominium can be far less expensive than rented shelter. It will also offer a tax advantage as well as an equity buildup.

In some resort areas, motel and hotel owners have converted rooms to condominium ownership. The owner of a unit may use it for specified periods of time during the year; the rest of the time, management rents the unit to tourists. All of the condominium rooms become a part of a common rental pool that is run for the benefit of its participants. Such arrangements are regulated through the Securities and Exchange Commission, and therefore a detailed prospectus must be supplied in advance of purchase.

In buying vacation shelter, consider the following:

1. Don't count on the income from rentals to cover your costs. If there is a slow season, you must be prepared to pay all costs for your share of the common expenses.
2. Beware of old buildings that are converted without extensive rehabilitation. They may be unattractive to vacationers.
3. Be sure that the managing agent is experienced in renting to transients. Without proper supervision, your property may be damaged or stolen.

Buying any cooperative or condominium is a sizable investment, which requires thorough analysis prior to purchase. The investigation method set forth in this book may be easily adapted to vacation shelter. If you are planning to purchase with other partners, you may want to divide the research. Just be certain that your partners are responsible and have the means to meet their share of the obligations.

SHOULD I RENT OR BUY?

There are no hard and fast rules to enable people to decide between owning and renting shelter. However, it is helpful to examine the question from three aspects. First, there are your personal preferences and needs and those of your family. Second, you should consider the prudence of investing your money for a long period of time. Third, the cost of ownership should be calculated and compared to the cost of renting.

If you look at the preferences and needs of your family it will be apparent that personal factors will change over time. You will want to consider the ages of members of your family, stability of employment of all members, likelihood of additional persons coming into your family unit, possibility of moving from one location to another, and impact of mortgage-payment responsibility on competing interests (e.g., vacations, education, cars, entertainment).

Beyond these factors are some highly subjective decisions: do you like to maintain a home? do you wish to become part of a community? There are numerous designs for cooperatives and condominiums, and you should investigate the types available before you choose.

Remember that it is usually impossible to add space onto an existing cooperative or condominium unit. Thus, it is wise to anticipate future needs and

perhaps purchase more shelter than you currently need. Although this will increase the amount you spend, it could prove an intelligent decision in the long run when you consider moving and settlement costs (see Chapter 7) and uprooting members of your family.

The second aspect to consider in deciding whether to rent or buy is the prudence of being responsible for a long-term mortgage commitment. For most people, the purchase of their home constitutes the single largest investment in a lifetime. Home ownership requires a large down payment, and a substantial amount of monthly cash flow will be diverted from other investments such as stocks, bonds, and savings accounts. In addition, real estate is not easy to dispose of on short notice. Owners may have to wait for a certain season of the year or for an improvement in the availability of financing to sell their homes at the maximum value.

One advantage that is often overlooked in buying shelter is the forced savings that a mortgage produces. You should consider whether you save regularly for the future and whether those savings are invested attractively. A mortgage forces the buildup of equity over a long period of time. In the early years, most of the monthly payments are applied toward paying interest. As time goes on, however, more and more of the money is used to repay the principal amount borrowed. Each dollar that is repaid is forced savings put into ownership. Table 1.1 indicates how you accumulate savings when you pay down your mortgage.

TABLE 1.1 PERCENTAGE OF MORTGAGE LOAN REMAINING

Interest Rate	Loan Remaining After					
	5 years	10 years	15 years	20 years	25 years	30 years
Life of mortgage, 30 years						
7%	94%	86%	74%	57%	33%	0%
7½	95	87	75	59	34	0
8	95	88	77	60	36	0
9	96	89	79	63	39	0
10	97	91	82	66	41	0
Life of mortgage, 25 years						
7%	91%	79%	61%	36%	0%	
7½	92	80	62	37	0	
8	92	81	64	38	0	
9	93	83	66	40	0	
10	94	85	69	43	0	
Life of mortgage, 20 years						
7%	86%	67%	39%	0%		
7½	87	68	40	0		
8	87	69	41	0		
9	89	71	43	0		
10	90	73	45	0		

Worksheet 1

You can get a basic idea of the cost of renting versus the cost of owning shelter by making the computations on Worksheet 1. Some common rules of thumb suggest that a person should spend about one-quarter of his or her income for housing and should purchase a unit with a market price approximately 2.5 times total annual income. If you can reasonably expect your earning power to increase in the near future, strict application of such rules may not be suitable. It is often best to consider rising income and to extend these rules of thumb into larger and more attractive shelter that you believe you can afford and will want in the future.

Worksheet 1 should not be used until you have read this handbook and understand the concepts in it. You may wish to work through the exercise for a series of hypothetical purchase prices (i.e., 2, 2.5, and 3 times your annual income). Your bank will be able to tell you about terms of financing, such as required down payment, duration of mortgage, monthly mortgage payments of principal and interest, approximate legal costs, and settlement costs. Appendix II will allow you to calculate the monthly installment payment of a mortgage for a term of from 15 to 30 years at various interest rates. Remember that this payment will include principal and interest costs. Settlement costs needed to make the comparison on Worksheet 1 can be calculated from the material in Chapter 7.

Tax Benefits

In examining the costs of owning versus renting shelter, don't forget to consider the benefit of ownership tax deductions when you file an itemized

WORKSHEET 1
RENT OR BUY?

1. Basic information on cooperative or condominium

Purchase price $_____

Amount of mortgage   _____

Interest rate on mortgage   _____%

Square feet of living space   _____sq ft

2. Cash invested in shelter

Renting		Owning	
Deposit on lease	$_____	Down payment	$_____
Moving expense	_____	Moving expense	_____
Necessary repairs	_____	Necessary repairs	_____
	_____	Settlement costs	_____
Initial cash invested	$		$

3. Monthly cash outlay

Renting		Owning	
Rent	$_____	Common charges	$_____
Apartment dweller insurance	_____	Homeowners insurance	_____
		Mortgage interest payment	_____ [a]
		Mortgage principal payment	_____ [a]
		Recreation charges	_____
		Taxes	_____
Total monthly cash outlay	$		$

4. Overall comparison

	Rent	Own
Initial cash invested	$_____	$_____
Total monthly cash outlay	$_____	$_____

9

Monthly cash outlay as percent of monthly income	____%	____%
Total square feet of living space	____sq ft	____sq ft
Cost per square foot per month	$_____	$_____
Yearly mortgage interest deduction	None	$_____
Taxes and other yearly deductions	None	$_____
Mortgage forced savings after:[b]		
5 Years	None	$_____
10 Years	None	$_____
15 Years	None	$_____
20 Years	None	$_____
25 Years	None	$_____
30 Years	None	$_____

5. Future market value of unit

Purchase price $_____

Appreciation rate per year   _____%

Estimated future market value

    5 Years $_____

    10 Years $_____

    15 Years $_____

    20 Years $_____

---

[a]Appendix II will allow computation of the combined monthly mortgage cost. Assume that 10% of your payment is for mortgage principal and 90% is for mortgage interest.
[b]Table 1.1 indicates the balance still outstanding on your mortgage after each 5-year interval.

return. Amounts spent on interest, school taxes, and real-estate taxes are deductible items on federal and many state and local tax returns. Such tax savings lower the cost of owning and provide an indirect government subsidy that renters do not enjoy. We will cover tax advantages of cooperative and condominium ownership in some detail when we compute net monthly cost. At this point, you should simply be aware that tax advantages exist and are an important element in your decision to rent or buy.

HOW TO DEAL WITH THAT DOWN PAYMENT

You have decided that cooperative or condominium ownership is for you. Your desires—and your family's—and the monthly cash flow seem to permit such an investment. However, the initial down-payment requirements appear to be beyond your financial abilities. Here are some tips to either help you accumulate the necessary cash or dispense with a down payment altogether.

The Federal Housing Administration insures loans made by conventional lenders. These insured loans often permit the buyer to obtain better terms and a lower down payment than would otherwise be available. To benefit the buyer initially, a condominium must be constructed or rehabilitated with an FHA blanket commitment. As units are sold, then individual mortgages are spun off to the buyers. In the case of condominiums with less than 12 units, which are not FHA-constructed or -rehabilitated, the FHA may appraise the completed project and guarantee a specific buyer's mortgage. As a practical matter, FHA assistance is not available to cooperative purchasers.

When a condominium mortgage is spun off from the blanket FHA commitment, the buyer will have a lower down payment than would be obtainable through conventional borrowing. A down payment of only 3% is required of the first $25,000 of FHA-appraised value and a 5% down payment thereafter, up to a $60,000 FHA appraisal value. The FHA-insured mortgage would only require a $3000 down payment, while an uninsured mortgage might require a $15,000 down payment.

Whereas most conventional condominium mortgages are written for a period of 20 or 25 years, the FHA generally allows a 30-year repayment term on a mortgage. The longer term permits lower monthly mortgage payments for families with cash-flow problems. In addition, interest rates on FHA-guaranteed mortgages are usually less, and prepayment provisions are less restrictive.

If you or your spouse are a veteran, then the Veterans Administration can assist you in buying a condominium. Unfortunately, VA restrictions on purchasing cooperatives effectively remove this avenue as a source of help. For a condominium, the VA will guarantee mortgage loans for 60% of the purchase price or $17,500, whichever is less. Lenders find such a mortgage a better credit risk because they are assured of recovering at least $17,500 if the buyer defaults. In rural areas where there is a scarcity of conventional lenders, the VA will lend money directly, up to a maximum of $17,500.

Saving is the primary method most people use to amass the down payment on a home. Under normal circumstances, you should ideally save 10% or more of your total monthly income. If your goal has been set, and you intend to purchase a cooperative or condominium, you may have to discipline yourself to save as much as 50% of your monthly income. Of course, this will mean doing without many of the things that compete for your money, until you have saved the down payment.

What if you have located the home of your dreams, but you don't have enough saved to cover the down payment and closing costs? The first thing you might do is liquidate any long-term assets such as savings bonds or stocks. If this is not sufficient, consider selling some of your personal property such as an unnecessary car, stereo equipment, an expensive camera, or a coin or stamp collection.

The second recourse is to borrow money against a coming tax refund, an anticipated bonus, or an inheritance. You should also determine if your life insurance policy has built up enough cash-value equity to cover the down payment shortfall. Finally, you might ask your parents or other relatives

for a low-cost or interest-free loan. Chances are that they did the same thing when they first purchased a home.

If you borrow part of the down payment, work out a method to pay it back on terms you can live with. Be realistic, and allow for unforeseen expenses such as medicine and repairs. Nevertheless, try to pay back these funds as quickly as possible. This will leave you with the peace of mind that your home is properly financed with your own equity.

FUTURE MARKET VALUE

It is not entirely unrealistic to calculate the future market value of a cooperative or condominium that will be sold some years after purchase. Such an estimate serves, not as a certainty of profit, but rather as a yardstick of expected return on an investment. To calculate the future market value, first choose a rate of appreciation per year. Earlier statistics indicated that from 1970 through 1976, the median price of existing housing rose at a compounded rate of approximately 9% per year, and the median price of new housing rose almost 11% per year. These rates would probably be too high for reliable results starting from today's market.

A more conservative approach would be to choose an appreciation rate of 2 to 5% per year. Your estimate of the rate should be based on local market conditions, stability of the neighborhood, previous increases in selling prices, and the condition and size of your unit in relation to the entire development. Most licensed brokers have a good idea of what you can expect in yearly appreciation, and you should poll several to get a consensus of opinion. For example, a $50,000 unit might appreciate as shown in Table 1.2.

TABLE 1.2 FUTURE MARKET VALUE OF A $50,000 UNIT.

Appreciation per year (%)	Future Market Value After			
	5 years	10 years	15 years	20 years
0	$50,000	$50,000	$50,000	$50,000
1	52,551	55,231	58,048	61,620
2	55,204	60,950	67,293	74,297
3	57,964	67,196	77,898	90,306
4	60,833	74,012	90,047	109,556
5	63,814	81,445	103,946	132,665

WHAT IS MY FIRST STEP?

The first step in buying a cooperative or condominium is to determine where you want to live. The proper neighborhood will add to your satisfaction as well as improve the value of your investment. Take some weekend drives through areas that appeal to everyone in the family. Then get down to business, and assemble the following information.

FOR MOST FAMILIES THE PURCHASE
OF THEIR HOME CONSTITUTES THE
SINGLE LARGEST INVESTMENT IN
A LIFETIME!

Local history: Usually obtainable from chamber of commerce or town
hall.

Local map: This should indicate local points of interest. You can use this
map to determine the proximity of individual developments to shopping
areas, schools, factories, and the fire department.

Zoning regulations: Find out how the residential neighborhoods are protected. The change over of residential land near your home to commercial use can harm the value of your investment.

Population and income levels: Available from the United States Bureau
of the Census. Many libraries also have this information.

Taxes: Speak to the local taxing authority, and get rates for school and
property taxes for the last 5 years.

Market prices of shelter: Many local real-estate boards or associations
of brokers can furnish the market prices of shelter. If they cannot help,
speak to the title insurance company.

Doing this kind of homework is dull and time-consuming. However, considering the magnitude of the investment you contemplate, it is time well spent. Armed with the preceding information, you will be able to deal more effectively with real-estate brokers, appraise neighborhoods more accurately, and generally feel more secure with the shelter you purchase.

2

USING THE NEWSPAPERS

The best source of information about housing in a particular area is the newspapers. Most local papers have a real-estate section, which lists offerings of property under the heading of "Cooperatives and Condominiums." It may be necessary to make inquiry to find out which local paper has the most extensive real-estate coverage. Often, the paper that publishes a large, multisection, Sunday edition will be your best guide.

Start to review the real-estate listings on a daily basis, and form a library of the Sunday real-estate sections. From this, you will learn the names of brokers who advertise on a regular basis as well as the kinds of property they handle. (Brokers often specialize in a certain area of the community or in a particular type of housing.)

Make notes on buildings that have a large number of apartments for sale, and keep track of how quickly they are sold. This could be a barometer of the desirability of the particular cooperative building or condominium development. Naturally, a larger building or project will have more turnover than a smaller one. However, beware of many units in one complex that are up for sale but don't find ready buyers. This indicates that something is wrong with the underlying value of the units.

Become familiar with the different types of financing packages advertised. In many cooperatives or condominiums, the promoter offers very attractive terms on the mortgage and a low down payment to boot. Don't hesitate to make telephone calls to inquire about the details of such plans. This research will give you an excellent picture of the comparative cost of borrowing in the area.

When you do find a cooperative or condominium unit that interests you, check back through the collected newspapers to determine the prices of comparable housing in the area. You might even discover the selling price of another unit in the same project. If you find that a unit has been sold in a

CHECK NEWSPAPERS, DOORMEN...
SPEAK WITH RESIDENTS.

project that interests you, call or visit the new owners. Ask about the price they paid and the availability of financing, and find out if they are happy with their new home.

The purpose of this sort of research is to ensure that you don't overpay. Once you have submitted a formal bid, you may be forced to proceed with the purchase or else pay expenses for your failure to close the transaction.

USING YOUR FEET

Never underestimate the value of plain old footwork. The best bargains rarely show up in the newspaper because they are snapped up by aggressive buyers.

If you are looking for a cooperative in an urban area, speak to the doormen or managers of the buildings that appeal to you. They often know about units that have not yet been given to a broker but that will be put up for sale in the near future. In such a case, you may save yourself a broker's fee by approaching the owner directly. A real-estate broker earns a commission fee based on a percentage of the sales price when a buyer purchases property that the broker has shown. In most cases, the seller pays the brokerage fee, which reduces the net proceeds he or she receives from the sale. If a unit owner, who is anxious to sell, discovers your interest in the particular project, he or she will be anxious to sell to you directly and thus save several thousand dollars in brokerage fees. You may even be able to reduce the purchase price by splitting the savings with the seller. So, even when nothing is currently coming up for sale, it doesn't hurt to leave your name and telephone number at buildings that you find desirable.

If you don't know anyone living in a development that interests you, try to locate friends who do. Ask them to supply telephone numbers so that you can call these people directly. Such calls can yield a wealth of information on the management of the project and give you early notice of a coming sale. If you are extremely interested in buying in a particular project, find out the names of members of the House Committee or Board of Directors, and then telephone them. If they know you are interested, the word should get around soon enough.

USING YOUR BROKER'S SERVICES

A broker is a trained real-estate salesperson, not a mind reader. Therefore, before you telephone a single broker, write down a detailed description of your housing needs and desires and those of your family. The more specific your description, the less time you will spend viewing unsuitable homes and the less chance you will have of buying the wrong cooperative or condominium. Some of the things to consider before you write your description are:

> How many bedrooms do you need?
> Do you plan to have (more) children?
> Is a family room or den important?
> How many bathrooms are necessary?
> Is a shower, a bathtub, or both necessary for comfort?
> Do you want an eat-in kitchen?
> Do you want a fireplace?
> What recreation facilities do you want?
> Do you want a terrace or a ground-floor patio?
> What floor would you wish to live above or below in a large building?
> Do you prefer old and quaint, or modern buildings?
> How important to you is the availability of parking? At what cost?
> What communities interest you and your family?
> How much money do you want to spend?
> When will you be able to move into a new home?

Gather the preceding information on Worksheet 2, and from it type up a brief description to give to brokers. Good brokers act as a clearing center for marketable cooperatives and condominiums. When they have a specific description of what you wish to buy, they will perform a screening process, which can save you many a wild-goose chase.

When you are out looking with a broker, don't trust what you see to memory. Take along a spiral notebook, and in it keep a record of:

1. Asking price

WORKSHEET 2
DESCRIPTION FOR BROKERS

Maximum purchase price $ _____

Maximum monthly carrying costs $ _____

Number of bathrooms   _____

Number of bedrooms   _____

Approximate floor desired (for high-rise)   _____

Occupancy date desired   _____

Positive Attractions (Check and number in order of importance)

☐ Bright apartment for plants _____

☐ Corner apartment   _____

☐ Commuting convenience   _____

☐ Den   _____

☐ Doorman   _____

☐ Eat-in kitchen   _____

☐ Elevator building   _____

☐ Fireplace   _____

☐ Gardens and grounds   _____

☐ Handyman's special   _____

☐ Large complex   _____

☐ Modern appearance   _____

☐ Older building   _____

☐ Parking   _____

☐ Recreation facilities   _____

☐ Small building   _____

☐ Terrace   _____

☐ Younger families   _____

Information Requested From Broker

☐ Local street map

☐ History of local community

☐ Names of local banks

_____

_____

_____

_____

Other Comments:

2. Monthly maintenance
3. Percent tax deduction of maintenance
4. Other taxes (when applicable)
5. Owner's name
6. Location
7. Number of bedrooms
8. Number of bathrooms
9. Special features.

This basic information will aid you in narrowing down your choice. Then, you should perform the detailed inspection that will be discussed in Chapter 3.

A word of advice: remember, people usually work hardest for the party who pays them. Real-estate brokers work for a commission, which is usually paid by the seller. (Normally, commissions are in the range of 5% to 7% of the sales price.) So be cautious in accepting brokers' oral advice yet do try to get the basic information from them.

PRICE AND MAINTENANCE

The marketplace for available cooperatives and condominiums usually has a trade-off between monthly maintenance and purchase price. Maintenance is the proportionate share of operating expenses assigned to each unit. Mortgage and other payments are other costs over and above monthly maintenance charges. As a rule, the higher the monthly maintenance, among comparable units, the lower the market purchase price. In other words, you can get more of better-quality shelter for less investment if you are prepared to pay a larger amount of money each month for maintenance.

Apartment A, a two-bedroom, two-bathroom townhouse unit in a luxury building, has maintenance of $450 per month and is currently priced at $36,000. The many improvements put in by the previous owner should logically increase its value. Instead, it could be selling for less than comparable units that have a significantly lower maintenance. Apartment B, a two-bedroom, two-bathroom townhouse in a luxury building nearby, with a maintenance of $285 per month, might be priced at $56,000. And Apartment B might have none of the valuable improvements in Apartment A.

Is Apartment B overpriced? Perhaps, but there are more buyers willing to put down a larger down payment and assume a larger mortgage if their monthly cash flow appears to be lower. But there is a catch here that is often overlooked: the units must be compared on an *after-tax* basis.

For example, suppose that Apartment A's maintenance of $450 per month is 62% tax-deductible and Apartment B's maintenance is 25% tax-deductible. (Information on tax deductions is available from the broker, the offering prospectus, or the building manager.) Furthermore, assume that in each case the purchaser must make a down payment of 25% of the purchase price and can obtain a 25-year mortgage at $8\frac{1}{4}\%$. Now we may compare the two apartment units to determine the net cost of each after tax.

MAINTENANCE HIGHER   PRICE LOWER

As might be expected, the monthly mortgage payment will be considerably higher on the larger mortgage balance (i.e., Apartment B). Using Appendix II, we can calculate that the total monthly mortgage payment for Apartment A is $213.03 and for Apartment B is $331.38. If we assume that 90% of this total monthly mortgage payment is interest that is deductible, then for Apartment A $191.72 ($213.03 × 90%) is a tax deduction and for Apartment B $298.24 ($331.38 × 90%) is a tax deduction. Next, we examine maintenance costs. Apartment A offers a monthly maintenance deduction of $279 ($450 × 62%), whereas Apartment B offers only $71.25 ($285 × 25%). If the buyer's federal taxable income is in the 35% tax bracket, then 35% of each of these monthly deductions will be returned to the buyer at tax time. So, for Apartment A the savings is $164.75 ([$191.72 + $279] × 35%) per month, and for Apartment B the savings is $129.32 ([$298.24 + $71.25] × 35%).

Our next step is to calculate the after-tax costs of Apartment A and Apartment B. From Table 2.1, we see that Apartment A requires a total monthly cash flow of $633.03, from which we subtract $164.75 of tax savings, thus, Apartment A has a net monthly cost of $498.28. Apartment B requires a total monthly cash flow of $616.38, from which we subtract $129.32 of tax

TABLE 2.1 ACTUAL MONTHLY COSTS.

	Apartment A		Apartment B	
Down payment	$ 9,000.00		$14,000.00	
Mortgage balance	27,000.00		42,000.00	
Monthly maintenance	450.00		285.00	
Monthly mortgage payment	213.03		331.38	
Total monthly cash flow	663.03	663.03	616.38	616.38
Monthly maintenance deduction	279.00		71.25	
Monthly mortgage interest deduction	191.72		298.24	
Total monthly deductions	470.72		369.49	
Multiply by tax bracket	×.35		×.35	
Total monthly tax savings	164.75	−164.75	129.32	−129.32
Net monthly cost[a]		$498.28		$487.06

[a]This example does not include any real-estate taxes paid directly by the owner of unit.

savings to arrive at a net monthly cost of $487.06. If we examine these results, they demonstrate that the tax savings involved actually make Apartment A only slightly more expensive than Apartment B! This is true even though Apartment A has a monthly maintenance of $450 compared to Apartment B's maintenance of $285 per month.

Monthly Cash Flow and Net Monthly Cost

Monthly cash flow is the amount of actual dollars you will have to pay out each month to cover your maintenance, taxes, and mortgage. When you purchase a cooperative, the monthly maintenance will generally include your local taxes. In a condominium, the unit owner ordinarily pays taxes directly, so you must include this monthly expense to correctly calculate total monthly cash flow. *Net monthly cost* is what you actually pay per month during the year, after all available tax savings are subtracted from monthly cash flow.

Monthly Cash Flow, Consisting of:		**Tax Savings, Included in:**	
1. Maintenance		1. Maintenance	**NET**
2. Mortgage	Minus	2. Mortgage interest	= **MONTHLY COST**
3. Local taxes		3. Local taxes	

Let us compare another set of apartments. Apartment C is a one-bedroom unit with maintenance of $210 per month, which is 50% deductible; it has a purchase price of $20,000. The building in which Apartment C is located will provide a 30-year, 7% interest mortgage with a down payment of only 10% of the purchase price. Apartment D is a comparable one-bedroom unit in a building where maintenance is $115 per month, which is 40% deductible, and

TABLE 2.2 ACTUAL MONTHLY COSTS.

	Apartment C		Apartment D	
Down payment	$2,000.00		$5,750.00	
Mortgage balance	18,000.00		17,250.00	
Monthly maintenance	210.00		115.00	
Monthly mortgage payment	119.88		139.04	
Total monthly cash flow	329.88	329.88	254.04	254.04
Monthly maintenance deduction	105.00		46.00	
Monthly mortgage interest deduction[a]	107.89		125.13	
Monthly real-estate tax paid directly	61.00		57.00	
Total monthly deductions	273.89		228.13	
Multiply by tax bracket[b]	×.35		×.35	
Total monthly tax savings	95.86	−95.86	79.84	−79.84
Net monthly cost		234.02		174.20

[a]Assumes that 90% of monthly payment goes to interest expense.
[b]Assumes that buyer is in 35% tax bracket.

the purchase price is $23,000; however, the building provides no financing. Conventional financing is available with a 25% down payment at 8½% for a term of 25 years. Table 2.2 compares the actual monthly cost.

Apartment D seems to be a better buy than Apartment C because it has a lower net monthly cash flow, even though it has a lower-percentage deduction of monthly maintenance. Here is where a buyer must consider the availability of attractive financing. If the buyer is having difficulty accumulating the $5750 down payment required to finance Apartment D, then the smaller down payment of Apartment C—$2000—might convince the buyer to choose this unit. The buyer must be certain to have a reserve for closing costs and be sure that monthly income will safely cover the higher net monthly cash flow.

CALCULATING NET MONTHLY COST

Use Worksheet 3 to calculate the net monthly cost of any cooperative or condominium unit you might consider buying. The results will give you an excellent idea of the comparative financial commitment of different units.

Note that in the calculation of tax savings on Worksheet 3, there is a line for the interest portion of your mortgage. Use Appendix II to calculate the total monthly mortgage cost including principal and interest. As shown in Table 1.1., in the early years of mortgage repayment, most money goes toward servicing interest costs. To simplify using the worksheet, assume that 90% of the monthly mortgage payment will go toward paying interest. The other 10% will be the monthly principal repayment. This assumption will work well enough to give you a fairly reliable estimate of the net monthly cost of a particular unit. If you wish to calculate it more exactly, then complete Worksheet 3 for each 5-year interval of your mortgage. Take the fig-

WORKSHEET 3
CALCULATING NET MONTHLY COST

Monthly Cash Flow

Add

1. Monthly maintenance $ _____
2. Mortgage payment   _____
3. Taxes paid directly per month   _____
4. Recreation charges   _____
   Total monthly cash flow $ _____

Tax Savings

Add

1. Maintenance × Percent deductible $ _____
2. Interest portion of mortgage[a]   _____
3. Taxes paid directly   _____
   Total monthly deductions $ _____

To Determine Tax Savings, Multiply

   Total monthly deductions × Tax bracket $ _____

Net Monthly Cost

Subtract

1. Total monthly cash flow $ _____
2. Tax savings   -$ _____
   Net monthly cost $ _____

[a]Assume that 90% of your mortgage payment is interest portion.

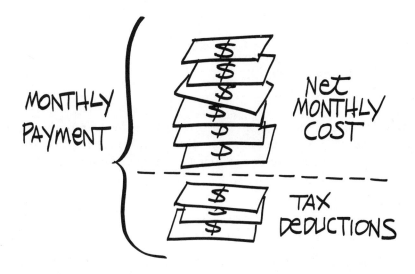

ures from Table 1.1 as the percentage of the monthly mortgage payment that is interest cost for each 5-year period.

Let's look at an example of how to use Worksheet 3. If a prospective buyer in a 31% federal tax bracket will buy a $40,000 unit that will give a monthly mortgage of $231.10 and a monthly maintenance of $370 (which is 53% tax-deductible), and if the buyer will pay $1092 per year in local taxes (which are not included in maintenance), then the calculations on Worksheet 3 would be as follows:

Monthly Cash Flow

Add

1. Monthly maintenance	$ 370.00
2. Mortgage payment	231.10
3. Taxes paid directly per month ($1092/12)	91.00
4. Recreation charges	0.00
Total monthly cash flow	$ 692.10

Tax Savings

Add

1. Maintenance × Percent deductible ($370 × 53%)	$ 196.10
2. Interest portion of mortgage ($231.10 × 90%)	207.99
3. Taxes paid directly	91.00
Total monthly deductions	$ 495.09

To Determine Tax Savings, Multiply

Total monthly deductions × Tax bracket ($495.09 × 31%)	$ 153.48

Net Monthly Cost

Subtract

1.	Total monthly cash flow	$ 692.10
2.	Tax savings per month	−153.48
	Net monthly cost	$ 538.62

Review Worksheet 3 until you are able to calculate the net monthly cash flow for any cooperative or condominium. However, remember that recreation costs charged to owners are not included in the preceding example.

3

INSPECTING THE APARTMENT

If you are purchasing in an area where there are building codes, be certain that the builder has received a Certificate of Occupancy. This will ensure you that an inspector has examined the structure and found it in conformity with the building codes. (During the Closing of Title, you will receive a copy of the Certificate of Occupancy for your records.) Nevertheless, building codes vary greatly in the kind of construction and materials they require. Your own inspection will be your primary indicator of the quality of construction.

When you go to inspect an apartment, take along the following tools:

1. A 10-foot retractable tape measure with a stop button that can lock it in an open position.
2. Clipboard or hard-backed pad to facilitate taking notes.
3. Mechanical pencil.
4. Red pencil.
5. Graph paper on which you can draw a floor plan to scale.
6. A ruler appropriate for making a scale drawing.
7. A copy of Worksheet 4.
8. Camera (optional).
9. Light meter (optional).

As you inspect the unit, fill in the appropriate information on Worksheet 4. Pay close attention to the overall quality of construction and to the layout of the unit. Remember, it is unlikely that you will ever find a unit with every feature you want. Instead, you should look for overall quality, with as many outstanding points as possible.

When a particular cooperative or condominium interests you enough to consider buying it, then you should obtain a copy of the floor plan. Ask the broker or the building manager for a floor plan of the particular unit. Verify the dimensions given by measuring the width and length of every

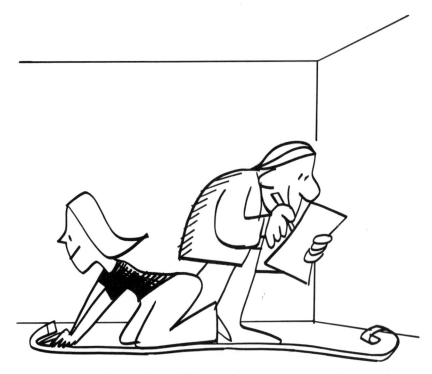

MAKE A DETAILED FLOOR PLAN
AND AN OVERALL INSPECTION.

room. Also, locate on the floor plan the windows in the rooms (if they are not already shown), and mark in red pencil the location of electrical outlets.

If no such floor plan is available, draw one on graph paper. An easy scale to work with is 0.5 inch equals 1 foot. Thus, if a room is 13 feet long and 12 feet wide, you should draw a box 6.5 inches long and 6 inches wide. Sketch the outlines of each room until you have a complete scale drawing of all floor space. If there is more than one floor (i.e., a duplex or townhouse), draw each layout on a separate page, noting the location of stairways. (See Fig. 3.1.)

The purpose of an accurate floor plan is twofold. First, it allows you to calculate the square footage of living space required on Worksheet 1. This in turn gives you the correct per-square-foot cost of shelter when you rent and when you buy. Second, you can use the scale drawing to plan how to fit your furniture into your new home. This should facilitate moving and perhaps save time and moving costs.

In the following sections, we will discuss how to examine such features as walls, windows, and electrical, heating, and plumbing systems. Bear in mind that replacing any one of these items can be as expensive as buying a new car. Proper examination before buying a cooperative or condominium should assure you of getting the best value for the money you spend.

WORKSHEET 4
INSPECTION

Address _____ Date _____

_____

Unit Description _____

Attic (where applicable)

   Evidence of roof leaks _____

   Insulation _____

   Ventilation opening _____

   Flooring _____

   Exhaust fan _____

Interior

   Walls

      Type _____

      Condition _____

      Insulation _____

   Ceilings

      Condition _____

      Height _____

   Type of heating _____

   Plumbing _____

   Fireplace _____

   Placement of electrical outlets _____

   Light level in rooms _____

   Floors creaking _____

   Closet space _____

   Storage space _____

   Air conditioning _____

   Dehumidifier _____

   Handrail on staircase _____

Bathrooms

   Condition of fixtures _____

   Separate shower stall _____

   Tile _____

Scale for Condition: E = excellent, G = good, F = fair, P = poor.

Medicine cabinets _____

Water pressure _____

Dripping faucets _____

Electrical outlets _____

Condition of bathtubs _____

Type of piping _____

Electricity

Number of amperes _____

Circuits in use _____

Breakers or fuses _____

Voltage _____

Kitchen

Cabinets _____

Formica countertops _____

Range _____

   Type _____

   Model year _____

Oven _____

   Type _____

   Model year _____

Dishwasher _____

   Type _____

   Model year _____

Refrigerator _____

   Type _____

   Model year _____

Disposal _____

Exhaust fan _____

Flooring _____

Lighting _____

Eat-in kitchen _____

Windows

Difficulty of operation _____

Broken panes _____

Worn sash cords _____

Scale for Condition: E = excellent, G = good, F = fair, P = poor.

Windowsills _____

Aluminum windows badly pitted _____

Exposure of apartment (N,S,E,W) _____

Exterior

Type of foundation _____

Roofing _____

Storm windows _____

Screens _____

Paint condition _____

Miscellaneous

Parking _____

Recreation facilities _____

Lawns _____

Transportation _____

Shopping _____

Floor of building _____

Location of elevators _____

Views from windows _____

Built-in features _____

Noise from other apartments _____

Overall Comment: _____

_____

_____

_____

_____

_____

_____

_____

_____

_____

_____

_____

_____

Scale for Condition: E = excellent, G = good, F = fair, P = poor.

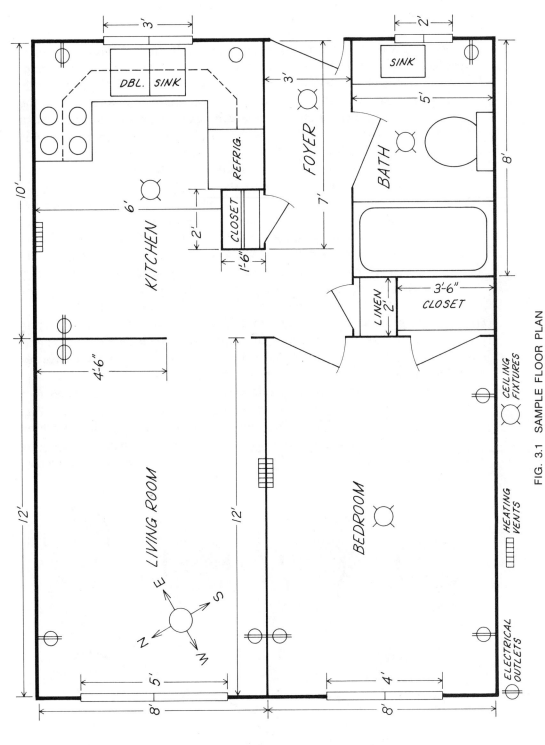

FIG. 3.1 SAMPLE FLOOR PLAN

THE ELECTRICAL SYSTEM

The electrical wiring that travels through the walls and ceilings of a house is divided into circuits. Each circuit is protected by its own *fuse* or *circuit breaker*. There is generally a a *panel box*, the purpose of which is to centrally contain these fuses or circuit breakers. In case too many appliances are on the same circuit or if bare electric wires are touching due to problems such as worn insulation, a fuse or circuit breaker will "blow." This means that the circuit will be interrupted, and electric current will not pass through the wires until either the problem is corrected or the circuit is reset. Without such safety devices, the hazard of an electrical fire exists.

When you inspect a cooperative or a condominium, always check the panel box. Older buildings usually have fuse boxes (see Fig. 3.3). A fuse, which looks like a small, round glass bulb, screws into the panel box (see Fig. 3.2). On its top is a small window, which has a flat metal strip inside. When there is trouble in the electrical system, the fuse discolors and the metal strip melts. One disadvantage of a fuse box is that spare fuses must be kept handy in case one has to be replaced. Since fuses come in several different sizes and shapes, this is something of an inconvenience. Also, fuse systems may not be able to handle heavy-duty appliances such as electric ranges, clothes dryers, air conditioners, and ovens. In such a case, an expensive rewiring job might be required to improve the electrical system.

Circuit breakers are a more modern type of protection than fuses (see Fig. 3.4). When electrical trouble causes them to "blow," circuit breakers simply switch to the "off" position. Once the cause of the problem has been determined and corrected, a circuit breaker has only to be reset—by flipping the switch back to the "on" position. From the standpoint of convenience,

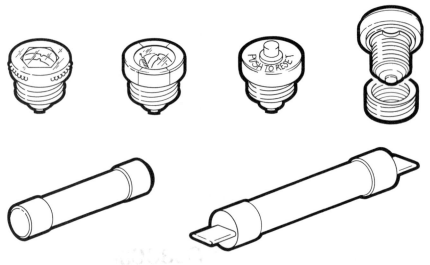

FIG. 3.2 COMMON TYPES OF FUSES

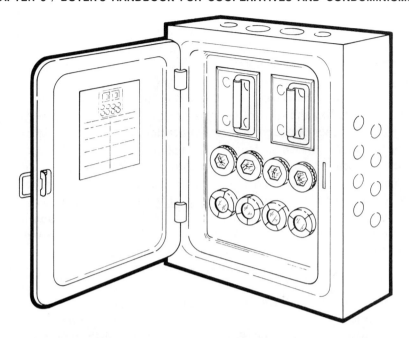

FIG. 3.3 FUSE BOX WITH MAIN DISCONNECTS AT TOP

circuit breakers are easy to use; unlike fuses, they do not have to be replaced. When inspecting a unit, remember that circuit breakers also indicate a more up-to-date electrical system.

When you examine the panel box, check to see that there are sufficient circuits for convenient and safe use of electrical lighting and appliances. Heavy-duty appliances should have their own separate circuit. Inadequate

FIG. 3.4 CIRCUIT BREAKERS OF 15 AND 20 AMPERES, AND PANEL BOX

wiring does not mean that you must completely replace all wiring. In most instances, additional circuits can be added to the existing system. If you believe this might be the case, get a cost estimate from a licensed electrician before you buy.

While examining the panel box, check the amperage at which electricity is delivered. Just like the flow of water through a pipe, the flow of electricity is larger if it comes through a larger-diameter wire. Current is measured in amperes. Ideal service is from 100 to 200 amperes. If the cooperative or condominium unit is equipped with an electric hot-water heater, electric range, electric washer and dryer, or several air-conditioning units, then 150-ampere service is the minimum acceptable current. Note too that three-wire service is better than two-wire, and it indicates that higher-quality materials were used in construction. You can identify the type of service by examining the electrical outlets. In three-wire service, all outlets have a round hole in addition to the two rectangular slits that accommodate the prongs of a plug.

Frequently overlooked during inspection of a unit is the adequacy of electrical outlets and switches in every room. It is very expensive to route wire inside walls, ceilings, and floors—either to establish new outlets or to install more convenient switches—after a building has been completed. Locate each electrical outlet on your scale drawing in red pencil, and then analyze the adequacy of the total system for your needs.

WALLS

Walls are an important point to consider during an inspection. They do not serve merely as background for furniture but also provide insulation, noise barriers, and sometimes fire protection. Ask the building manager about the general construction of ceilings and walls. In colder climates, find out how well the walls are insulated.

There are two types of wall construction: *dry-wall*, which includes gypsum board, Sheetrock, paneling, and plastic-type covering; and *wet-wall*, which includes plaster, masonry, and brick. Wet-wall construction is substantially more expensive than dry-wall, because the walls are more time-consuming to complete and the price of materials is much higher. Wet-walls are usually sturdier and are better barriers to noise and fire.

Gypsum board or Sheetrock is the leading dry-wall material applied to interior walls. It is relatively inexpensive and comes in 4-by-8 foot panels, which cost about $4 each. Tape and compound are used to join the sheets to create a complete wall, which is then painted or wallpapered. Flame-resistant finishes are available in higher-quality Sheetrock; however, such details might only be available when the cooperative or condominium is being sold prior to or during construction.

Kitchens should have proper wall covering. Water- and dirt-resistant wallpaper made of vinyl keep a kitchen clean and new-looking for a long time. Also, it is a good idea to have tile or some other protection such as metal or

WALLS ARE IMPORTANT
WHEN YOU ARE MAKING
AN INSPECTION.

glass on the wall behind a cooking range. Check for these features when inspecting a unit.

Cracks in walls, common in older buildings, usually occur because of the foundation settling. Small cracks are easy to repair in preparation for painting. However, be cautious if whole sections of a painted wall appear loose or flaky. This usually indicates that water is leaking from either the plumbing or the roof. Discolorations in the paint also indicate leaks, and you should feel any discolored areas with your palm to detect dampness.

If there's a fireplace, be sure that fireproof brick or stone has been used in a sufficient area. Check for cracked bricks and loose cement in any case. Open and close the flue several times to be certain it is working.

HEATING SYSTEMS

In certain parts of the United States, gas and electric fuels are relatively cheap and in plentiful supply. In other areas, however, they would be the last energy sources to consider for heating. Therefore, determine the suitability of the fuel used in the building for the area in which you will live.

In a newly constructed cooperative or condominium, it is probably not necessary to have a heating company inspect the heating system. But in older buildings, it is wise to have a professional evaluate the system for any hidden, needed repairs. A qualified heating specialist might be able to suggest alterations that could significantly reduce the yearly fuel bill. In such cases, the expense of repairs would be recouped in a short period of time.

Remember, the cost of fuel will be a major component in the monthly maintenance costs. Try to get a good estimate of what the yearly fuel costs have been and will be in the near future. Also, if you are on a limited budget and purchasing a cooperative or condominium in a tropical climate, consider whether you even need the added expense of a heating system.

In the following pages, several common types of heating systems are described so that you may become familiar with their benefits and disadvantages.

1. In **gravity warm-air systems,** the furnace utilizes the fact that warm air is lighter than cold, so hot air rises and cold air settles. The heat rises through ducts and passes through registers into various rooms.

Pro

- This is an easy system in which to install central air conditioning.
- There are no large, exposed radiators.

Con

- There must be a considerable difference in temperature between rising hot air and descending cold air to obtain good air movement.
- Many people complain that it dries out their sinuses and throats.

2. In **hot-water systems,** water is heated and then employed as the medium for transmitting heat principally by a gravity system or a forced hot-water system.

Pro

- This method is generally less drying for those suffering from sinus trouble.

Con

- It requires large radiators or convectors, which take up wall and floor space.

3. In **radiant systems,** heat generated by hot water is conveyed to pipes, which are hidden in surfaces such as floors and ceilings. These surfaces then radiate energy in automatically controlled amounts.

Pro

- Heat sources are invisible—no radiators, convector cabinets, or grills are apparent.

- It can be used to warm basementless homes when other types of heat cannot completely warm floors.

Con

- Large pieces of furniture and carpeting can intercept the heat.

4. In **steam systems,** water is heated in the boiler until it turns to steam and rises through pipes to radiators. As the steam contacts the radiators, it condenses and returns to the boiler to be reheated.

Pro

- Steam radiators can be smaller than—and yet supply the same heat as— a hot-water system, because steam is hotter than water.
- Steam runs more rapidly through pipes than does hot water, and so a steam system heats up faster.

Con

- The pressure of steam is more dangerous, and more service may be required to operate the system safely.

5. In **electric heat systems,** any electrical conductor with a resistance to electricity will become hot when current is passed through it. Baseboard units are the most popular form.

Pro

- Electrical systems have no moving parts to wear out, and thus are virtually maintenance-free.
- Fuel does not have to be delivered or stored.
- There is no combustion, and thus no expensive chimney need be installed.

Con

- In some places, the high cost of electric power makes this type of heating too expensive to be practical.

6. In **solar heating systems,** the energy of the sun is used to heat water, which may be used to heat the home or simply to supply hot water.

Pro

- The fuel source is free.

Con

- Most solar heating systems require a backup conventional system for use during sunless periods, thus making the initial cost somewhat higher.
- Finding qualified repair personnel may be difficult.

PLUMBING SYSTEMS

Local building codes regulate the design and materials that may be used in plumbing systems. Check to be certain that the plumbing installed in your

INSPECT THE PLUMBING AND WATER PRESSURE.

prospective cooperative or condominium conforms to the local code. You can do this either by asking to see a certificate of compliance in the manager's office or by calling the local building inspector. Be alert to the quality of the plumbing work in a cooperative or condominium. Because plumbing is a major construction cost, how the work is done, and its present condition, reflect on the basic value of the unit. So, test for pressure in every faucet, and fill the sinks and bathtubs to judge how well they drain. Once you own a unit, correcting faulty plumbing work will be an expensive proposition.

Should you be concerned with the *type* of pipes that supply water? Yes. The following list describes what to look for in four different types:

1. **Steel,** a common type of piping, is found in older structures. It cannot be bent to make turns and thus requires numerous fittings (however, this allows easy replacement). Over time, steel pipes rust, and so, when the water is first turned on, it may appear brownish for the first few moments. Rust can also accumulate inside steel pipes and reduce the waterflow to certain facilities.

Pitfalls

- When inspecting, check to see if pipes appear rusty on the outside. Such pipes may have to be replaced.
- Test the water pressure of every bathtub, shower, sink, and toilet.

2. **Copper** piping is more expensive than steel and is often used to replace rusted steel pipes. It is very common throughout newer homes. It is easily bent to make turns, and thus there are fewer fittings in a copper system. Since copper joints are usually sweat-soldered, they cannot be unscrewed to replace a damaged pipe. Copper offers less resistance to waterflow, and more pressure is delivered at the tap.

Pitfall

- Most copper pipes cannot be serviced with a pair of open-end wrenches, and so repair costs are higher.

3. **Plastic** piping is generally used for cold-water supply, and most local codes prevent its use within walls. It is the least expensive type of plumbing— a fact that you should consider when you evaluate the overall construction of the building.

Pitfalls

- Plastic piping is the least desirable plumbing system because it is difficult to service and is easily damaged.
- In the event of a fire, some plastic piping gives off harmful fumes.

4. **Brass**, the most expensive and least common piping, is primarily used in areas with severe water problems. Brass pipe is rigid and must be joined and threaded in the same manner as steel pipe. As a general rule, although brass plumbing reflects a high-quality construction job, it adds so much cost that it should only be used where absolutely necessary. The more common copper piping should perform just as satisfactorily where water problems do not exist.

Ideally, each sink, bathtub, shower, water heater, washing machine, and toilet should have its own shutoff valve. Then, if an emergency arises, you can close off the flow of water to a specific area and still use the rest of the plumbing system. So be sure to check for adequate shutoff valves during the inspection.

INSPECTING THE KITCHEN

One of the most important assets of a home is a functional kitchen. A fully equipped and modern kitchen in your cooperative or condominium will be important to the comfort of your family. In addition, it is often a primary attraction to buyers should you later wish to sell your unit.

It is sometimes wise to purchase a unit with an outdated kitchen and then modernize it to your own household's taste. The cost of complete renovations, however, ranges from $4000 to $10,000. So, if you don't plan on doing that much work, look at the following features during your inspection:

1. *Cabinets*
   - ☐ What material are they made of? Metal cabinets are cheaper than wood and less attractive to most people.
   - ☐ Are they well surfaced and easy to clean? or discolored and in need of repainting or recoating with Formica?
   - ☐ Are the shelves deep enough to accommodate plates lying flat? Depth should be at least 13 inches.
   - ☐ Is there sufficient storage space for food, pots, dishes, and small appliances?
   - ☐ Are cabinets located where they are convenient to use?

2. *Countertops*
   - ☐ How high are the countertops? In most kitchens, 36 inches is the standard height.
   - ☐ Do they have splash guards?
   - ☐ Are there convenient electrical outlets where countertop appliances would be connected?
   - ☐ Is the Formica self-edged, or is it cheaply edged with metal?
   - ☐ Is there sufficient preparation space (at least 30 inches) near the sink and stove?
   - ☐ What kind of sink is installed? If it is enamel, check for discoloration or chips. Does it drain well?

3. *Floor*
   - ☐ Is it easy to care for, or does it require constant waxing?
   - ☐ Are there holes, scratches, or tears?
   - ☐ Is the floor level?

4. *Layout*
   - ☐ Is the overall layout awkward?
   - ☐ Is there adequate ventilation for normal cooking purposes? One or more windows?
   - ☐ Are the working and eating areas adequately lit?
   - ☐ When opened, does the refrigerator door block other areas?
   - ☐ Do you want an eat-in kitchen *plus* a separate dining room?

5. *Appliances*
   - ☐ Does the kitchen have all the appliances you normally need?
   - ☐ Is the built-in oven too high for convenient access?
   - ☐ Is the cooking range vented to remove cooking odors and moisture?
   - ☐ Do the appliances run on electricity or gas? Which do you prefer?

When you are purchasing a cooperative or condominium that has not yet been built, or one that will replace kitchen appliances for new owners, carefully look at the models that will be supplied. If these are not satisfactory, offer to pay the developer for the appliances you desire. It is far simpler to

KNOW WHAT
YOU ARE BUYING.

do such work in the beginning than to change major appliances at a later date because they don't suit your household's needs.

WINDOWS

When inspecting a cooperative or condominium unit, open and close all windows to make certain that they work properly. Take note of broken panes of glass and windows that do not close tightly. Give the unit a plus if it has either double-pane thermal windows, which provide excellent insulation in cold months, or storm windows, which perform the same function. Don't forget to look for window screens, which are needed during the warmer months. If you don't see them, ask.

The following paragraphs describe the four types of windows you are likely to find in a condominium or cooperative.

The most prevalent type of window is the *double-hung window*, which has an upper portion that slides down and a lower portion that slides up (Fig. 3.5). Although the frame can be made of aluminum, in most windows it is wooden. A very common problem is that these windows are painted shut by careless painters. In an old building where many coats of paint have been

FIG. 3.5 DOUBLE-HUNG WINDOW

FIG. 3.6 CASEMENT WINDOWS

applied, it may be impossible to open a window without damaging it. Another problem is that the sash is made of rope, which has become rotten or frayed over time. Such sash cords must be replaced to enable proper use of the windows for ventilation and for escape in case of fire.

Casement windows have metal frames and are hung on hinges at either side of the window frame (Fig. 3.6). They are sometimes opened through the operation of a crank. (Be certain that all cranking mechanisms work!) The main problem with casement windows is that they rust and are eventually ruined if not properly painted. If casement windows are in an older building, there may be a draft due to uneven fit of the closed windows. This will affect heating costs for the entire building. However, corrective measures can be taken to reduce drafts, and most managing agents will properly maintain the window frames.

Horizontal sliding windows are constructed of aluminum and move along a fitted track at the top and bottom (Fig. 3.7). Sometimes, they have nylon guides that reduce friction and allow the window to operate more smoothly. Cheap horizontal sliding windows will warp and fail to operate properly in

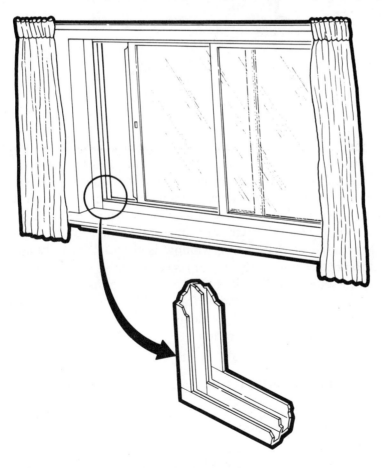

FIG. 3.7   SLIDING WINDOWS

FIG. 3.8   AWNING WINDOW

a short time. Keep in mind that it would require a special assessment of all owners to replace such poor-quality windows in all units.

Awning windows are hinged at the top and swing out at the bottom (Fig. 3.8). They are usually operated by a crank or a manual linkage connected to scissors-type metal arms on the window bottom. Be certain that each window fits snugly into the exterior frame so that there are no large air leaks. One disadvantage of the awning window is that it may only be opened a certain distance because of the control mechanism.

In a high-rise cooperative, it is an especially expensive proposition to replace broken panes or redo window frames. Check with the managing agent to see if such expenses are paid by the owner or fall into the category of general maintenance by the corporation.

PROFESSIONAL INSPECTORS AND APPRAISERS

In most areas, you can hire professional inspectors and expert appraisers. Inspectors merely look for defects in the physical property, whereas appraisers give an estimate of the current market value of property. Fees for each service range from $25 to $100. The quality of inspectors' opinions varies greatly, and the best precaution against shoddy workmanship and needed repairs is still your own diligent inspection.

Nevertheless, it is a good idea in the stages before signing a contract to hire an appraiser if your bank or lending institution has not already done so. Most times, an appraiser will be automatically engaged before a mortgage is extended. If you need to hire your own, they are listed in the Yellow Pages.

4

INSPECTING THE BUILDING AND THE COMMUNITY

Location and surface topography are important measures of value for land. For example, in the Rocky Mountains, land sells for $50 per acre while, in downtown Chicago, San Francisco, and other urban settings, it may sell for as much as $1 million per square block. Rocky Mountain land is hilly and not desirable for residential development, while urban land is readily usable and conveniently located.

Before you sign anything, get a good idea of the quality of land included with your particular cooperative or condominium. It may appear that you are buying into a small complex when in fact the sponsor has extensive property holdings, which will be developed over time. Because land is one of the major factors in the cost of constructing shelter (land accounts for about 25% of the purchase price), you should be satisfied that what you buy is located on desirable property.

Determine whether certain improvements or recreational facilities will be built only if a specific number of units are sold. Check up on the builder to see if previous projects were successfully sold out and whether promises to build specific amenities were carried out. Such information may be obtained from local banks, brokers, or real-estate boards. If you find that the builder has been unreliable, it is best to shy away from the purchase. If several different projects are being built in the surrounding or adjacent area, find out their prices and evaluate their attractiveness. It is never wise to buy the most expensive unit in an area, because it makes resale difficult. Also, don't move into a complex with high-income residents who may demand common services beyond your resources. The Board of Directors, who review financial information on prospective buyers, may be able to furnish some guidelines on the income level of the residents.

Analyze the building and your prospective unit for safety. Locate the nearest fire exits and fire extinguishers. The overall type of construction is

also important in considering the hazard a fire would pose. For example, brick or concrete fire walls between the units indicate that a building was constructed with fire safety in mind. In multiple-unit buildings, consider how a fire in your neighbor's apartment would affect you—and remember, damage can be caused by water draining through ceilings, not just by smoke and flames. Concrete floors, steel stairways, and appropriate fire walls and doors add safety as well as value to a home.

Examine the physical layouts of the structure to see if individual entrances and grounds permit privacy. The windows should not allow anyone to look directly into the bedrooms or living areas of the unit. Noise and sounds from neighboring units should not filter easily into your unit. In well-designed buildings, the architect will have taken such matters into account.

Following is a checklist of points that you should know about the overall community surrounding any style of cooperative or condominium. Much of this informaton can be marked on a map of the local area to give an overview of the community.

Fire Department
  Where is the nearest firehouse?
  Is there a fire-hydrant system? (This will affect fire insurance premiums.)
  Where is the nearest fire-alarm box?
  Has the fire department inspected the building recently?

Police Department
   Is the area adequately patrolled?
   Is there a history of crime in the area?

Food Stores
   Can you walk to shopping areas?
   Is there adequate competition?

Laundry Facilities
   Are they convenient to your unit?
   Can you have a washer and dryer in your home?
   To reach the laundry facilities, must you go up and down steps carrying
      laundry?

Schools
   Are there quality schools in the area?
   Is the school district planning to build any structure that will raise school
      taxes?

General Shopping
   Is there a full-service business district nearby? Department stores?

Parking
   Can your car be left near your unit?
   Is indoor parking available?

Sanitation
   How hidden and efficient is garbage disposal?
   Does the town cart the garbage away, or is a private firm employed?

General
   Where is the nearest appropriate house of worship?
   Is there a theater or other entertainment nearby?
   Are there parks and recreation facilities?
   Does the state require substantial and detailed disclosure by the sponsor?
   Where is the nearest hospital?

EMPLOYMENT

The most overlooked factor in the purchase of shelter is the employment prospects in the area. Before you commit yourself to long-term mortgage payments, assess the scope of industry in the local community. Since buying a cooperative or condominium is a decision to "put down roots" in a particular place, be sure it offers you opportunities for attractive employment. Settling in a "company town" where there is one major employer can endanger your entire investment if that employer's business turns sour. Not only might you be unemployed, but there may also be no buyers for your home. So, when buying in a company town, satisfy yourself as to the size and stability of the main industry.

THE TOWNHOUSE DEVELOPMENT

In inspecting a townhouse complex, look at all of the grounds covered by the master deed. If there are wet or swampy areas, sharp drops in elevation, poor topsoil, landfill, or otherwise unusable portions of land, consider it when deciding what price to bid. Natural beauty such as ponds or shade trees, which make the land desirable for living, are plus factors in a buying decision. Nevertheless, find out how much it costs for the upkeep of the grounds. Large lawns and numerous bushes are lovely, but they require constant attention. All such services will be reflected in higher monthly maintenance.

If you are buying during the early stages of a townhouse development, remember that future construction will create noise and inconvenience. Many sponsors are aware of this and so give early buyers concessions on maintenance and even mortgage financing. Don't hesitate to ask for such concessions if they are not immediately offered. This is part of negotiating a good purchase.

When you purchase a townhouse that has yet to be built, be sure that what will be constructed is identical to the model unit. Obtain experienced legal counsel. Have the building materials itemized by the selling agent, and tell your attorney exactly what you think you are buying. The inspection details on Worksheet 4 will give your lawyer an excellent idea of the townhouse interior, and a photograph of the exterior of the model will also aid him or her in protecting your investment.

HIGH-RISE LIVING

In a high-rise, there are many small factors that affect the quality of life. Following is a list of do's and don'ts, which can help you decide which unit to purchase.

Do

- Live on an upper floor if there is street noise.
- Choose as good a view as possible.
- Pay the premium for a corner apartment, if possible.
- Choose a windowed kitchen.
- Purchase in a building with central air conditioning.
- Choose a balcony or terrace.
- Look for a separate service elevator.
- Expect a live-in handyman or superintendent to be on the premises.
- Evaluate the doormen.
- Look for a safety system of locked doors and routine inspections.
- Judge the adequacy of laundry facilities.
- Look for cleanliness and the general state of repairs of carpeting, elevators, and walls.

- Observe the people entering the building.
- Inspect the unit several times, at various hours of the day, to check for noise filtering through from other units.

Don't

- Choose a unit directly in front of noisy elevator doors.
- Choose a unit near a garbage chute.
- Buy in a complex where electricity for all units is included in common maintenance charges.
- Choose a unit at the bottom of a deep light shaft between high-rise units.
- Buy if the lobby wastes space and is extremely ornate. This costs money to maintain and will increase maintenance charges.
- Buy a unit located next to a doctor's or dentist's office.
- Buy without adequate off-street parking in the area.

In the case of a high-rise building, land linkage (the land between units) is important. If the owner of property between large buildings is an outside party and not under the control of the Board of Directors, the owner might bring undesirable development on the land and hurt the values of all units. If there are streets in the complex, ask whether the town or the residents are responsible for maintenance. Such information should be contained in a schedule of actual or estimated expenses, which you should obtain from the sponsor seller or the broker.

RECREATION FACILITIES

It is important to examine all recreation facilities to assess their quality and safety. These items are an important element of what you are purchasing.

Look around. Does the playground have sturdy equipment? Adequate protection under swings and monkey bars? Is the setting appealing? Is the playground located away from streets or adequately fenced in? Are there sufficient tennis courts for the number of residents? Is the swimming pool big enough? Is there a lifeguard on duty? Are recreation facilities kept in usable condition? If the complex is not fully constructed, will these facilities be adequate when all units are inhabited?

Never assume that use of recreation facilities comes automatically with the purchase of a unit. In some states, buyers have found that monthly charges for recreation facilities, which they had believed were free, exceed the maintenance on their units. Get all the facts, and note the recreation costs on Worksheets 1, 3, and 4.

CONVERSIONS

The U.S. Department of Housing and Urban Development estimates that over 100,000 rental units were converted to cooperatives and condominiums

from 1970 through 1975. In many cases, conversions were due to rent control regulations, which destroyed the income potential of some rental buildings. Owners who wished to sell such buildings had to sell it either to another investor at a low price (because it produced little net rental income) or to their tenants.

It is frequently argued that conversions aggravate the housing shortage in urban areas because they force many people, who would not otherwise do so, to move. There have been numerous confrontations between tenants' groups and sponsors. So, when you speak to present occupants about a building, determine their bias. Tenants who are being forced to move because they failed to buy will often present an unfavorable picture that is not realistic.

In three states—California, New York, and Virginia—the seller is required to furnish to prospective buyers a qualified engineer's report on the condition of the building. In most other areas, the tenants' association will have such an examination carried out at its own expense. These reports are especially useful because they give a professional opinion of the condition of heating, electrical, plumbing, and other systems.

Advantages

When considering a converted building, there are the following possible advantages:

- Conversions are usually done in older buildings, which have superior construction.
- There is a more accurate budget based on previous operating costs, so maintenance figures furnished to buyers should be more reliable.
- When a large number of renters choose to purchase, it indicates a well-run building with satisfied tenants.
- A local bank will probably have experience with the building and can advise you on its suitability.
- You can speak with tenants who have lived there to get an excellent idea of the merits and faults of the building and area.
- You can contact local enforcement officials to see if the building is in conformity with the building-code requirements.

Disadvantages

Converted buildings also have several disadvantages:

- Local laws may permit some tenants to stay without buying, and they may be less concerned with maintaining the property.
- The conversion plan may never become completely effective.
- Older buildings may have outmoded heating, electrical, and elevator systems. Make sure the converter-seller furnishes you with an inspection report prepared by a professional engineer.

5

PROTECTION OF THE BUYER

As a general rule, the law in most states offers little protection to consumers who purchase a cooperative or condominium. The main constraints on deceptive selling practices seem to come from the reputation of a particular builder in the marketplace and from individual lawsuits.

New York State is an exception. Most experts consider its consumer law on cooperatives and condominiums to be the strongest in the country. In New York, a developer must furnish buyers with a detailed disclosure statement that has been approved in advance by the state attorney general. Other states that rank close to New York in protection against deception are California, Hawaii, Michigan, and Virginia.

After you have decided to buy, it is a good idea to check on the general status of your state's protection for buyers. An attorney, broker, or bank can probably tell what kind of disclosure to expect from the developer or selling agent. Even though the large majority of cooperative and condominium developments are built by ethical real-estate people, the best approach is still "Buyer beware."

WHAT DOCUMENTS TO REQUEST

It is amazing how many people purchase real estate without having all the facts. The first rule in buying shelter is: *don't hesitate to ask anything.* For some reason, when many people are making one of the largest investments of their life, they become timid. They are embarrassed to make the seller answer their questions. The best approach is to ask any questions that come to mind. There are no foolish questions when your hard-earned money is on the line.

When you have narrowed the search to a few choice units, start gathering detailed information. You have a right to receive copies of all of the basic documents (see following lists), as well as any other material that would dis-

DON'T HESITATE TO ASK QUESTIONS!

close terms of the sale. This material should be read and studied before you sign anything.

Following is a list of the documents to request and what to look for in each of them. Remember not to make a decision to buy before you fully understand this information.

Cooperatives

When looking at a cooperative, ask about the following items:

Conversion Plan

- If the cooperative was on an ordinary lease basis and converted to a cooperative occupancy through the efforts of a sponsor-seller, a plan was drawn up.

Pitfalls

- How many tenants elected to purchase their apartments?
- What is the reputation of the sponsor-seller who converted?
- Carefully review how the shares were allocated to each apartment, because this determines price and maintenance.

Schedule of Available Apartments

Pitfalls

- Analyze the entire building to be certain that few or no apartments have excessive maintenance or selling prices. This might make them unmarketable, and if so they will remain vacant, causing problems when other owners have to contribute their share of expenses.

- Has any particular unit layout been difficult to sell? Avoid buying it without additional concessions on price or down payment.

Proprietary Lease

Pitfalls

- Are all tenant stockholders subject to substantially the same lease? Guard against special concessions to the sponsor-controlled apartments while they are vacant. (For instance, in some projects, the first few owners have paid full costs of maintenance and upkeep on their units, while sponsors have contributed only a fraction of their share for units not yet sold.)
- In some publicly assisted cooperatives, the occupancy agreement only covers a few years in order to protect against the cutoff of government subsidies. Such leases are really nonproprietary and should be avoided.
- What degrees of family relationship are permitted in subleasing? Be certain that permitted occupants include children and grandchildren.
- The lease should be inseparable from the stock, so that there are no owners who are not also occupants.

READ THE LANGUAGE IN YOUR DECLARATION OR PROPRIETARY LEASE. UNDERSTAND WHAT IT MEANS.

- Does the lease include parking space?
- Is there control by the Board of Directors on the future resale of units? You want to be certain that future owners are able to live up to their financial responsibilities.

Bylaws

Pitfalls

- Is voting by number of shares, not by one stockholder per one vote? If you buy a more expensive unit with higher maintenance, you should have more of a voice in governing the cooperative.
- Check specific percentage of votes needed to approve the yearly budget, discharge the managing agent, and perform other important functions. If a 100% vote is required to do anything, then the sponsor will maintain control as long as he or she owns a single unit.
- Who may inspect books and records of the corporation? Residents should be authorized to inspect such material in the office of the corporation.

Counsel's Tax Opinion

Pitfall

- Have you or the sponsor-seller obtained a reputable law firm's opinion on the tax deductions of the cooperative? You don't need trouble at tax time.

Details of Mortgage Indebtedness

Pitfalls

- If the common mortgage must be renewed soon, maintenance will skyrocket if the old mortgage was at an abnormally low rate. Get a list of all current mortgages with amounts, interest rates, and maturity dates.
- The wide use of "balloon" mortgages, where a large principal amount suddenly comes due, can mean trouble. Ask your banker and lawyer their opinion of the mortgage financing of the building.

Floor Plan of Unit

Pitfalls

- Do the dimensions of the rooms include closet space?
- Are dimensions omitted on seller's drawings in areas that would be considered inadequate by most people?
- How high is the ceiling in each room? (Many drawings omit this dimension.)

Financing Arrangement for Purchasers

Pitfalls

- The cost of attractive financing may be hidden in inflated unit prices. Know the real market value of your unit before you decide to buy.
- Has your attorney reviewed all financing papers for problems hidden in the fine print?

Financial Details

- There are many pitfalls, which we will explore in detail later in this chapter.

Management Agreement (See Exhibit 5.1)

Pitfalls

- Is the sponsor also the managing agent? Is the fee for management excessive?
- Can the managing agent be fired if he or she does not perform the assigned duties satisfactorily? The Bylaws should indicate what percentage of the vote is necessary to fire or hire a new manager. If 100% is needed, it could be difficult to discharge an inept agent.
- Does the agent have previous experience? Ask for references, and check them out. See what the experience of other owners has been in buildings the agent has managed.

Contract of Sale

Pitfalls

- Don't try to be your own lawyer. No one should purchase a cooperative or condominium apartment without proper representation by counsel.
- Under what conditions will your deposit be refunded?

House Rules

Pitfalls

- Are pets permitted?
- Are barbecues allowed on terraces?
- How are radio and television aerials attached? How are they used? Is there a monthly service charge?
- Are there storage facilities? What can be stored?

EXHIBIT 5.1

MANAGEMENT AGREEMENT

THIS AGREEMENT, made and entered into this _____ day of _____, 19___, Dade County, Florida, by and between:

SUN CLUB, INC., A nonprofit Florida
corporation, herein called "Condominium"
AND

WITNESSETH:

For and in consideration of these premises and of the mutual promises and covenants herein contained, Condominium and Manager agree as follows:

In this Agreement, the following definitions shall prevail:

1. Employment. The Condominium does hereby employ the Manager as the exclusive manager of the property of the Condominium, and the Manager does hereby accept such employment.

2. Term. The commencement date of this agreement when the Manager will be required to begin performance of its duties hereunder shall be
Unless sooner terminated as elsewhere herein provided this agreement shall be in effect until the 31st day of December, 1978.

3. Duties of Manager. Manager shall have the duty to perform and supply all of the following services, manpower and materials and shall be reimbursed by the Condominium for all costs and expenses thereof.

(a) Manager shall provide at least one supervisory management person who shall devote full time employment to the management of the Condominium property and the Condominium, and he shall be available to the owners within the Condominium and the persons directly employed by the Condominium and the persons dealing with the Condominium.

(b) Manager shall select, employ and supervise employees to work in, about and around the Condominium property. Except for the supervisory employees of Manager, the wages of such other employees shall be paid by the Condominium.

(c) Manager shall collect all common expenses, charges and assessments and monies and debts of every nature and description which may become due the Condominium from its members. The Condominium does hereby authorize the Manager, and the Manager is obligated to request, demand, collect, receive and receipt for any and all such common expenses, charges, assessments and other monies which may become due the Condominium and to take such action in the name of the Condominium, with the approval of the Board of Directors of the Condominium, as may be required for the collection of the same.

(d) Manager shall cause the grounds, lands, appurtenances and those portions of the buildings and improvements on the property required by the terms of the By-Laws and the Declaration of Condominium to be maintained and repaired by the Condominium, to be maintained and repaired. The same shall include landscaping, re-landscaping, elevator maintenance, painting, roofing, cleaning, and such other ordinary and extraordinary maintenance and repair work as may be necessary or found desirable by the Manager. For any one item of repair, replacement or refurbishing the expense incurred shall not exceed the sum of $2,500.00, unless specifically authorized by the Directors of the Condominium, excepting emergency repairs involving manifest danger to persons or property immediately necessary for the preservation and safety of the property or the safety of persons or required to avoid the suspension of any necessary service to the property, may be made by the Manager, irrespective of the above cost limitation. Notwithstanding this authority as to emergency repairs, it is understood that the Manager will, if at all possible, confer immediately with the Directors of the Condominium regarding emergency expenditures.

(e) Manager shall take such action as may be necessary to comply with all laws, statutes, ordinances, rules and of all appropriate government authority, and the rules and regulations of the National Board of Fire Underwriters, or in the event it shall terminate its present functions, those of any other body exercising similar functions, subject to the limitations set forth in the foregoing paragraph. The Manager, however, shall not take any action so long as the Condominium is contesting or has affirmed its intention to contest any such law, statute, ordinance, rule, regulation or order or requirement pursuant thereto.

(f) Manager shall purchase equipment, tools, vehicles, appliances, goods, supplies and materials as shall be reasonably necessary or desirable to perform its duties including the maintenance, upkeep, repair, replacement, refurbishing and preservation of the property, as aforesaid. Purchases shall be made in the name of the Manager, or in its discretion, in the name of the Condominium. When making purchases, the Manager shall make reasonable effort to obtain the best price available, all factors considered, and shall pass on to the Condominium all discounts, commissions and rebates received in the purchase. It is the intention of this Agreement that the Manager shall always use the Condominium funds in the purchases above referred to for the Condominium. In the event the Manager shall ever advance its own funds for any such purposes, then the Condominium shall, as part of its common expenses, reimburse Manager for the actual cost of such purchases. Manager shall always endeavor to keep costs to a minimum and never to order or purchase any materials or supplies or services which are not necessary for the reasonable operation of the building.

(g) (i) Manager shall cause to be placed or kept in force all insurance required in the By-Laws, and the Declaration of Condominium or requested by the Board of Directors; to adjust all claims arising under insurance policies purchased by the Condominium; to bring suit thereon in the name of the Condominium and deliver release upon payment of claims; to otherwise exercise all of the rights, powers and privileges of the Condominium; to receive on behalf of the Condominium all insurance proceeds and pay the same to the Insurance Trustee.

(ii) Manager shall keep in force insurance on itself protecting the Condominium in all respects against any liability arising out of any wrongful or negligent acts of the Manager or any other actions of the Manager which might cause the Condominium to incur liability; and the Condominium shall carry insurance which will protect the Manager from any liability arising out of its faithful performance of its duties on behalf of the Condominium, in sum both the Condominium and the Manager, shall name the other as an additional insured in such liability insurance.

(h) Manager shall maintain the Condominium's minute books, membership lists, give notice of membership and Director's meetings, and maintain all financial record books, accounts and other records required to be kept by the Condominium. Such records shall be kept at the office of the Manager and shall be available for inspection at all reasonable times by the Condominium's officers and Directors. As a standard procedure, the Manager shall render to the Condominium a statement of its receipts and accounts for each calendar year no later than the April 1st next thereafter. The Manager shall perform a continual internal audit of the Condominium's financial records for the purpose of verifying the same but no independent or external audit shall be required of it. The Condominium shall have the right to an external independent audit provided the costs for the same and the employment of such auditor be by the Condominium directly and not through the Manager and the external independent auditor is acceptable to the Manager whose acceptance may not be unreasonably withheld. Such independent audit shall be at the office of the Manager.

(i) Manager will maintain records with respect to services and materials and expenses provided to the Condominium, which records will be sufficient to describe the services rendered and shall be kept in accordance with prevailing accounting procedures and shall identify the source and expenditure of all funds. Such records shall be kept at the Manager's office and shall be freely available for inspection by the Condominium's officers and directors on a reasonable basis and the records shall be subject to an independent audit as set forth in paragraph (h) above.

(j) Manager shall deposit all funds collected of the Condominium otherwise accruing to the Condominium, in a special bank account or accounts of the Manager, in banks and/or savings and loan associations in Broward or Dade Counties, Florida, with suitable designation indicating their source, separate from and not comingled with any other funds of any other Condominium, Property or building managed by Manager. Said funds, or as much of it as is reasonably possible, shall be kept in a separate interest-bearing account, which interest shall accrue to the benefit of the Condominium.

(k) Manager shall prepare an operating budget setting forth an itemized statement of the anticipated receipts and disbursements for the new year based upon the then current schedule of monthly assessments and charges and taking into account the general condition of the Condominium and the Property, which budget shall comply to the requirements of By-Laws, together with a statement from the Manager outlining a plan of operation and justifying the estimates made in every important particular, shall be submitted to the Condominium in final draft at least forty-five (45) days prior to commencement of the new year for which it has been made. The budget shall serve as a supporting document for the schedule of monthly assessments proposed for the new year. It shall also constitute a major control under which the Manager shall operate and there shall be no substantial variances therefrom except as may be incurred or commitments made by the Manager in connection with maintenance and operation of the Property, in excess of the amounts allocated to the various classifications of expense in the approved budget without prior consent of the Condominium except that, if necessary because of a lack of sufficient time to obtain such prior consent, an overrun may be experienced provided it is brought promptly to the attention of the Condominium in writing.

(l) Any vending machines, pay telephones, or other coin operated equipment or other type machinery which may be installed by the Manager or at Manager's request upon the Condominium premises shall be for the benefit of the Condominium, and any profits arising therefrom shall accrue to and be allocated to the maintenance, administration, upkeep and repair of the Condominium. Under any circumstances, the Board of Directors of the Condominium shall first approve the installation of any such machines.

4. Powers of Manager. Manager is and shall have general authority and the powers necessary to carry out the intent of this Agreement and to act therefor on behalf of the Condominium. Manager is authorized in the name of and at the expense of the Condominium to make reasonable contracts for electric, gas, steam, telephone, window cleaning, extermination and other such services as shall be necessary. Nothing in this Agreement shall prohibit the Manager from managing other properties, condominium or commercial. It is contemplated that the Manager may also be the manager of the commercial areas of this condominium apartment building and a reasonable pro-ration of all charges, costs and expenses shall be made by the Manager in such case.

5. Employees. Each of Manager's employees shall be suitably bonded by a fidelity bond in an amount of not less that $100,000.000 securing their faithful performance of their duties and their honesty.

6. Reimbursement of Expenses. Condominium shall reimburse the Manager upon demand for any monies which the Manager becomes obligated and required to pay for services or materials purchased or obtained under this Agreement for the benefit of the Condominium.

7. Compensation. In compensation for the management services rendered hereunder, Condominium agrees to pay Manager the sum of $45,000.00 per year, payable in equal monthly installments. Manager shall begin earning its fee on the commencement date of this Agreement, and the first payment shall become due the last day of that month. Thereafter, payments shall come due on the last day of each month for the services performed during the preceding month. The Manager shall be provided with office space, without cost or expense to the Manager, on the Lobby Floor.

8. Default.

(A) If the Manager shall fail to satisfactorily perform its duties and obligations under this Agreement or shall default in any of the particulars provided herein, then the Condominium shall, after the giving of not less than thirty days written notice, in which the default is defined and specified, after which time the default remains uncured or if Manager has not undertaken reasonable steps to cure a default which cannot be cured within such thirty (30) days, then the Condominium shall have the right to cancel this Agreement, and such cancellation shall be effective, and Manager shall be removed from the premises and shall have handed over to the Condominium all monies, records, papers, etc., not less that fifteen (15) days after the giving of notice of cancellation.

(B) In the event that the Condominium defaults in failing to make the payments required to be made hereunder or by continuing to violate any law, ordinance or statute after notice from the appropriate governmental authority, and after having failed to commence to resist or test such ordinance or statute by appropriate legal action, then upon the giving of thirty (30) days written notice by Manager, after which time such default remains uncured, of it the default involves violation of such statute or ordinance and reasonable steps have not been taken to comply with this paragraph, then Manager shall have the right, upon the giving of fifteen (15) days' written notice, to cancel this Agreement and this Agreement will be cancelled on a date not less than fifteen (15) days after the giving of such notice.

9. Notice. Notice which either party desires to give or is required to give to the other under this Agreement shall be given by Certified Mail, return receipt requested, and it shall be deemed given when it shall have been deposited in the United States Mails, addressed to the party for whom it is intended as follows

For the Condominium

For Manager

IN WITNESS WHEREOF, the parties hereto have caused these presents to be executed on the day and year first hereinabove written.

Signed, sealed and delivered   SUN CLUB, INC., a
in the presence of: nonprofit Florida Corporation

_____

_____   By _____
(As to Condominium)   (CONDOMINIUM)

_____

_____   By _____
(As to Manager)   (MANAGER)

Condominiums

When looking at a condominium, ask about the following items:

Declaration

Pitfalls

- Are there any clauses that lock the developer into long-term, self-serving agreements? One good measure is: how much authority does the Board of Directors have to replace a developer who fails to perform specific services?
- Is there any action that requires 100% of the owners to effect change? If so, developers could purchase a single unit and prevent changes not to their liking.
- If the condominium is not yet built, is there a specific date on which the deposit is returnable if the completed unit is not delivered?
- Do you understand any right of first refusal on resale that is included? (This means that you must first offer the unit to the Board of Directors and that they must refuse to purchase it before you can sell to an outside buyer.)

LOOK IN THE DECLARATION FOR A COMPLETE DESCRIPTION OF THE LAND.

- If the common estate contains streets, check restrictions on their use.
- Avoid condominiums that would allow unit ratios to change at a future date. This would cause a shift in maintenance charges among units.

Financial Details

- There are many pitfalls, which we will explore in detail later in this chapter.

Building Schedule

Pitfall

- If the condominium is under construction, get a written timetable of its completion. This will avoid your being the sole inhabitant of the land while construction goes on for months or years.

Management Agreement

Pitfall

- Same as for cooperatives, p. 61.

Floor Plan of Unit

Pitfall

- Same as for cooperatives, p. 60.

Bylaws

Pitfalls

- Are the powers of the Board of Directors dictatorial? Is everything couched in terms of reasonableness?
- Check the specific percentage of votes needed to approve the yearly budget, terminate the managing agent, and perform other important functions.
- Who may inspect books and records of the corporation?
- Is there a right to petition for change in the government of the condominium—for example, to remove an ineffective Board of Directors?

Recreation Leases

Pitfalls

- Do you know what you're paying for? Is there a charge to *use* the recreation facilities?
- Who owns the land under the recreation facility? Can the land be built on when the lease expires?
- Carefully review recreation lease charges, which are tied into automatic increases based on the cost-of-living or other index.
- Is the yearly lease cost reasonable in light of the facilities rented?

Details of Mortgage Indebtedness

Pitfall

- Same as for cooperatives, p. 60.

Contract of Sale

Pitfall

- Same as for cooperatives, p. 61.

Summary

After you have become familiar with all of the preceding information, go see your attorney. An attorney will thoroughly review all of the detailed information in the selling documents. Don't let a salesperson convince you that all documents are the same for everyone and that they cannot be changed by a lawyer. Only the Declaration, Bylaws, and House Rules are the same for everyone. Unquestionably, all purchasers need advice regarding which specific provisions must be negotiated during the purchase to obtain maximum satisfaction from their new home.

FINANCIAL STATEMENTS

Exhibit 5.2 shows projected receipts and expenses for the first year of operation of Two Main Street Corporation, a cooperative in New York City. Since New York State has one of the strictest disclosure laws, we can expect that the amount of information given to the buyer is a good basis for judging maintenance costs. Exhibit 5.3 is a disclosure of the estimated operating budget of Sun Club, Inc., a condominium development in Dade County, Florida. There are no accompanying footnotes to explain the charges set forth in the document given prospective purchasers.

An important item that should appear in any operating budget is a *Reserve for Contingencies*, in which money is put aside for unexpected expenses. It is impossible to predict when, for example, elevators or oil burners will break down, forcing the spending of large sums not anticipated in the normal budget. The amount of money set aside usually depends on both the size of the building and its insurance coverage. In Exhibit 5.2, Two Main Street Corporation has a $25,446 Reserve for Contingencies in a building with 186 apartments. In Exhibit 5.3, Sun Club, Inc. has an $11,820 reserve in a building with 446 units (which is probably not adequate).

Reasonable management fees vary from 2% to 6% of the annual operating budget. Earlier, we noted that it is important to study the Management Agreement to see if it is unreasonable. As we can see from the sample budgets, Two Main Street Corporation will pay a management fee of $20,342 (1.6% of its budget), and Sun Club, Inc. will pay $45,000 (7.5% of its budget). Thus, we should question exactly what services are being performed by building management in Sun Club to justify such a large fee.

When reviewing budgets, it is also a good policy to review the terms of the income-producing commercial leases and the quality of large commercial tenants. In Two Main Street Corporation, there are parking and laundry leases, which together contribute $38,500 toward the expense budget. As a buyer, you should feel reasonably secure that this income will continue. It will reduce the overall maintenance and benefit all unit owners. Unlike Two Main Street Corporation, Sun Club, Inc. has no commercial tenants to help offset expenses.

All footnotes to budgets should be read with care. In Exhibit 5.2, we learn the basis on which projected expenses for Two Main Street Corporation for 1974 have been calculated (notes 4–6). In addition, the names of service and maintenance companies, insurance coverage on the building, number of employees by occupation, assessed valuation, and the terms of the first mortgage are clearly detailed. This kind of information enables buyers to judge the quality of their investment.

Don't expect budget expenses to be carried out to the penny. Rounding off is acceptable since the expenses are really projections for the coming year. On the other hand, read any qualifiers given along with estimates of expenses. If the qualification is put in such broad terms that it almost absolves the preparer from liability, be especially careful. Then, form your own judgment of

EXHIBIT 5.2

TWO MAIN STREET CORPORATION
June 1, 1974

Schedule of Projected Receipts and Expenses for First Year of Cooperative Operation

Receipts:

Annual Rent (Maintenance Charges) (60,119 shares at $20.526 per share) $1,234,000

Miscellaneous Income (Note 1) 31,500

    Total Estimated Receipts (Note 2) $1,265,500

Expenses:

Labor Charges (Including wages, Workman's Compensation & Disability Insurance, Welfare and Pension costs & Payroll taxes) (Note 3) .... $ 180,475

Heat and Hot Water—Fuel Oil (Note 4) 31,500

Power, Light, and Gas (Note 5) 39,000

Water Charges and Sewer Rent (Note 6) 15,000

Maintenance of Building (Including General Repairs and Maintenance, Elevator Maintenance, Supplies and Sundries, and Building Services) (Note 7) 46,000

Management Fee (Including other charges) (Note 8) ... 20,342

Building Insurance (Note 9) 6,600

Legal and Auditing 2,000

Taxes:

Real Estate (Note 10) 382,500

Franchise, Etc. (Note 11) 2,000

Reserve For Contingencies 25,446

    Total Operating Expense .... $ 750,863

Mortgage, Indebtedness (Note 12)

Interest .... $ 424,597

Amortization 90,040

Total Mortgage Indebtedness .... $ 514,637

    Total Estimated Expenses (Note 13) $1,265,500

1. Miscellaneous Income consists of:

(a) $21,000 per annum from the garage concessionaire, Joy Parking, Inc. under a lease expiring on December 31, 1982.

(b) $7,500 per annum from the laundry equipment, based on an agreement with Washer Operating Corp. for a term ending on October 31, 1976, unless extended.

(c) $3,000 per annum from the ground floor office based on the undertaking by the Sponsor-Seller to pay to the Apartment Corporation, for the first two fiscal years after the Closing Date, to the extent that the actual income received from such office during each such fiscal year following the Closing Date is less than

$3,000 (such payment to be made within 60 days after the first and second anniversaries of the Closing Date).

2. This does not include any interest income that may be received by the Apartment Corporation from the Reserve Fund to be retained at the closing of title. It may be expected that all or part of the Reserve Fund will be expended during the first or subsequent years of operation. Accordingly, such interest income cannot be determined with exactitude. For the foregoing reason and because such income does not reflect the normally anticipated receipts from operations, same has not been included in the estimated receipts for the first year of operation.

3. This amount includes the increase in the union wage rates effective on April 21, 1974 and April 21, 1975 for 15 employees, which includes 1 superintendent, 1 handyman, 4 doormen, 3 hallmen, 2 service elevator operator/porters, 2 porters and 2 relief personnel.

4. Based on an increase of approximately 10.4% above 1972 costs.

5. Based on an increase of 7% above 1972 costs and 9% above the average costs for the past three calendar years ending 1972, 1971, and 1970.

6. Predicated on an increase of approximately 4% above current rates.

7. Based approximately on the costs incurred in the 1972 calendar year. Includes the following service and maintenance agreements:
- (i) elevator maintenance agreement with Elevator Maintenance Corp. for an initial term ending on September 1, 1974, and from year to year thereafter until terminated by either party on thirty (30) days' written notice, at a monthly fee of $500.00 (adjustable in accordance with the rate scale for mechanics in the event same increases or decreases over the amount paid on April 20, 1973);
- (ii) air conditioning service contract with Air Conditioning Company for a term ending on May 15, 1974, at an annual charge of $2,676.00;
- (iii) alarm system contract with Eye Security Service, Inc., for a term ending on August 16, 1976 at a monthly fee of $10.00;
- (iv) master television antenna agreement with Television, Inc., for a term ending on September 30, 1974, at an annual fee of $230 plus tax;
- (v) water treatment agreement with Water, Inc., on a month to month basis, for a charge equal to the cost of chemicals used for treating the various water systems (not to exceed $825.00 per annum);
- (vi) exterminator agreement with Exterminating Corp., on a month-to-month basis, at a monthly fee of $19.

8. The management fee consists of $20,000 (which is less than the rates recommended by the Real Estate Board of New York, Inc.) and customary charges of $1.90 per employee per month for processing employee benefits (in accordance with said Board's rates). Refer to "Management Agreement" below for full discussion.

9. Multi-peril policy covering all risks of direct physical loss on the following coverages in the amounts shown:

Item Covered	Amount	Exposures Insured Against
Building	$6,000,000	All risk of direct physical loss or damage (80% co-insurance)
Rents	1,264,000	All risk of direct physical loss or damage

Public Liability	1,000,000 Per Occurrence	Personal injury and property damage
Water Damage Legal Liability	25,000 Per Occurrence	Damage to property of tenants by water
Elevator Collision	25,000 Per Elevator	Collision damage
Boiler and Machinery	1,000,000	Cracking, burning and explosion of boilers, etc. and machinery break-down

10. Based on the current 1973/1974 assessed valuation of $5,100,000 (comprising land at $825,000 and building at $4,275,000) at a projected rate of $7.50 per $100 of assessed valuation.

11. Includes the New York City and State franchise taxes and miscellaneous fees and permits.

12. The first mortgage is held by The Whole Life Insurance Company and provides for constant monthly payments of $42,886.39, to be applied first to interest at the rate of 7⅛% per annum and the balance in reduction of principal. The loan will self-liquidate over its term of 25 years.

13. The foregoing estimates assume the first fiscal year of cooperative operation will begin on or about June 1, 1974.

each expense item. Remember, unrealistically low budgets will mean a large jump in maintenance costs when actual expenses have to be paid.

There are several other points that you should keep in mind when reviewing budgets:

1. Look for subsidies that are given by the sponsor and which keep maintenance unrealistically low. When the subsidy ends, you must be prepared for a substantial maintenance hike.
2. If a building is being converted to a cooperative, try to acquire an old budget and compare it with the projected one.
3. Beware of an expense budget that is much lower than the budget of comparable buildings in the area.
4. There is an argument that, because a building depreciates, a building replacement fund should be established to provide funds in the future to remodel or replace most of the project. Not many buildings have such a fund, and the counterargument is that inflation will cover depreciation as long as the complex is constantly upgraded to halt physical obsolescence.
5. Determine whether employees receive excessively high salaries.

EXHIBIT 5.3

SUN CLUB, INC.

ESTIMATED OPERATING BUDGET

	Monthly	Annually
Accounting and Legal	$ 500	$ 6,000
Insurance	6,000	72,000
Maintenance and Repairs	2,500	30,000
Management	3,750	45,000
Payroll	21,065	252,780
Supplies	1,700	20,400
Utilities	9,750	117,000
Taxes	3,750	45,000
Reserve	985	11,820
	$50,000	$600,000

ESTIMATED ASSESSMENTS FOR EACH UNIT

	Monthly	Annually
A Units	$129.80	$1,557.60
B Units	108.80	1,305.60
C Units	102.30	1,227.60
D Units	81.85	982.20
E Units	116.80	1,401.60

MONTHLY EXPENSE SCHEDULES

Whenever a cooperative or a condominium is formed, a detailed monthly expense schedule is drawn up for all units. This columnar chart sets forth the percentage of common ownership, and estimated monthly expenses associated with that ownership, for individual units. In a cooperative, the ownership in the cooperative corporation is designated by the number of shares of stock assigned to a unit, whereas a condominium expresses common ownership as a percentage of all the common areas. Additional columns give the selling price of each unit, information on sponsor mortgage financing, estimated real-estate taxes, estimated monthly maintenance, and estimated monthly tax deduction available to the purchaser.

As was the case with the financial statements, the notes are very important and should be studied. The notes may indicate such basics as the tax rate used to determine monthly real-estate charges, qualifications given for estimates, and whether gas or electric is included in monthly maintenance. Determine who prepared the estimate of monthly expenses, and weigh the preparer's ability to make such projections.

How the number of shares or percent of common areas is assigned to each unit is quite important. It is supposed to be accomplished on the relative value of the units in relation to the whole complex. If assignment is poorly managed, units may remain unsold, and thus they cannot contribute to the cost of maintaining common areas. We can analyze assignment from the monthly expense schedule.

Exhibit 5.4 shows the financial details of expenses for Two Main Street Corporation. The schedule reveals that we are reviewing the conversion of an existing rental building to a cooperative. Previous rental tenants have the right to purchase their apartments at $96 per share, while the public will have to pay $119 per share. Note that from the third floor up to the 14th floor, the number of shares assigned to each unit increases by floor in a regular three-

EXHIBIT 5.4

TWO MAIN STREET CORPORATION

Purchase Price and Other Expense Details for Each Apartment

Apartments (1)	Rooms and Baths (1)	Number of Shares	Shares Purchase Price at $1.00 per Share (2)	Additional Cash Payment by Tenant Purchasers at $95 per Share (3)	Total Cash Payment by Tenant Purchasers at $96 per Share (2)	Additional Cash Payment by Non-Tenant Purchasers at $110 per Share (3)	Total Cash Payment by Non-Tenant Purchasers at $120 per Share (3)	Approximate Amount of Mortgage Applicable to Shares ($99.00 per Share) (3)	Estimated First Year Maintenance Charges ($20.526 per Share) (4)	Estimated Monthly Maintenance Charges ($1.710 per Share) (4)	Estimated First Year Income Tax Deduction ($13.107 per Share) (5)
1-F	3½-1	200	200	$19,000	$19,200	$23,800	$24,000	$19,960.40	$ 4,105.18	$342.08	$2,621.36
2-F	5-2	298	298	28,310	28,608	35,462	35,760	29,741.00	6,116.72	509.70	3,905.83
3-F	5-2	300	300	28,500	28,800	35,700	36,000	29,940.60	6,157.77	513.12	3,932.04
4-F	5-2	303	303	28,785	29,088	36,057	36,360	30,240.01	6,219.35	518.25	3,971.36
5-F	5-2	305	305	28,975	29,280	36,295	36,600	30,439.61	6,260.40	521.67	3,997.57
6-F	5-2	308	308	29,260	29,568	36,652	36,960	30,739.02	6,321.98	526.80	4,036.89
7-F	5-2	310	310	29,450	29,760	36,890	37,200	30,938.62	6,363.03	530.22	4,063.11
8-F	5-2	313	313	29,735	30,048	37,247	37,560	31,238.03	6,424.61	535.36	4,102.43
9-F	5-2	315	315	29,925	30,240	37,485	37,800	31,437.63	6,465.66	538.78	4,128.64
10-F	5-2	318	318	30,210	30,528	37,842	38,160	31,737.04	6,527.24	543.91	4,167.96
11-F	5-2	320	320	30,400	30,720	38,080	38,400	31,936.64	6,568.29	547.33	4,194.18
12-F	5-2	323	323	30,685	31,008	38,437	38,760	32,236.05	6,629.87	552.46	4,233.50
14-F	5-2	325	325	30,875	31,200	38,675	39,000	32,435.65	6,670.92	555.88	4,259.71
15-F	5-2	330	330	31,350	31,680	39,270	39,600	32,934.66	6,773.55	564.43	4,325.24
16-F	5-2	340	340	32,300	32,640	40,460	40,800	33,932.68	6,978.81	581.54	4,456.31
17-F	5-2	350	350	33,250	33,600	41,650	42,000	34,930.70	7,184.07	598.64	4,587.38
18-F	5-2-T	365	365	34,675	35,040	43,435	43,800	36,427.73	7,491.95	624.30	4,783.98
19-F	5½-2-T	538	538	51,110	51,648	64,022	64,800	53,693.48	11,042.93	920.20	7,051.46
20-F	5½-2	475	475	45,125	45,600	56,525	57,000	47,405.95	9,749.80	812.44	6,225.73

Legend: "T" denotes Terrace.

(1) Each apartment should be inspected to determine present layout.

(2) Tenants of the Building on the date of presentation of the Plan have the exclusive right for a period of ninety (90) days from said date of presentation to purchase the shares allocated to their apartments for a Total Cash Payment of $96 per share. During said ninety (90) day period, such tenants may finance up to 75% (i.e., up to $72 per share) of said Total Cash Payment under either a five year or a ten year financing plan (see "Financing Arrangements For Tenants in Occupancy" for full details). Prices to non-tenants of the Building are subject to change without prior notice or amendment to the Plan. Prices to tenants in occupancy of the Building are subject to change only by a duly filed amendment to the Plan.

(3) Tenant-shareholders will have no personal liability for the mortgage for payment of the Apartment Corporation's mortgage indebtedness. Interest and amortization payments to be made by the Apartment Corporation are included in the monthly maintenance charges. The amount of mortgage indebtedness shown in this column will be reduced by amortization.

(4) Estimated maintenance charges include the cost of gas furnished to apartments. Tenant-shareholders will be responsible for the cost of electricity in their apartments which is separately metered and for the cost of interior repairs in, and decoration of, their respective apartments, including appliances. These estimates were prepared by Management Corp. for the first year of co-operative operation, assuming same to be the fiscal year from June 1, 1974 to May 31, 1975.

(5) The first year tax deductions are estimated at $13.107 per share, which is equivalent to 64% of the total estimated first year's maintenance charges shown below on the Schedule of Projected Receipts and Expenses for the First Full Year of Cooperative Operation. The estimated tax deductions are based on the full twelve months operation commencing June 1, 1974 and will vary in later years because of changes in the amount of real estate taxes on the Apartment Corporation's property and interest on the Apartment Corporation's mortgage indebtedness. These figures were computed by the Selling Agent and have not been verified by counsel to either the Apartment Corporation or Sponsor-Seller.

two progression. So Apartment 4F has three more shares than 3F; 5F has two more shares than 4F; 6F has three more shares than 5F; and so on. We might ask if 14F is worth 25 more shares than 3F, which is an identical apartment. Those additional shares raise the monthly maintenance $42.76 per month, and the purchase price at least several thousand dollars.

We can also see that the jump in shares from 14F to 16F is 15 shares. The layout and location are identical. We should assess whether the view or some other factor contributes to the higher purchase price and substantially higher maintenance given to the 16th floor. The terraced apartments show a substantial jump in shares, which should reflect the relative value of these units.

In addition, we should consider that outside purchasers pay $23 per share more for their stock than do the tenant purchasers. We should also acquire a copy of the budget for the building when it was still a rental. It should indicate how close the estimated maintenance charges are to the real expenses in previous years. A conversion building can supply much more helpful financial information than a new building, for which all operating costs are strictly estimates.

Exhibit 5.5 shows the monthly expense schedule for a condominium called Sun Club, Inc. If, by simply dividing the square footage of each apartment into the percentage of common elements, we determine that there was no apparent uniform assignment on the basis of square footage, we must then conclude that there was a more subjective method. In a building not assigned on a specific formula basis, you should view several styles of apartments to determine whether the more costly apartments with higher common charges are worth their pricetag. If not, they may remain unsold.

Finally, check the real-estate tax rate in the community where the complex is located. (To locate the appropriate tax information, contact the local town hall.) It is also a good idea to ask the local tax authority about the rates for the last 5 years. This will indicate how you might expect the real-estate taxes on your unit to increase in the future. If the current tax rate differs from that set forth in the monthly charges, calculate the correct maintenance based on the actual tax rate.

COMMON AREA MORTGAGES

Generally, the single largest operating expense of a cooperative or condominium is the servicing of its mortgage. Thus, the terms and conditions of mortgage financing can dramatically affect monthly maintenance charges. If the mortgage is at an interest rate well below the market, it is a form of subsidy. For example, a 5% mortgage when the present going rate is 9% provides a four-point advantage to residents. However, there is a catch. If that 5% mortgage is due to expire in several years, then a purchaser should be aware that maintenance must jump sharply when the mortgage rate returns to the market rate of 9%.

For example, let us consider a building with a $4 million mortgage at 5% interest, which is due in 7 years. At the present time, interest costs are $200,000

EXHIBIT 5.5

SUN CLUB, INC.

Schedule of 446 apartment units; percent of interest in common elements; square foot unit areas; selling price; down payment; maximum mortgage; monthly mortgage payments; estimated monthly charges for common expenses; estimated monthly real estate taxes; total estimated monthly mortgage payments; common expenses and real estate taxes; estimated income tax deductions on monthly basis for the first year of operation.

Floor Apt. No.	Type and Plan Designation	Percent of Common Element	Area (sq. ft.)	Selling Price[1]	25% Down Payment	Maximum Mortgage	Monthly Mortgage Payments 8½% 30 Years[2]	Estimated Monthly Real Estate Taxes[3]	Estimated Monthly Common Charges[4]	Estimated Total Monthly Carrying Charges Including Mortgage Charges and Real Estate Taxes	Estimated Amount of Carrying Charges Deductible for Income Taxes Averaged on a Monthly Basis[5]
7A	2-bdrm-2-bath (Plan A)[6]	.985402	1,700	$75,000.	$18,750.	$56,250.	$432.53	$178.	$ 91.69	$677.67	$576.44
7B	1-bdrm-w/den or 2nd bdrm-2-bath (Plan B)	.906570	1,610	69,000.	17,250.	51,750.	397.93	163.	84.36	622.81	529.56
7C	3-bdrm-2½-bath (Plan C)	1.156205	2,003	88,000.	22,000.	66,000.	507.49	208.	107.58	794.26	675.50
7D	3-bdrm-2½-bath (Plan D)	1.169343	2,003	89,000.	22,250.	66,750.	513.27	211.	108.81	803.94	683.81
7E	1-bdrm-w/den or 2nd bdrm-2-bath (Plan E)	.998541	1,715	76,000.	19,000.	57,000.	438.29	180.	92.91	686.38	583.75
7F	2-bdrm-2-bath (Plan F)	.998541	1,715	76,000.	19,000.	57,000.	438.29	180.	92.91	686.38	583.75
7G	1-bdrm-1-bath (Plan G)	.722628	1,181	55,000.	13,750.	41,250.	317.19	130.	67.24	496.45	422.18
7H	2-bdrm-2-bath (Plan H)	.945985	1,637	72,000.	18,000.	54,000.	415.22	170.	88.02	649.69	552.50
7J	2-bdrm-2½-bath (Plan J)	1.103650	1,864	84,000.	21,000.	63,000.	484.42	199.	102.69	758.61	645.25
7K	1-bdrm-1-bath (Plan K)	.762044	1,315	58,000.	14,500.	43,500.	334.48	137.	70.91	523.42	445.12
7L	2-bdrm-2-bath (Plan L)	.998541	1,732	76,000.	19,000.	57,000.	438.29	180.	92.91	686.38	583.75
7M	1-bdrm-1½-bath (Plan M)	.787393	1,403	60,000.	15,000.	45,000.	346.02	142.	73.27	541.75	460.75

[1]Sponsor reserves the right to change the selling price as initially established.

[2]Based on maximum mortgage for 30 years at 8½% interest per annum: The monthly payments may be larger than as set forth should the interest rate be greater than 8½% or if the term is less than 30 years.

[3]Based on 1975 tax rate of $5.23 per $100 of assessed valuation.

[4]Based on estimates of the various items set forth in Schedule B hereof. These do not include painting, decorating of apartment units or electricity for heating, lighting and cooling of the apartment units which are to be paid separately by the owner of each unit.

[5]This is a total of the estimated annual mortgage interest for the first year, based upon the maximum amount set forth in the column "Maximum Mortgage," averaged on a monthly basis, and the monthly real estate taxes.

[6]Indicates plan designation for individual apartment unit as shown on floor plans.

per year, and principal payments are additional. When the mortgage expires in 7 years and the building must refinance itself at 9% interest, the yearly interest cost alone will be $360,000. Even if there are 320 units in the building, the average maintenance increase from this single item is $500 per unit! Of course, the exact increase will depend on the number of shares allocated to a particular unit in a cooperative, and the percent of ownership in the common elements assigned to a particular unit in a condominium.

Therefore, it is best to purchase in a building that has a long-term mortgage (20 to 25 years) at a favorable interest rate. However, this does not mean that all complexes whose mortgages will shortly be refinanced are a bad buy. You should examine the mortgage to see how closely it resembles current rates. If it is at an abnormally low percentage, recalculate interest costs in the budget to reflect what current costs should be. Then, figure out the impact this would have on your particular unit.

6

NEGOTIATING THE PURCHASE

A thing is worth whatever someone is willing and able to pay for it at the time it is sold. Clearly, buyers are in an inherently better position than sellers. Buyers can determine what they are willing to pay, whereas sellers can only attempt to hit that target without going beyond the abilities and interest of their customers. In addition, buyers can choose the time to purchase.

When you are making an investment as large as a cooperative or condominium, use your position as the buyer to your advantage. Your negotiating success or failure can mean thousands of dollars on the purchase price. This in turn affects the amount of down payment and the net monthly cost. Although it is impossible to discuss the entire art of negotiating in this chapter, below are some helpful hints for your strategy:

Rule 1

Fix the maximum price that you will pay, and stick to it. Don't agree immediately to pay the price the seller is asking. It is customary for a seller to add 5% to 10% to a satisfactory price in anticipation of negotiating downward. Make your bid lower than this, and anticipate having to move upward. But never go beyond the maximum price you fixed in the beginning.

Rule 2

Don't discuss your whole strategy with the broker. Brokers make commissions from completing sales, and they may not always keep a confidence. Don't take it for granted that a broker is correct when he or she states that the seller will not accept less than a particular price.

Rule 3

Supply the broker with a sales pitch to give the seller. Explain to the broker the major flaws you have found in the cooperative or condominium. Never debate these flaws with the broker. Instead, tell the broker to inform the seller that these flaws make your bid quite reasonable.

Rule 4

Find out how much the seller paid—and when. This information is almost always available from local recording records. Most brokers can supply you with the price the seller paid, but will do so only if you ask. Once you know the extent of the seller's profit, it will give you a notion of his or her flexibility. For example, a seller who purchased a condominium unit 8 years ago for $25,000, and is asking $60,000 for it now, is apt to be flexible. On the other hand, a seller who paid $40,000 for a cooperative 2 years ago, spent $5000 on a new kitchen, and is asking $52,000 now, may only be slightly flexible.

Rule 5

Never argue with the seller. You'll lose your advantage if insignificant points turn into matters of honor. If the seller says a new floor cost $1000 but you know from experience that it should cost only $250, be silent. Make a mental note of it, and take the real cost into account when you are formulating your bid. People are attached to where they live and want to sell their home to someone who appears to appreciate their efforts.

Rule 6

Conduct yourself in a businesslike manner. Don't exhibit undue enthusiasm. This does not mean that you should appear to be as hard as stone. It means that you should not make numerous positive statements in earshot of the seller. Such statements only encourage the seller to be less flexible because you seem very eager. Appear to be interested—but only at the right price.

Rule 7

Think everything through overnight. It is amazing how tired one can become during serious negotiations. When you are tired, your mind is not at its best. Try to "sleep on" a proposed counteroffer, and ignore the pressured sales pitch of brokers or sellers who insist that there are other buyers waiting.

Rule 8

Don't bring along children if you are going to discuss purchasing terms with the seller. Children can be a great distraction. They may pressure you, and they may make encouraging comments to the seller, thus making the seller less flexible. For instance, the seller will recognize that buyers want to please their 8-year-old daughter who has already picked out her new room.

Rule 9

Accommodate the seller's needs at the right price. If a seller must move quickly and you can take possession rapidly, use it as a bargaining chip. Likewise, if the seller wishes to remain for several months, use it to your advantage. The seller may choose to accept your bid over a slightly higher bid submitted by a purchaser who won't meet the seller's immediate needs.

Rule 10

Try to include expensive improvements in the sale price. A seller will often include wall-to-wall carpeting, custom-made furniture, and certain appliances in the sale price, if you ask. If not, you can probably purchase them from the seller at a fraction of their replacement cost because of the expense of moving them.

Rule 11

Find out why the seller is moving. In most cases, a seller has a logical reason for wanting to move. If the reason seems far-fetched, however, or if you don't think it fits the seller's circumstances, investigate. This may be your tip-off that something is wrong with the entire cooperative or condominium. On the other hand, it may be your tip-off that the seller has an urgent need to move quickly and will accept a lower price.

Rule 12

Buy in late fall if you possibly can. In many parts of the country, the price of shelter peaks in spring and dips lowest in late fall. One reason for this is that most families want their children settled in a new school before the end of September. Thus, by late fall, many once-potential buyers have completed their purchase. When sellers see fewer potential customers, they may develop a sense of urgency—especially in areas where the winter is quite severe. Spring, on the other hand, marks the beginning of a long selling season, and buyers may feel then that they can afford to wait for their price.

ALLOWING A LAWYER TO NEGOTIATE

If your own skills as a negotiator are not particularly effective, consider allowing an attorney to negotiate the purchase. Chances are that the attorney has experience in real estate as well as in negotiating contracts. There are several subtle advantages to having a third party negotiate with the seller. First, a third party must always consult the actual buyer before agreeing to any offer proposed by the seller. This time lag allows an opportunity for reflection and helps avoid hasty decisions. Second, you gain the insight of an objective observer who is not tied up in the emotion of desiring a particular cooperative or condominium.

7

COMPLETING THE PURCHASE

You should engage a lawyer *before* you decide on a particular cooperative or condominium unit. Provide the lawyer with all of the documents you have gathered and the research data from the worksheets so that he or she can act as an independent adviser as well as a legal representative. Most lawyers are experienced in real-estate transactions, so their opinion of what you are buying is valuable.

Finding a good lawyer is relatively easy. Ask a real-estate broker, a relative, or a banker to make some recommendations. Or, since lawyers are now permitted to advertise, you can also check the advertising in a local newspaper. Then, interview your prospective lawyer to make certain he or she is experienced and knowledgeable. Ask questions about previous experience handling real-estate transactions.

Generally, legal fees for a completed transaction run from 0.5% to 1% of the purchase price. Once you've chosen an attorney, establish a fee, and be certain you understand what will be done for that fee. Try to specify two separate prices: one for reading documents and giving advice, the other for completing the closing.

Finally, don't sign anything without first consulting your lawyer. And remember, skimping on legal counsel is taking a chance on financial ruin.

BINDERS

Avoid signing a binder if you possibly can. Many real-estate brokers prepare a binder that sets forth enough details (i.e., price, parties, date) of the proposed sale that a court may enforce the binder as though it were a contract. In such cases, the parties to the sale are deprived of any opportunity to include necessary language to protect their individual interests. Therefore, never sign a binder before you have shown it to your attorney.

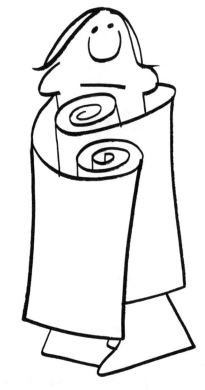

DON'T GET TIED INTO
A CONTRACT UNLESS
YOU COMPLETELY
UNDERSTAND IT!

CONTRACT OF SALE

Documents used in the transfer of ownership such as Contracts of Sale or Deeds are professionally known as *instruments*. Such instruments vary not only because of the different purposes of the seller and buyer, but also because of differences in state, county, and municipal laws. Thus, to avoid problems with the Contract of Sale, it is a good idea to select a local attorney who is aware of the laws and customs of the area where you wish to buy.

The Contract of Sale fixes the obligations of the parties with respect to purchase price, the premises to be conveyed, and the terms of sale. Your attorney will specify any personal property included in the sale and may condition your obligation on certain events, such as the ability to obtain mortgage financing. You can also negotiate with the seller about who pays various settlement fees and other charges, and put it in the contract. Otherwise, much of the language in a Contract of Sale is often found on a printed form. You should read the Contract of Sale and ask your attorney to explain any language that is not clear to you.

805. *Lender's inspection fee* covers inspections, often on newly constructed housing, made by personnel of the lending institution or an outside inspector. The quality and suitability of construction is important if the lender must foreclose, take title, and resell the property.

806. *Mortgage insurance application fee* covers processing the application for private mortgage insurance, which may be required on certain loans. It may cover both the appraisal and application fee.

807. *Assumption fee* is charged for processing papers for cases in which the buyer takes over payments on the prior loan of the seller.

900. *Items required by lender to be paid in advance* include such items as interest, mortgage insurance premium, and hazard insurance premium that the buyer may be required to prepay at the time of settlement. Prepayment gives the lender assurance that adequate insurance is in effect.

901. *Interest* accrues on the mortgage from the date of settlement to the beginning of the period covered by the first monthly payment. Lenders usually require that borrowers pay the interest at settlement. For example, suppose the settlement takes place on April 16, and the first regular monthly payment, to cover interest charges for the month of May, is due May 11. On the settlement date, the lender will collect the interest for the period from April 16 to May 11. So, if the amount borrowed is $30,000 at 9% interest, the interest item would be $184.93. (This amount would be entered on Worksheet 5, line 901.)

902. *Mortgage insurance* protects the lender from loss due to payment default by the owner. The lender may require the buyer to pay the first premium in advance, on the day of settlement. The premium may cover a specific number of months or a year in advance. With this insurance protection, the lender is willing to make a larger loan, thus reducing the down-payment requirements. This type of insurance should not be confused with mortgage life, credit life, or disability insurance, designed to pay off a mortgage in the event of physical disability or death of the borrower.

903. *Hazard insurance* protects the buyer and the lender against losses due to fire, windstorm, and natural hazards. This coverage may be included in a homeowners policy, which insures against additional risks such as personal liability and theft. Lenders often require payment of the first year's premium at settlement.

1000. *Reserves deposited with lenders* (sometimes called *escrow* or *impound* accounts) are funds held in an account by the lender to assure future payment for such recurring items as real-estate taxes and other insurance.

Buyers usually have to pay an initial amount for each of these items to start the reserve account at the time of settlement. A portion of the regular monthly payments required by the lender is added to the reserve account. Thus, when the recurring expense becomes due, the buyer will have saved sufficient funds to pay for it.

1001. *Hazard insurance*. The lender determines the amount of money that must be placed in the reserve in order to pay the next insurance premium when due.

1002. *Mortgage insurance*. Mortgage insurance pays off the remaining balance of the mortgage obligation if the buyer should die. The lender may require that part of the total annual premium be placed in the reserve account at settlement.

1003/1004. *City/county property taxes*. The lender may require a regular monthly payment to the reserve account for property taxes. This payment is added to the monthly mortgage payment amount and raises the total paid each month. However, the lender does not keep the additional portion. Instead, it is escrowed and paid to the appropriate tax authority when property taxes fall due.

1005. *Annual assessments* is a reserve item covering assessments that may be imposed by subdivisions or municipalities for special improvements (such as sidewalks, sewers, or paving) or fees.

OTHER CLOSING COSTS

The settlement fees and services required by a particular lender are not the only expenses paid at closing. In addition to the closing costs just listed, there may be the following:

1. *Survey fee* for a professional survey to determine the exact location of the unit on the property as well as if others have easements or rights-of-way on the property. (See line 1301 on Worksheet 5.)

2. *Termite or pest inspection* determines if there has been any damage to the property that should be corrected. Some lenders require such an inspection, but generally it is the buyer who insists on a right to inspect for insect or pest damage. (See line 1302 on Worksheet 5.)

3. *Mortgage taxes* are required by some state and local authorities at the time a new mortgage is issued by a lending institution. The amount can be quite substantial. (See lines 1202 and 1203 on Worksheet 5.)

4. *Adjustments* are usually made between the buyer and seller for property or other taxes that are paid annually or semiannually. For example, if property taxes are paid once each year on December 31 and the closing occurs on August 1, the seller owes the buyer money. The seller has lived there for 7 months, yet on December 31 the buyer will have to pay a whole year's taxes. In such a case, the seller will either pay or credit to the buyer seven-twelfths of the taxes that must be paid.

5. *Cooperative or condominium processing fees* are often charged by a development to cover the cost of interviewing and investigating prospective buyers. Such fees vary from $25 to $150.

6. *Personal property* such as rugs, draperies, washing machines, and built-in shelving not included in the sales price are paid for by the purchaser.

When you sign the Contract of Sale, it is customary to give the seller or the seller's attorney a deposit of "earnest money," which is about 10% of the purchase price. This money is evidence of your good faith; it should be returnable if you or the seller cannot fulfill all conditions of the contract. For example, if you are unable to obtain mortgage financing at the specific rate, amount, or full term of years set forth in the Contract of Sale, then the monies given upon the signing of the Contract of Sale would be returned, and no rights or obligations would continue under the contract.

SOME WORDS ABOUT TITLE

Title is a legal concept that confers the claim of ownership and possession to property. It also gives owners recourse to legal power to defend their property from others. When you plan to purchase a specific cooperative or condominium, your attorney should do a title search on the premises to determine the chain of ownership. If defects such as lack of clear title are discovered (i.e., there is doubt about the right of the seller to transfer marketable title to you), they are either corrected or the terms of sale are not completed. Defects that cannot be corrected make property less marketable and so less valuable. Even a reasonably thorough title search can fail to discover certain defects in title, such as forgery. Therefore, your attorney will probably advise that you purchase a title insurance policy to guard against any hidden risks. The cost for title search and insurance should be entered next to "1100. Title Charges" on Worksheet 5.

COMMITMENT LETTERS

Most Contracts of Sale, are conditioned on the ability of the purchaser to obtain mortgage financing. They specify a period of time in which the purchaser must find a lending institution willing to extend a mortgage for a particular term of years, at a specific interest rate, and in a certain dollar amount. Purchasers unable to obtain the requisite mortgage have the right to cancel the contract. The lending institution that receives the mortgage application will check up on the credit, employment, and assets of the purchaser and will usually appraise the property. When the lender is satisfied that the loan is worthwhile, a Commitment Letter is issued to the purchaser for a specific mortgage. This completes the condition and assures the parties that a sale will take place according to the terms of the Contract of Sale.

THE CLOSING

Closing is the time when the buyer and seller are ready to complete transfer of the deed to the property and when all of the parties must carry out the terms of the Contract of Sale. If there is an existing mortgage by the seller, it must be satisfied before the lender will issue a new first mortgage. The purchase price due the seller is divided into a portion that satisfies the existing mortgage, and the balance is given to the seller. The following parties are usually present at the closing:

Seller(s)
Attorney of seller
Lending institution of seller
Purchaser(s)
Attorney of purchaser
Lending institution of purchaser
Title insurance company
Broker.

At the closing, all of the settlement services are paid for, the mortgage bond or note is begun, a Deed is given, and the keys are delivered by the seller to the buyer.

Many papers are signed and exchanged between all of the parties. Don't hesitate to ask questions or read documents before you sign them. Expect to write checks to the title insurance company, your lending institution, your attorney, and other parties.

EXHIBIT 7.1

FORM APPROVED OMB NO. 63-R-1501

A.		B. TYPE OF LOAN	

A.

U.S. DEPARTMENT OF HOUSING AND URBAN DEVELOPMENT

SETTLEMENT STATEMENT

X 88 p. 1, Julius Blumberg, Inc., NYC 10013

B. TYPE OF LOAN

1. ☐ FHA 2. ☐ FMHA 3. ☐ CONV. UNINS.
4. ☐ VA 5. ☐ CONV. INS.

6. FILE NUMBER: 7. LOAN NUMBER:

8. MORTGAGE INSURANCE CASE NUMBER:

C. NOTE: This form is furnished to give you a statement of actual settlement costs. Amounts paid to and by the settlement agent are shown. Items marked *"(p.o.c.)"* were paid outside the closing; they are shown here for informational purposes and are not included in totals.

D. NAME OF BORROWER:	E. NAME OF SELLER:	F. NAME OF LENDER:

G. PROPERTY LOCATION:	H. SETTLEMENT AGENT:	PLACE OF SETTLEMENT
	I. SETTLEMENT DATE:	

J. SUMMARY OF BORROWER'S TRANSACTION		K. SUMMARY OF SELLER'S TRANSACTION	
100. GROSS AMOUNT DUE FROM BORROWER:		**400. GROSS AMOUNT DUE TO SELLER:**	
101. Contract sales price		401. Contract sales price	
102. Personal property		402. Personal property	
103. Settlement charges to borrower *(line 1400)*		403.	
104.		404.	
105.		405.	
Adjustments for items paid by seller in advance		*Adjustments for items paid by seller in advance*	
106. City/town taxes to		406. City/town taxes to	
107. County taxes to		407. County taxes to	
108. Assessments to		408. Assessments to	
109.		409.	
110.		410.	
111.		411.	
112.		412.	
120. GROSS AMOUNT DUE FROM BORROWER		**420. GROSS AMOUNT DUE TO SELLER**	
200. AMOUNTS PAID BY OR IN BEHALF OF BORROWER:		**500. REDUCTIONS IN AMOUNT DUE TO SELLER:**	
201. Deposit or earnest money		501. Excess deposit (see instructions)	
202. Principal amount of new loan(s)		502. Settlement charges to seller *(line 1400)*	
203. Existing loan(s) taken subject to		503. Existing loan(s) taken subject to	
204.		504. Payoff of first mortgage loan	
205.		505. Payoff of second mortgage loan	
206.		506.	
207.		507.	
208.		508.	
209.		509.	
Adjustments for items unpaid by seller:		*Adjustments for items unpaid by seller:*	
210. City/town taxes to		510. City/town taxes to	
211. County taxes to		511. County taxes to	
212. Assessments to		512. Assessments to	
213.		513.	
214.		514.	
215.		515.	
216.		516.	
217.		517.	
218.		518.	
219.		519.	
220. TOTAL PAID BY/FOR BORROWER		**520. TOTAL REDUCTION AMOUNT DUE SELLER**	
300. CASH AT SETTLEMENT FROM/TO BORROWER		**600. CASH AT SETTLEMENT TO/FROM SELLER**	
301. Gross amount due from borrower *(line 120)*		601. Gross amount due to seller *(line 420)*	
302. Less amounts paid by/for borrower *(line 220)*	(	602. Less reductions in amt. due to seller *(line 520)*	(
303. CASH (☐ FROM) (☐ TO) BORROWER		**603. CASH (☐ TO) (☐ FROM) SELLER**	

EXHIBIT 7.1 *(Continued)*

HUD-1 REV. 5/76

L. SETTLEMENT CHARGES		PAID FROM BORROWER'S FUNDS AT SETTLEMENT	PAID FROM SELLER'S FUNDS AT SETTLEMENT
700. TOTAL SALES/BROKER'S COMMISSION based on price $ @ % =			
Division of Commission (line 700) as follows:			
701. $ to			
702. $ to			
703. Commission paid at Settlement			
704.			
800. ITEMS PAYABLE IN CONNECTION WITH LOAN			
801. Loan Origination Fee %			
802. Loan Discount %			
803. Appraisal Fee to			
804. Credit Report to			
805. Lender's Inspection Fee			
806. Mortgage Insurance Application Fee to			
807. Assumption Fee			
808.			
809.			
810.			
811.			
900. ITEMS REQUIRED BY LENDER TO BE PAID IN ADVANCE			
901. Interest from to @ $ /day			
902. Mortgage Insurance Premium for months to			
903. Hazard Insurance Premium for years to			
904. years to			
905.			
1000. RESERVES DEPOSITED WITH LENDER			
1001. Hazard insurance months @ $ per month			
1002. Mortgage insurance months @ $ per month			
1003. City property taxes months @ $ per month			
1004. County property taxes months @ $ per month			
1005. Annual assessments months @ $ per month			
1006. months @ $ per month			
1007. months @ $ per month			
1008. months @ $ per month			
1100. TITLE CHARGES			
1101. Settlement or closing fee to			
1102. Abstract or title search to			
1103. Title examination to			
1104. Title insurance binder to			
1105. Document preparation to			
1106. Notary fees to			
1107. Attorney's fees to			
(includes above items numbers;)			
1108. Title insurance to			
(includes above items numbers;)			
1109. Lender's coverage $			
1110. Owner's coverage $			
1111.			
1112.			
1113.			
1200. GOVERNMENT RECORDING AND TRANSFER CHARGES			
1201. Recording fees: Deed $; Mortgage $; Releases $			
1202. City/county tax/stamps: Deed $; Mortgage $			
1203. State tax/stamps: Deed $; Mortgage $			
1204.			
1205.			
1300. ADDITIONAL SETTLEMENT CHARGES			
1301. Survey to			
1302. Pest inspection to			
1303.			
1304.			
1305.			
1400. TOTAL SETTLEMENT CHARGES *(enter on lines 103, Section J and 502, Section K)*			

We, the undersigned, identified as Borrower in section D hereof and Seller in section E hereof, hereby acknowledge receipt of this completed Uniform Settlement Statement (pages 1 & 2) on 19

Borrower: **Seller:**

_____   _____

_____   _____

UNIFORM SETTLEMENT STATEMENT

Exhibit 7.1 is an example of a *Uniform Settlement Statement*, which is provided to the buyer at the closing. Observe that Sections A through I contain information about the loan and the parties involved in the settlement. Sections J and K summarize all monies that are adjusted between the purchaser, who is called the *borrower*, and the seller. Section L has a part on broker's commission and lists the information gathered in Worksheet 5 on settlement services required by the lending institution you have chosen.

ESCROW CLOSINGS

In some parts of the United States, there is no actual meeting for a closing. Instead, an escrow agent such as a lender, title company, attorney, or escrow company completes the sale under the terms of an escrow agreement. The escrow agent requests title reports, drafts documents, pays off loans, acquires insurance, settles costs of services, and records the appropriate documents. When all papers and monies have been properly deposited and executed, the escrow is *closed*. In such cases, the escrow agent sends the Uniform Settlement Statement to the buyer by mail.

8

The following chapter presents nine common situations that confront the buyers of condominiums and cooperatives. If you have absorbed the material presented so far, you should be able to spot the potential pitfalls in each situation. These are all actual cases, although each has been simplified to illustrate important points.

EXAMPLE 1

One summer, Pam, a suburban school teacher, bought a condominium that was under construction. The sales agent promised that the unit would be completed by early fall. Nothing in the contract of sale guaranteed occupancy on a specific date. In October, Pam gave up her apartment so that she would not have to renew the lease, put her furniture in storage, and moved into a hotel. In March, the condominium was still not available for occupancy, yet Pam risked losing her $3700 down payment if she tried to rescind the contract.

Conclusion: Don't depend on oral promises for a date of occupancy. Have a firm date specified in the contract of sale, with the option to rescind if it is not met.

EXAMPLE 2

Bob and Fran saw a model townhouse unit that had everything they'd always wanted—beautiful carpeting, high-quality kitchen appliances, built-in hardwood shelves in several rooms, carved wooden doors, customized bathrooms, and a magnificent fireplace. The exterior had a slate roof with copper gutters and drainpipes. The agent said that the developer was only going to build 12 condominium townhouses and that only one more could be sold. Since the developer was providing financing, they were told they could save a legal fee for their own lawyer, and the bank's. Since Bob and Fran had already saved the down payment, they decided on the spot to buy. When the townhouse was finally constructed, however, it had none of the luxury amenities shown in the model, and the kitchen appliances were strictly bottom of the line. In the meantime, the mortgage that Bob and Fran signed had been sold to a local bank so they could not hold up their payments.

Conclusions: Know what you are buying, and have it specified in detail in the sales contract. Include model numbers and names for all kitchen appliances.

Never buy without consulting your own attorney.

EXAMPLE 3

Jim and Paula had enough of renting and decided to take advantage of the luxury and tax breaks of an urban high-rise cooperative. Since their taste tends toward the modern, they were fascinated by a new, strikingly designed building, which had a very different shape. Moreover, they just loved a particular apartment. The sales agent told Jim and Paula that they had to act immediately to beat other buyers who were interested in the same unit. They hired a lawyer and closed on the apartment within a month. Two years later, half of the building was still not sold, and the maintenance costs were twice as high as Jim and Paula had wanted to pay. The far-out design of the building had produced numerous apartments that were unsalable except at distressed prices. In addition, upkeep on the exterior of the building proved very expensive because the construction materials were more aesthetically pleasing than practical.

Conclusions: Beware of high-styled buildings unless you make a complete inspection and are sure that the entire structure is practical.

Remember, high-styled architecture often requires expensive upkeep.

EXAMPLE 4

The Muccinos were getting on in years and wished to retire to a warm southern climate. Since they had a limited income, they chose a Florida condominium with maintenance charges within their means. The project had a swimming pool and a clubhouse with exercise machines, which were also important features in the Muccinos' decision to buy.

To save money, the Muccinos engaged a local lawyer who was recommended by the developer for his low fees. The condominium was purchased, and the couple moved in. When Mr. Muccino went to use the pool, however, he was informed that the recreational facilities were not owned by the condominium. The developer owned the pool and clubhouse, and charged a monthly membership fee that was almost equal to the monthly maintenance charge. The Muccinos could not afford to pay the extra cost.

Conclusion: Find out all of the details about recreational facilities.

EXAMPLE 5

Steven and Karen always wanted a penthouse in Manhattan. After much searching, they finally found exactly what they desired located on the 20th floor in a cooperative apartment building. The elevator buttons indicated that the 20th floor was the last stop, which was how they wanted it. Steven and Karen showed the Proprietary Lease, Bylaws, prospectus, and financing instruments to their attorney, who advised them that all was in order. Thus, they purchased the penthouse.

After they moved in, they discovered that a salable studio apartment was located over their bedroom.

Why hadn't they discovered the studio *before* moving in? It was not serviced by any elevators. In addition, it was listed in an obscure manner in the schedule of details on all apartments.

Conclusion: Nothing takes the place of a thorough physical inspection of a cooperative's building.

EXAMPLE 6

Don and Jenny both worked full-time. Because they had no deductions, they paid sky-high taxes. So, they decided to look at a condominium. The sales agent stressed all of the deductions available to condominium owners. Without investigating further, Don and Jenny bought an $85,000 unit, with 10% down and the balance financed by the seller at 8% per year. Delighted with their interest and maintenance deductions, they broke their existing lease and moved into their condominium. Three years later, when Jenny left her job to care for their first baby, Don's salary barely covered the carrying costs. In addition, they paid $20,000 too much on their impulsive purchase and had to sell the condominium at a huge loss.

Conclusions: Look into the future before you buy something that requires two incomes to maintain it.

Take the time to shop around. Do not act on impulse.

Tax savings are not as important as the real value of a cooperative or condominium. Don't be so swayed by the immediate tax advantages that you forget the importance of the purchase price.

EXAMPLE 7

Al and Judy were loaded with cash after selling their family home in Connecticut. They wanted a winter apartment in Florida, in a building with prestige. Without consulting their lawyer, they signed a binder and put a $15,000 deposit on a unit in a building in which a well-known actor was on the board of directors. The aura of prosperity made them feel that they were making a sound investment.

For the summer, Al and Judy wanted a lakeside condominium in New Hampshire. Judy located the perfect townhouse development, which was being constructed by a friendly local builder. The basement was not completed, some doors were missing, and the driveway had to be paved. Nevertheless, the builder said that he needed a deposit immediately because other buyers were interested in the unit. Al and Judy gave him a $10,000 deposit, expecting to close the deal and be given title on the townhouse in about 2 months.

Al and Judy then retained an excellent attorney who carefully examined the various documents. The attorney discovered that the prestige building in Florida had its owners locked into a 25-year management agreement at an exorbitant price. It also rented its pool and recreation facilities on a 99-year lease from the developer at an unreasonable price. When the attorney tried to get the deposit refunded, the seller refused. The binder spelled out all of the necessary terms for a sale of the condominium. The lawyer will have to sue, and Al and Judy may lose their deposit or be forced to go through with the purchase.

On the New Hampshire townhouse, all of the documents seemed in order. When the attorney tried to phone the builder to proceed with the purchase, however, it was discovered that the builder had filed for bankruptcy. Al and Judy's deposit money was lost.

Conclusions: Never sign anything unless your attorney has approved it.

Prominent people do not necessarily assure a good investment.

Don't give a deposit directly to a builder. Put it in an escrow account pending completion of the sale.

EXAMPLE 8

Bert and George are bachelors who like to ski. Since they go to the same ski area almost every winter weekend, they decided to purchase a condominium in a development near the slopes. They believed this would save them from having to make motel reservations every week. They would also build up some equity. The sales agent told them that, if they bought, they could rent out the unit for one month during the winter and all summer, thus covering all the expenses. George thought that his half of the $350 per month carrying costs was too high for his budget, but Bert talked him into buying, reminding him of the sales agent's assurances about the ease of rental. A year later, however, there were no renters in sight. George had problems making the payments on his share of the condominium, and Bert had to put up the shortfall. In addition, it was a bad winter for skiing, and so they got little use out of the condominium.

Conclusions: Never buy a vacation cooperative or condominium if you cannot afford to maintain it without rental income.

It is usually best not to have multiple owners.

EXAMPLE 9

Art and Marcia were a busy couple who spent 12 hours a day in their own business. When they decided to buy a home, they contacted one broker and spent only two weekends searching. The condominium unit they chose was lovely, but the couple failed to allot the time to explore the surrounding community. Within 2 years, a factory had been built directly across the street, and zoning had been downgraded to accommodate commercial enterprises. As a result, the value of units in their condominium development fell dramatically.

Conclusions: When buying shelter, remember that its value can decline rapidly if the character of the neighborhood changes.

A thorough inspection of a community will usually give advance warning of any imminent changes from residential to commercial zoning.

APPENDIX I

COOPERATIVE AND CONDOMINIUM VOCABULARY

Abstract of Title
A document ordered by the buyer's attorney for a closing of the sale. It contains a list of all instruments, legal claims, and encumbrances on the property that occurred because of previous Chain of Titles.

Acceleration Clause
A clause in the mortgage contract that serves to make the entire balance outstanding due and immediately payable if there has been a breach of the mortgage contract by the purchaser.

Adjustments at Closing
The apportionment between the buyer and the seller, as of the date of the Closing of Title, of expenses such as maintenance, taxes, prepaid charges, and oil.

Amortization
The gradual repayment of a mortgage debt on a payment schedule, which is usually once per month.

Apartment Corporation
The corporation that supervises the operation of a cooperative building or project.

Apartment Corporation Bylaws
The rules governing the rights, powers, and duties of officers, directors, and stockholders of the Apartment Corporation of a cooperative. The Bylaws provide for annual meetings, voting, inspection of elections, filling vacancies on the Board of Directors, compensation, indemnification of directors,

fiscal years, and other such procedural problems.

Assessed Value The value placed on realty by an elected or appointed local official. It is usually reported as value of the land and value of the improvements on the land. The assessed value is used to determine the taxes that the community will place on the property.

b

Binder An agreement, drawn up between the buyer and seller of property, which secures the sale until the parties can go to contract. Most often, the binder is not refundable if the buyer decides not to go ahead with the purchase.

Blanket Mortgage A mortgage covering the entire property. In a condominium, when an apartment is sold, the individual unit will be released from the overall lien of the blanket mortgage when a required payment is made to the owner of the mortgage. The individual unit then will usually have its own mortgage.

Board of Directors The group of individuals chosen by the owners of a cooperative or condominium to supervise the affairs of the project.

Broker's Agreement A written agreement between the seller and broker that specifies the commission to be paid and length of time of the agreement. There are three kinds of broker's agreements:
1. Nonexclusive agency: The broker will not be the only broker showing the property and able to earn the commission.
2. Exclusive agency: The broker will be the only broker to show the property and earn a commission. The seller may also show the property, and, if the seller locates a buyer without the aid of the broker, no commission is earned.
3. Exclusive right to sell: Regardless of who sells the property, the broker will earn the commission.

Building Code   The details of how a building is to be erected in a specific community. Since requirements vary, the ordinance is usually enforced by a local building inspector.

Chain of Title   A history of all prior owners up to the present owner who have been recorded in public records.

Closing   The final completion of the sale of real property where the balance of money above the down payment is exchanged for the deed. In the case of a cooperative, there is an assignment of stock and the proprietary lease to the purchaser.

Closing Statement   A detailed presentation, drawn by an attorney, that explains the details of a transfer of title.

Commitment Letter   A letter from a bank or other financial institution that states that a mortgage loan will be extended under specific terms and conditions.

Common Areas   Property held jointly with one or more other persons.

Condominium   A form of co-ownership over multiple-unit property where the owner-occupier owns an undivided ownership of the grounds and common areas with other unit owners. The purchaser of a condominium receives a separate deed for a specific apartment unit and a prorated interest in the common property.

Contract of Sale   A contract that fixes the obligations of the seller and purchaser for the transfer of title to real estate.

Conversion Plan   The plan by which a building on an ordinary lease basis converts to cooperative occupancy.

Cooperative Apartment   The purchaser of a cooperative apartment buys shares of the Apartment Corporation which owns the building or project in which his or her apartment is located. Ownership of the prorated shares in the total project entitles the purchaser to a special lease of the apartment which is commonly known as a Proprietary Lease. As a shareholder, he or she will have the right to vote annually for the Board of Directors who will conduct the affairs of the Apartment Corporation.

d

Declaration

The instrument that creates the condominium form of ownership. See also **Master Deed.**

Deed

The legal instrument that embodies ownership of property and passes title from the seller to the purchaser.

Down Payment

The amount of money (usually 10% of the purchase price) paid or escrowed on signing of a Contract of Sale. The contract usually contains conditions which must be fulfilled or else the seller must refund the down payment to the purchaser. Some common conditions are: the obtaining of a mortgage, termite inspection, engineering inspection, and getting clear title.

Easement

The right of one party to use the property of another.

Equity

The money interest that an owner holds in a property. Thus, a condominium worth $80,000 on the open market, with a mortgage debt of $50,000, would have an owner's equity of $30,000.

Escalator Clause

A clause in a lease that provides for increased rental payments in accordance with an index such as the consumer price index. These clauses must be carefully considered because they can dramatically affect monthly charges during an inflationary period.

Escrow Agreement

An agreement in which an agent, usually a bank, broker, or attorney, holds on to a down payment while the conditions in the Contract of Sale are being acted upon. It is generally best to escrow a down payment and thus avoid problems that may arise from try-ing to force the seller to return money because a condition cannot be met.

Fee Simple	Outright ownership of land in the highest degree. The only limitations on this type of ownership are governmental limitations.
Financial Statements	A detailed listing of the income and expenses for a given year of operation of a cooperative or condominium. There are usually accompanying notes explaining the details of all money flows.
Fixtures	Property that is attached to realty in a way that would cause substantial damage if it were removed.

Going to Contract	The formal signing of a written contract for sale of real property. All of the terms and conditions of the sale are specified in detail, and a date is set for a closing where monies will be exchanged for the deed or other evidence of ownership. At the time of going to contract, a down payment of 10% of the purchase price is given to the seller or an escrow agent.
Ground Lease	A lease in which the underlying land is rented and an annual ground rent paid for the use of the land. Many cooperatives and condominiums are built on rented ground. This is an essential element to consider before purchase. An Escalator Clause in a ground lease can increase maintenance charges to a level that might decrease the value of the home.

House Committee	In many cooperatives and condominiums, the house committee is an advisory group selected to consider matters relating to quality of life. The house committee solicits the opinions of owners on decorating ideas in common areas, convenience expenses, and a wide range of other topics. Membership is usually voluntary according to the interest of individual unit owners.

	House Rules	The rules adopted by the Apartment Corporation and contained in the Proprietary Lease of a cooperative. The owner of the cooperative is responsible for compliance with these rules as though they were part of a lease contract.

i

	Indenture	A legal term for a formal, written instrument.

j

	Joint Tenancy	Two or more individuals hold equal title to real property whereby, if one owner dies, his or her interest goes to the surviving owner(s). There is personal liability for all expenses.

l

	Lessee	The tenant in leased space.
	Lessor	The landlord in leased space.
	Lien	A legal claim on another's property as security for the payment of a mortgage or other debt. If necessary, the property may be seized and sold to satisfy the debt.

	Maintenance	The rent payable under a Proprietary lease to the Apartment Corporation or to a condominium. Maintenance charges are a proportionate share of the cash requirements for the operation and maintenance of the building or project assigned to each unit in it.
	Management Agreement	A contract between the owners and an outside agent, which outlines the obligations and compensation of the agent. This is an important part of the operating expenses of most cooperatives and condominiums. The management agreement should be studied to determine if it will excessively raise monthly maintenance charges.
	Master Deed	The overall declarations of legal right, title obligation, and immunity for those who participate in condominium ownership. Sometimes called the *declaration*.

Mechanic's Lien	A legal claim on property by a person who furnishes labor and materials that have improved the property.
Monthly Cash Flow	The amount of actual dollars needed to pay maintenance, taxes, mortgage, and other expenses on a cooperative or condominium.
Monthly Expense Schedule	A chart with a series of columns that indicate the number of shares assigned to a cooperative unit, or the percent of common areas assigned to a condominium unit, and the monthly charges that arise from common ownership. Financial information on mortgage financing is often included.
Mortgage	An instrument that pledges property to a financial institution or a person as security for a loan.
Mortgagee	The lender of funds that are secured by a mortgage.
Mortgagor	The borrower of funds secured by a mortgage.
Net Monthly Cost	The actual cost for maintenance, taxes, mortgage, and other expenses on a cooperative or condominium after all available tax benefits are subtracted from monthly cash flow.
Prepayment Penalty Clause	A clause in a mortgage contract that requires the mortgagor to pay a penalty if the mortgage is prepaid prior to its maturity. Most mortgage contracts have such a dollar penalty in the first year of the mortgage.
Points	A disguised form of interest, when a lender requires a set fee from the borrower in advance of the mortgage loan. One point is 1% of the amount of the loan.
Proprietary Lease	The document providing for occupancy of a unit in a cooperative apartment. It provides for payment of maintenance, services, House Rules, repairs, use of the premises, subletting, assignment, alterations, notices, and many other basic functions that affect a unit in a cooperative. A Proprietary Lease is often

quite long and should be studied in detail. All tenant-stockholders should be subject to substantially the same Proprietary Lease.

Pro Rata	Divided or assessed proportionally.
Prospectus	The offering document in a condominium or cooperative, which sets forth the terms for purchase of a unit.
Purchase Money Mortgage	A mortgage given by the seller at the time of closing, which takes the place of cash due at the closing.

Recording	Having a written instrument, placed in the public records. Deeds, mortgage liens, and other instruments are usually recorded in the county clerk's office or in the county courthouse.
RESPA	Real Estate Settlement Procedures Act, which requires a lender to give a good-faith estimate of settlement costs and an informational booklet at the time of submission of a loan application.
Restrictive Covenant	A limitation in a deed that requires property to be used or not to be used in some stipulated manner.
Right of First Refusal	A right that provides that prior to any transfer of shares in a cooperative, or deed in a condominium, to a prospective buyer, the shares or deed must be offered to the Board of Directors at the price that the prospective buyer is willing to pay.
Satisfaction of a Mortgage	A legal instrument that discharges a mortgage lien. It is often publicly recorded.
Settlement Costs	The costs paid at a closing to enable the completion of the sale. They include legal fees, recording of mortgage fee, mortgage tax, cost of title search and title insurance, the purchaser's reimbursement of seller's prepaid taxes and bank charges.
Special Assessment	A special charge to the stockholders in a cooperative or owners in a condominium for a particular repair or improvement.

Sponsor-Seller   The developer of a cooperative or a condominium building or project. Sometimes it is the builder, and other times it is simply an investor, who purchases an existing building and converts it into a cooperative or condominium.

Stock Pledge   The document that pledges the stock from a cooperative apartment as security for a loan.

Subject to a Mortgage   In the purchase of a piece of property that already has a mortgage, the purchaser assumes the mortgage obligation of the former owner.

Survey   An engineering examination of property that identifies its boundaries and the location of structures on the property.

Tenants-in-Common   A group of persons acquire interest in real estate at the same time under a single deed. They need not all have equal interests, and there is no survivorship feature as in Joint Tenancy. All tenants-in-common are liable for their proportionate share of expenses and are able to dispose of their interest as they see fit.

Tenant-in-Occupancy   A tenant living in an apartment that is converted to cooperative ownership.

Tenant-Stockholder   An individual who is a shareholder in a cooperative housing corporation.

Title Insurance   A special kind of insurance that protects the purchaser of real property against defects in title that may be passed from the seller of the property.

Title Search   An examination of the title of the owner of real property from the public records to determine if it is free and clear of liens and other encumbrances. Such a search is usually necessary before title insurance may be obtained to guard against taking imperfect title from the seller.

Townhouse   An attached or separate house in a row of two or more. Most townhouses are two or three stories high, with the living area on the main floor and the bedrooms upstairs. In certain parts of the country, they are called *villas* or *town-home apartments*.

 Voting Rights

The right of a stockholder in a cooperative or of an owner in a condominium to determine matters concerning operation of the property.

 Warranty Deed

A deed that contains specific promises, called *warranties*, made by the seller to the purchaser.

 Zoning

The wide variety of controls that are exercised over real property by the local community for protection of the public.

APPENDIX II

MONTHLY MORTGAGE COSTS PER THOUSAND DOLLARS INCLUDING INTEREST

To use these tables, locate the interest rate on your mortgage along the top line and the term of the mortgage in the left-hand column. The number at the intersection is your monthly cost per thousand dollars for principal and interest. Multiply the number times the thousands of dollars in your mortgage.

Example: A $51,000 mortgage at 8½% for a term of 20 years:

$$\$8.68 \times 51 = \$442.68/\text{month}.$$

Example: A $32,000 mortgage at 7¼% for a term of 30 years:

$$\$6.83 \times 32 = \$218.56/\text{month}.$$

AMORTIZATION TABLES

MONTHLY INSTALLMENT PER THOUSAND DOLLARS INCLUDING INTEREST AT—

Term of Mortgage Years	Months	No. of Payments	5%	5¼%	5½%	5¾%	6%	6¼%	6½%	6¾%	7%	7¼%	7½%	7¾%	8%	8¼%	8½%	8¾%	9%	9¼%	9½%	9¾%
40	0	480	4.83	4.99	5.16	5.33	5.51	5.68	5.86	6.04	6.22	6.40	6.59	6.77	6.96	7.15	7.34	7.53	7.72	7.91	8.11	8.30
39	11	479	4.83	5.00	5.17	5.34	5.51	5.69	5.86	6.04	6.22	6.40	6.59	6.77	6.96	7.15	7.34	7.53	7.72	7.91	8.11	8.30
39	10	478	4.83	5.00	5.17	5.34	5.51	5.69	5.86	6.04	6.22	6.41	6.59	6.78	6.96	7.15	7.34	7.53	7.72	7.91	8.11	8.30
39	9	477	4.84	5.00	5.17	5.34	5.52	5.69	5.87	6.05	6.23	6.41	6.59	6.78	6.96	7.15	7.34	7.53	7.72	7.92	8.11	8.30
39	8	476	4.84	5.01	5.17	5.35	5.52	5.69	5.87	6.05	6.23	6.41	6.59	6.78	6.97	7.15	7.34	7.53	7.73	7.92	8.11	8.31
39	7	475	4.84	5.01	5.18	5.35	5.52	5.70	5.87	6.05	6.23	6.41	6.60	6.78	6.97	7.16	7.35	7.54	7.73	7.92	8.11	8.31
39	6	474	4.85	5.01	5.18	5.35	5.52	5.70	5.88	6.06	6.23	6.42	6.60	6.78	6.97	7.16	7.35	7.54	7.73	7.92	8.11	8.31
39	5	473	4.85	5.02	5.18	5.35	5.53	5.70	5.88	6.06	6.24	6.42	6.60	6.79	6.97	7.16	7.35	7.54	7.73	7.92	8.12	8.31
39	4	472	4.85	5.02	5.19	5.36	5.53	5.70	5.88	6.06	6.24	6.42	6.60	6.79	6.97	7.16	7.35	7.54	7.73	7.92	8.12	8.31
39	3	471	4.86	5.02	5.19	5.36	5.53	5.71	5.88	6.06	6.24	6.42	6.61	6.79	6.98	7.16	7.35	7.54	7.73	7.92	8.12	8.31
39	2	470	4.86	5.03	5.19	5.36	5.54	5.71	5.89	6.06	6.24	6.43	6.61	6.79	6.98	7.17	7.35	7.54	7.74	7.93	8.12	8.32
39	1	469	4.86	5.03	5.20	5.37	5.54	5.71	5.89	6.07	6.25	6.43	6.61	6.79	6.98	7.17	7.36	7.55	7.74	7.93	8.12	8.32
39	0	468	4.87	5.03	5.20	5.37	5.54	5.72	5.89	6.07	6.25	6.43	6.61	6.80	6.98	7.17	7.36	7.55	7.74	7.93	8.12	8.32
38	11	467	4.87	5.03	5.20	5.37	5.54	5.72	5.89	6.07	6.25	6.43	6.62	6.80	6.99	7.17	7.36	7.55	7.74	7.93	8.13	8.32
38	10	466	4.87	5.04	5.21	5.38	5.55	5.72	5.90	6.07	6.25	6.43	6.62	6.80	6.99	7.17	7.36	7.55	7.74	7.93	8.13	8.32
38	9	465	4.88	5.04	5.21	5.38	5.55	5.72	5.90	6.08	6.26	6.44	6.62	6.80	6.99	7.18	7.36	7.55	7.74	7.94	8.13	8.32
38	8	464	4.88	5.04	5.21	5.38	5.55	5.73	5.90	6.08	6.26	6.44	6.62	6.81	6.99	7.18	7.37	7.56	7.75	7.94	8.13	8.33
38	7	463	4.88	5.05	5.22	5.38	5.56	5.73	5.91	6.08	6.26	6.44	6.62	6.81	7.00	7.18	7.37	7.56	7.75	7.94	8.13	8.33
38	6	462	4.89	5.05	5.22	5.39	5.56	5.73	5.91	6.09	6.26	6.45	6.63	6.81	7.00	7.18	7.37	7.56	7.75	7.94	8.13	8.33
38	5	461	4.89	5.05	5.22	5.39	5.56	5.74	5.91	6.09	6.27	6.45	6.63	6.81	7.00	7.19	7.37	7.56	7.75	7.94	8.14	8.33
38	4	460	4.89	5.06	5.23	5.39	5.57	5.74	5.91	6.09	6.27	6.45	6.63	6.82	7.00	7.19	7.38	7.56	7.75	7.95	8.14	8.33
38	3	459	4.90	5.06	5.23	5.40	5.57	5.74	5.92	6.09	6.27	6.65	6.63	6.82	7.00	7.19	7.38	7.57	7.76	7.95	8.14	8.33
38	2	458	4.90	5.07	5.23	5.40	5.57	5.74	5.92	6.10	6.28	6.46	6.64	6.82	7.01	7.19	7.38	7.57	7.76	7.95	8.14	8.33
38	1	457	4.90	5.07	5.24	5.40	5.58	5.75	5.92	6.10	6.28	6.46	6.64	6.82	7.01	7.19	7.38	7.57	7.76	7.95	8.14	8.34
38	0	456	4.91	5.07	5.24	5.41	5.58	5.75	5.93	6.10	6.28	6.46	6.64	6.83	7.01	7.20	7.38	7.57	7.76	7.95	8.15	8.34
37	11	455	4.91	5.08	5.24	5.41	5.58	5.75	5.93	6.11	6.28	6.46	6.64	6.83	7.01	7.20	7.39	7.57	7.76	7.95	8.15	8.34
37	10	454	4.92	5.08	5.25	5.41	5.58	5.76	5.93	6.11	6.29	6.47	6.65	6.83	7.01	7.20	7.39	7.58	7.77	7.96	8.15	8.34
37	9	453	4.92	5.08	5.25	5.42	5.59	5.76	5.93	6.11	6.29	6.47	6.65	6.83	7.02	7.20	7.39	7.58	7.77	7.96	8.15	8.34
37	8	452	4.92	5.09	5.25	5.42	5.59	5.76	5.94	6.11	6.29	6.47	6.65	6.84	7.02	7.21	7.39	7.58	7.77	7.96	8.15	8.35
37	7	451	4.93	5.09	5.26	5.42	5.59	5.77	5.94	6.12	6.29	6.47	6.66	6.84	7.02	7.21	7.39	7.58	7.77	7.96	8.15	8.35
37	6	450	4.93	5.09	5.26	5.43	5.60	5.77	5.94	6.12	6.30	6.48	6.66	6.84	7.02	7.21	7.40	7.58	7.77	7.96	8.16	8.35
37	5	449	4.93	5.10	5.26	5.43	5.60	5.77	5.95	6.12	6.30	6.48	6.66	6.84	7.03	7.21	7.40	7.59	7.78	7.97	8.16	8.35

SELECTING A LENDER

The first place to look for financing is to the sponsor of the cooperative or condominium, as sponsors often have several different financing packages available for qualified purchasers. Many times, sponsors use attractive financing with low down payments to aid in the sale of units. If you are purchasing a unit from an individual seller, see if the mortgage is assignable and whether its terms are attractive compared to those available from regular mortgage sources. If neither of these options is available, then you will have to seek a loan from a financial institution.

All lenders are not alike. The price of settlement services, which will be discussed in detail in this chapter, can vary greatly. In any case, the federal Real Estate Settlement Procedures Act (RESPA) will help protect you. When you submit a written application for a loan, the lender is required to give you a booklet on settlement costs. In addition, lenders must give you a good-faith estimate for each settlement charge that they anticipate you will pay. Since charges vary by locality, this service is extremely helpful.

You may also want to request a truth-in-lending statement when you apply for a mortgage loan. This will disclose the annual percentage rate you will pay on the outstanding balance. The annual percentage rate may be higher than the contract rate in your mortgage because it includes discount points, financing charges, and certain other fees that the lender requires.

You should use Worksheet 5 to compile loan information and to list settlement charges that you will have to pay to different lending institutions. The following items will enable you to complete the worksheet. The numbers for each item below correspond to a line number on Worksheet 5. Remember, this is a complete listing, and it is unlikely a single lender will require more than a few of these fees.

800. *Items payable in connection with a loan* are the fees that lenders charge to process, approve, and make a mortgage loan.

801. *Loan origination* covers the lender's administrative costs in processing the loan. Often expressed as a percentage of the loan, the fee will vary among lenders and from locality to locality. Generally, the buyer pays the fee unless another arrangement has been made with the seller and written into the sales contract.

802. *Loan discount* often called *points*, is a one-time charge used to adjust the yield on the loan to what the market conditions demand. It is used to offset constraints placed on the yield by state or federal regulations. Each point is equal to 1% of the mortgage amount. For example, if a lender charges 3 points on a $30,000 loan, the total charge is $900.

803. *Appraisal fee* pays for a statement of property value for the lender, which is made by an independent appraiser or by a member of the lender's staff. This charge may vary significantly from transaction to transaction. The lender needs to know if the value of the property is sufficient to secure the loan should the buyer fail to repay it according to the provisions of the mort-

ALL LENDERS ARE NOT ALIKE.

gage contract, thus forcing the lender to foreclose and take title to the cooperative or condominium.

In determining the value, the appraiser inspects the unit and the neighborhood, and considers sales prices of comparable units, as well as other factors. The appraisal report may contain photographs and other valuable information. It will provide the factual data upon which the appraiser based the appraised value. Ask the lender for a copy of the appraisal report, or review the original.

804. *Credit report fee* covers the cost of the credit report, which shows how the buyer has handled other credit transactions. The lender uses this report—in conjunction with information the buyer submitted with the application regarding income, outstanding bills, and employment—to determine (1) whether the buyer is an acceptable credit risk and (2) how much money to lend the buyer.

WORKSHEET 5
SETTLEMENT COSTS

	Lender 1	Lender 2	Lender 3
800. ITEMS PAYABLE IN CONNECTION WITH LOAN			
801. Loan Origination Fee %			
802. Loan Discount %			
803. Appraisal Fee			
804. Credit Report			
805. Lender's Inspection Fee			
806. Mortgage Insurance Application Fee to			
807. Assumption Fee			
808.			
809.			
810.			
811.			
900. ITEMS REQUIRED BY LENDER TO BE PAID IN ADVANCE			
901. Interest from to @ $ /day			
902. Mortgage Insurance Premium for months			
903. Hazard Insurance Premium for years			
904. years			
905.			
1000. RESERVES DEPOSITED WITH LENDER			
1001. Hazard insurance months @ $ per month			
1002. Mortgage insurance months @ $ per month			
1003. City property taxes months @ $ per month			
1004. County property taxes months @ $ per month			
1005. Annual assessments months @ $ per month			
1006. months @ $ per month			
1007. months @ $ per month			
1008. months @ $ per month			
1100. TITLE CHARGES			
1101. Settlement or closing fee			
1102. Abstract or title search			
1103. Title examination			
1104. Title insurance binder			
1105. Document preparation			
1106. Notary fees			
1107. Attorney's fees			
(includes above items numbers;			
1108. Title insurance			
(includes above items numbers;			
1109. Lender's coverage $			
1110. Owner's coverage $			
1111.			
1112.			
1113.			
1200. GOVERNMENT RECORDING AND TRANSFER CHARGES			
1201. Recording fees: Deed $; Mortgage $; Releases $			
1202. City/county tax/stamps: Deed $; Mortgage $			
1203. State tax/stamps: Deed $; Mortgage $			
1204.			
1205.			
1300. ADDITIONAL SETTLEMENT CHARGES			
1301. Survey			
1302. Pest inspection			
1303.			
1304.			
1305.			
1400. TOTAL SETTLEMENT CHARGES			

Yr	Mo	No.																			
37	4	448	4.94	5.10	5.27	5.43	5.60	5.78	5.95	6.13	6.30	6.48	6.66	6.85	7.03	7.21	7.40	7.59	7.78	7.97	8.16	8.35
37	3	447	4.94	5.10	5.27	5.44	5.61	5.78	5.95	6.13	6.31	6.49	6.67	6.85	7.03	7.22	7.40	7.59	7.78	7.97	8.16	8.35
37	2	446	4.94	5.11	5.27	5.44	5.61	5.78	5.96	6.13	6.31	6.49	6.67	6.85	7.03	7.22	7.41	7.59	7.78	7.97	8.16	8.36
37	1	445	4.95	5.11	5.28	5.44	5.61	5.79	5.96	6.14	6.31	6.49	6.67	6.85	7.04	7.22	7.41	7.60	7.78	7.97	8.17	8.36
37	0	444	4.95	5.12	5.28	5.45	5.62	5.79	5.96	6.14	6.32	6.49	6.67	6.86	7.04	7.22	7.41	7.60	7.79	7.98	8.17	8.36
36	11	443	4.96	5.12	5.28	5.45	5.62	5.79	5.97	6.14	6.32	6.50	6.68	6.86	7.04	7.23	7.41	7.60	7.79	7.98	8.17	8.36
36	10	442	4.96	5.12	5.29	5.46	5.62	5.80	5.97	6.14	6.32	6.50	6.68	6.86	7.05	7.23	7.42	7.60	7.79	7.98	8.17	8.36
36	9	441	4.96	5.13	5.29	5.46	5.63	5.80	5.97	6.15	6.33	6.50	6.68	6.86	7.05	7.23	7.42	7.61	7.79	7.98	8.17	8.37
36	8	440	4.97	5.13	5.30	5.46	5.63	5.80	5.98	6.15	6.33	6.51	6.69	6.87	7.05	7.23	7.42	7.61	7.80	7.99	8.18	8.37
36	7	439	4.97	5.13	5.30	5.47	5.64	5.81	5.98	6.16	6.33	6.51	6.69	6.87	7.06	7.24	7.42	7.61	7.80	7.99	8.18	8.37
36	6	438	4.98	5.14	5.30	5.47	5.64	5.81	5.98	6.16	6.33	6.51	6.69	6.88	7.06	7.24	7.43	7.61	7.80	7.99	8.18	8.37
36	5	437	4.98	5.14	5.31	5.47	5.64	5.81	5.99	6.16	6.34	6.51	6.69	6.88	7.06	7.24	7.43	7.61	7.80	7.99	8.18	8.37
36	4	436	4.98	5.15	5.31	5.48	5.65	5.82	5.99	6.16	6.34	6.52	6.70	6.88	7.06	7.25	7.43	7.62	7.81	7.99	8.18	8.38
36	3	435	4.99	5.15	5.31	5.48	5.65	5.82	5.99	6.17	6.34	6.52	6.70	6.88	7.07	7.25	7.43	7.62	7.81	8.00	8.19	8.38
36	2	434	4.99	5.15	5.32	5.48	5.65	5.82	6.00	6.17	6.35	6.52	6.70	6.88	7.07	7.25	7.44	7.62	7.81	8.00	8.19	8.38
36	1	433	5.00	5.16	5.32	5.49	5.66	5.83	6.00	6.17	6.35	6.53	6.71	6.89	7.07	7.25	7.44	7.62	7.81	8.00	8.19	8.38
36	0	432	5.00	5.16	5.33	5.49	5.66	5.83	6.00	6.18	6.35	6.53	6.71	6.89	7.07	7.26	7.44	7.63	7.81	8.00	8.19	8.38
35	11	431	5.00	5.17	5.33	5.50	5.66	5.83	6.01	6.18	6.36	6.53	6.71	6.89	7.08	7.26	7.44	7.63	7.82	8.01	8.20	8.39
35	10	430	5.01	5.17	5.33	5.50	5.67	5.84	6.01	6.18	6.36	6.54	6.72	6.90	7.08	7.26	7.45	7.63	7.82	8.01	8.20	8.39
35	9	429	5.01	5.17	5.34	5.50	5.67	5.84	6.01	6.19	6.36	6.54	6.72	6.90	7.08	7.26	7.45	7.63	7.82	8.01	8.20	8.39
35	8	428	5.02	5.18	5.34	5.51	5.68	5.85	6.02	6.19	6.37	6.54	6.72	6.90	7.08	7.27	7.45	7.64	7.82	8.01	8.20	8.39
35	7	427	5.02	5.18	5.35	5.51	5.68	5.85	6.02	6.19	6.37	6.55	6.72	6.90	7.09	7.27	7.45	7.64	7.83	8.02	8.20	8.39
35	6	426	5.03	5.19	5.35	5.52	5.68	5.85	6.02	6.20	6.37	6.55	6.73	6.91	7.09	7.27	7.46	7.64	7.83	8.02	8.21	8.40
35	5	425	5.03	5.19	5.35	5.52	5.69	5.86	6.03	6.20	6.38	6.55	6.73	6.91	7.09	7.28	7.46	7.65	7.83	8.02	8.21	8.40
35	4	424	5.03	5.20	5.36	5.52	5.69	5.86	6.03	6.20	6.38	6.56	6.73	6.91	7.10	7.28	7.46	7.65	7.83	8.02	8.21	8.40
35	3	423	5.04	5.20	5.36	5.53	5.69	5.86	6.03	6.21	6.38	6.56	6.74	6.92	7.10	7.28	7.47	7.65	7.84	8.02	8.21	8.40
35	2	422	5.04	5.20	5.37	5.53	5.70	5.87	6.04	6.21	6.39	6.56	6.74	6.92	7.10	7.28	7.47	7.65	7.84	8.03	8.22	8.41
35	1	421	5.05	5.21	5.37	5.54	5.70	5.87	6.04	6.22	6.39	6.57	6.74	6.92	7.10	7.29	7.47	7.66	7.84	8.03	8.22	8.41
35	0	420	5.05	5.21	5.38	5.54	5.71	5.88	6.05	6.22	6.39	6.57	6.75	6.93	7.11	7.29	7.47	7.66	7.84	8.03	8.22	8.41
34	11	419	5.06	5.22	5.38	5.54	5.71	5.88	6.05	6.22	6.40	6.57	6.75	6.93	7.11	7.29	7.48	7.66	7.85	8.04	8.22	8.41
34	10	418	5.06	5.22	5.38	5.55	5.71	5.88	6.05	6.23	6.40	6.58	6.75	6.93	7.11	7.30	7.48	7.66	7.85	8.04	8.23	8.42
34	9	417	5.07	5.23	5.39	5.55	5.72	5.89	6.06	6.23	6.40	6.58	6.76	6.94	7.12	7.30	7.48	7.67	7.85	8.04	8.23	8.42
34	8	416	5.07	5.23	5.39	5.56	5.72	5.89	6.06	6.23	6.41	6.58	6.76	6.94	7.12	7.30	7.49	7.67	7.86	8.04	8.23	8.42
34	7	415	5.07	5.23	5.40	5.56	5.73	5.90	6.07	6.24	6.41	6.59	6.76	6.94	7.12	7.31	7.49	7.67	7.86	8.05	8.23	8.42
34	6	414	5.08	5.24	5.40	5.57	5.73	5.90	6.07	6.24	6.42	6.59	6.77	6.95	7.13	7.31	7.49	7.68	7.86	8.05	8.24	8.43
34	5	413	5.08	5.24	5.41	5.57	5.74	5.90	6.07	6.25	6.42	6.59	6.77	6.95	7.13	7.31	7.49	7.68	7.86	8.05	8.24	8.43
34	4	412	5.09	5.25	5.41	5.57	5.74	5.91	6.08	6.25	6.42	6.60	6.77	6.95	7.13	7.31	7.50	7.68	7.87	8.05	8.24	8.43
34	3	411	5.09	5.25	5.41	5.58	5.74	5.91	6.08	6.25	6.43	6.60	6.78	6.96	7.14	7.32	7.50	7.68	7.87	8.06	8.24	8.43

AMORTIZATION TABLES (Continued)

MONTHLY INSTALLMENT PER THOUSAND DOLLARS INCLUDING INTEREST AT—

Term of Mortgage Years	Months	No. of Payments	5%	5¼%	5½%	5¾%	6%	6¼%	6½%	6¾%	7%	7¼%	7½%	7¾%	8%	8¼%	8½%	8¾%	9%	9¼%	9½%	9¾%
34	2	410	5.10	5.26	5.42	5.58	5.75	5.92	6.09	6.26	6.43	6.61	6.78	6.96	7.14	7.32	7.50	7.69	7.87	8.06	8.25	8.44
34	1	409	5.10	5.26	5.42	5.59	5.75	5.92	6.09	6.26	6.43	6.61	6.79	6.96	7.14	7.32	7.51	7.69	7.88	8.06	8.25	8.44
34	0	408	5.11	5.27	5.43	5.59	5.76	5.92	6.09	6.26	6.44	6.61	6.79	6.97	7.15	7.33	7.51	7.69	7.88	8.06	8.25	8.44
33	11	407	5.11	5.27	5.43	5.60	5.76	5.93	6.10	6.27	6.44	6.62	6.79	6.97	7.15	7.33	7.51	7.70	7.88	8.07	8.25	8.44
33	10	406	5.12	5.28	5.44	5.60	5.77	5.93	6.10	6.27	6.45	6.62	6.80	6.97	7.15	7.33	7.52	7.70	7.88	8.07	8.26	8.45
33	9	405	5.12	5.28	5.44	5.60	5.77	5.94	6.11	6.28	6.45	6.62	6.80	6.98	7.16	7.34	7.52	7.70	7.89	8.07	8.26	8.45
33	8	404	5.13	5.29	5.45	5.61	5.77	5.94	6.11	6.28	6.45	6.63	6.80	6.98	7.16	7.34	7.52	7.71	7.89	8.08	8.26	8.45
33	7	403	5.13	5.29	5.45	5.61	5.78	5.95	6.11	6.28	6.46	6.63	6.81	6.98	7.16	7.34	7.53	7.71	7.89	8.08	8.27	8.45
33	6	402	5.14	5.29	5.46	5.62	5.78	5.95	6.12	6.29	6.46	6.64	6.81	6.99	7.17	7.35	7.53	7.71	7.90	8.08	8.27	8.46
33	5	401	5.14	5.30	5.46	5.62	5.79	5.95	6.12	6.29	6.47	6.64	6.81	6.99	7.17	7.35	7.53	7.72	7.90	8.08	8.27	8.46
33	4	400	5.15	5.30	5.46	5.63	5.79	5.96	6.13	6.30	6.47	6.64	6.82	7.00	7.17	7.35	7.54	7.72	7.90	8.09	8.27	8.46
33	3	399	5.15	5.31	5.47	5.63	5.80	5.96	6.13	6.30	6.47	6.65	6.82	7.00	7.18	7.36	7.54	7.72	7.91	8.09	8.28	8.47
33	2	398	5.16	5.31	5.47	5.64	5.80	5.97	6.14	6.31	6.48	6.65	6.83	7.00	7.18	7.36	7.54	7.73	7.91	8.09	8.28	8.47
33	1	397	5.16	5.32	5.48	5.64	5.81	5.97	6.14	6.31	6.48	6.66	6.83	7.01	7.19	7.36	7.55	7.73	7.91	8.10	8.28	8.47
33	0	396	5.17	5.32	5.48	5.65	5.81	5.98	6.14	6.31	6.49	6.66	6.83	7.01	7.19	7.37	7.55	7.73	7.92	8.10	8.29	8.47
32	11	395	5.17	5.33	5.49	5.65	5.82	5.98	6.15	6.32	6.49	6.66	6.84	7.01	7.19	7.37	7.55	7.74	7.92	8.10	8.29	8.48
32	10	394	5.18	5.33	5.49	5.66	5.82	5.99	6.15	6.32	6.49	6.67	6.84	7.02	7.20	7.38	7.56	7.74	7.92	8.11	8.29	8.48
32	9	393	5.18	5.34	5.50	5.66	5.82	5.99	6.16	6.33	6.50	6.67	6.85	7.02	7.20	7.38	7.56	7.74	7.93	8.11	8.30	8.48
32	8	392	5.19	5.34	5.50	5.67	5.83	6.00	6.16	6.33	6.50	6.68	6.85	7.03	7.20	7.38	7.56	7.75	7.93	8.11	8.30	8.49
32	7	391	5.19	5.35	5.51	5.67	5.83	6.00	6.17	6.34	6.51	6.68	6.85	7.03	7.21	7.39	7.57	7.75	7.93	8.12	8.30	8.49
32	6	390	5.20	5.35	5.51	5.68	5.84	6.00	6.17	6.34	6.51	6.68	6.86	7.03	7.21	7.39	7.57	7.75	7.94	8.12	8.30	8.49
32	5	389	5.20	5.36	5.52	5.68	5.84	6.01	6.18	6.35	6.52	6.69	6.86	7.04	7.22	7.39	7.57	7.76	7.94	8.12	8.31	8.49
32	4	388	5.21	5.37	5.52	5.69	5.85	6.01	6.18	6.35	6.52	6.69	6.87	7.04	7.22	7.40	7.58	7.76	7.94	8.13	8.31	8.50
32	3	387	5.21	5.37	5.53	5.69	5.85	6.02	6.19	6.35	6.52	6.70	6.87	7.05	7.22	7.40	7.58	7.76	7.95	8.13	8.31	8.50
32	2	386	5.22	5.38	5.53	5.70	5.86	6.02	6.19	6.36	6.53	6.70	6.88	7.05	7.23	7.41	7.59	7.77	7.95	8.13	8.32	8.50
32	1	385	5.22	5.38	5.54	5.70	5.86	6.03	6.20	6.36	6.53	6.71	6.88	7.05	7.23	7.41	7.59	7.77	7.95	8.14	8.32	8.51
32	0	384	5.23	5.39	5.55	5.71	5.87	6.03	6.20	6.37	6.54	6.71	6.88	7.06	7.24	7.41	7.59	7.77	7.96	8.14	8.32	8.51
31	11	383	5.24	5.39	5.55	5.71	5.87	6.04	6.20	6.37	6.54	6.71	6.89	7.06	7.24	7.42	7.60	7.78	7.96	8.14	8.33	8.51
31	10	382	5.24	5.40	5.56	5.72	5.88	6.04	6.21	6.38	6.55	6.72	6.89	7.07	7.24	7.42	7.60	7.78	7.96	8.15	8.33	8.52
31	9	381	5.25	5.40	5.56	5.72	5.88	6.05	6.21	6.38	6.55	6.72	6.90	7.07	7.25	7.43	7.61	7.79	7.97	8.15	8.33	8.52
31	8	380	5.25	5.41	5.57	5.73	5.89	6.05	6.22	6.39	6.56	6.73	6.90	7.08	7.25	7.43	7.61	7.79	7.97	8.15	8.34	8.52

Yr	Mo	No.	5.26	5.41	5.57	5.73	5.89	6.06	6.22	6.39	6.56	6.73	6.91	7.08	7.26	7.43	7.61	7.79	7.97	8.16	8.34	8.53
31	7	379	5.26	5.41	5.57	5.73	5.89	6.06	6.22	6.39	6.56	6.73	6.91	7.08	7.26	7.43	7.61	7.79	7.97	8.16	8.34	8.53
31	6	378	5.26	5.42	5.58	5.74	5.90	6.06	6.23	6.40	6.57	6.74	6.91	7.08	7.26	7.44	7.62	7.80	7.98	8.16	8.34	8.53
31	5	377	5.27	5.43	5.58	5.74	5.91	6.07	6.23	6.40	6.57	6.74	6.91	7.09	7.26	7.44	7.62	7.80	7.98	8.16	8.35	8.53
31	4	376	5.28	5.43	5.59	5.75	5.91	6.07	6.24	6.41	6.58	6.75	6.92	7.09	7.27	7.45	7.62	7.80	7.99	8.17	8.35	8.54
31	3	375	5.28	5.44	5.59	5.75	5.92	6.08	6.24	6.41	6.58	6.75	6.92	7.10	7.27	7.45	7.63	7.81	7.99	8.17	8.36	8.54
31	2	374	5.29	5.44	5.60	5.76	5.92	6.08	6.25	6.42	6.59	6.76	6.93	7.10	7.28	7.45	7.63	7.81	7.99	8.18	8.36	8.54
31	1	373	5.29	5.45	5.61	5.77	5.93	6.09	6.25	6.42	6.59	6.76	6.93	7.11	7.28	7.46	7.64	7.82	8.00	8.18	8.36	8.55
31	0	372	5.30	5.45	5.61	5.77	5.93	6.10	6.26	6.43	6.60	6.77	6.94	7.11	7.29	7.46	7.64	7.82	8.00	8.18	8.37	8.55
30	11	371	5.30	5.46	5.62	5.78	5.94	6.10	6.27	6.43	6.60	6.77	6.94	7.12	7.29	7.47	7.65	7.82	8.01	8.19	8.37	8.55
30	10	370	5.31	5.47	5.62	5.78	5.94	6.11	6.27	6.44	6.61	6.78	6.95	7.12	7.30	7.47	7.65	7.83	8.01	8.19	8.37	8.56
30	9	369	5.32	5.47	5.63	5.79	5.95	6.11	6.28	6.44	6.61	6.78	6.95	7.13	7.30	7.48	7.65	7.83	8.01	8.19	8.38	8.56
30	8	368	5.32	5.48	5.63	5.79	5.95	6.12	6.28	6.45	6.62	6.79	6.96	7.13	7.30	7.48	7.66	7.84	8.02	8.20	8.38	8.57
30	7	367	5.33	5.48	5.64	5.80	5.96	6.12	6.29	6.45	6.62	6.79	6.96	7.13	7.31	7.48	7.66	7.84	8.02	8.20	8.39	8.57
30	6	366	5.34	5.49	5.65	5.80	5.97	6.13	6.29	6.46	6.63	6.80	6.97	7.14	7.31	7.49	7.67	7.85	8.03	8.21	8.39	8.58
30	5	365	5.34	5.50	5.65	5.81	5.97	6.13	6.30	6.46	6.63	6.80	6.97	7.14	7.32	7.49	7.67	7.85	8.03	8.21	8.39	8.58
30	4	364	5.35	5.50	5.66	5.82	5.98	6.14	6.30	6.47	6.64	6.81	6.98	7.15	7.32	7.50	7.68	7.85	8.03	8.22	8.40	8.58
30	3	363	5.35	5.51	5.66	5.82	5.98	6.14	6.31	6.47	6.64	6.81	6.98	7.15	7.33	7.50	7.68	7.86	8.04	8.22	8.40	8.58
30	2	362	5.36	5.51	5.67	5.83	5.99	6.15	6.31	6.48	6.65	6.82	6.99	7.16	7.33	7.51	7.68	7.86	8.04	8.22	8.41	8.59
30	1	361	5.37	5.52	5.68	5.83	5.99	6.16	6.32	6.49	6.65	6.82	6.99	7.16	7.34	7.51	7.69	7.87	8.05	8.23	8.41	8.59
30	0	360	5.37	5.53	5.68	5.84	6.00	6.16	6.33	6.49	6.66	6.83	7.00	7.17	7.34	7.52	7.69	7.87	8.05	8.23	8.41	8.60
29	11	359	5.38	5.53	5.69	5.85	6.01	6.17	6.33	6.50	6.66	6.83	7.00	7.17	7.35	7.52	7.70	7.88	8.06	8.24	8.42	8.60
29	10	358	5.39	5.54	5.70	5.85	6.01	6.17	6.34	6.50	6.67	6.84	7.01	7.18	7.35	7.53	7.70	7.88	8.06	8.24	8.42	8.60
29	9	357	5.39	5.55	5.70	5.86	6.02	6.18	6.34	6.51	6.67	6.84	7.01	7.18	7.36	7.53	7.71	7.89	8.06	8.24	8.43	8.61
29	8	356	5.40	5.55	5.71	5.87	6.02	6.19	6.35	6.51	6.68	6.85	7.02	7.19	7.36	7.54	7.71	7.89	8.07	8.25	8.43	8.61
29	7	355	5.41	5.56	5.71	5.87	6.03	6.19	6.35	6.52	6.69	6.85	7.02	7.19	7.37	7.54	7.72	7.90	8.07	8.25	8.43	8.62
29	6	354	5.41	5.57	5.72	5.88	6.04	6.20	6.36	6.53	6.69	6.86	7.03	7.20	7.37	7.55	7.72	7.90	8.08	8.26	8.44	8.62
29	5	353	5.42	5.57	5.73	5.88	6.04	6.20	6.37	6.53	6.70	6.86	7.03	7.21	7.38	7.55	7.73	7.90	8.08	8.26	8.44	8.63
29	4	352	5.43	5.58	5.73	5.89	6.05	6.21	6.37	6.54	6.70	6.87	7.04	7.21	7.38	7.56	7.73	7.91	8.09	8.27	8.45	8.63
29	3	351	5.43	5.59	5.74	5.90	6.06	6.22	6.38	6.54	6.71	6.88	7.05	7.22	7.39	7.56	7.74	7.91	8.09	8.27	8.45	8.63
29	2	350	5.44	5.59	5.75	5.90	6.06	6.22	6.38	6.55	6.71	6.88	7.05	7.22	7.39	7.57	7.74	7.92	8.10	8.28	8.46	8.64
29	1	349	5.45	5.60	5.75	5.91	6.07	6.23	6.39	6.55	6.72	6.89	7.06	7.23	7.40	7.57	7.75	7.92	8.10	8.28	8.46	8.64
29	0	348	5.45	5.61	5.76	5.92	6.08	6.24	6.40	6.56	6.73	6.89	7.06	7.23	7.40	7.58	7.75	7.93	8.11	8.29	8.47	8.65
28	11	347	5.46	5.61	5.77	5.92	6.08	6.24	6.40	6.57	6.73	6.90	7.07	7.24	7.41	7.58	7.76	7.93	8.11	8.29	8.47	8.65
28	10	346	5.47	5.62	5.77	5.93	6.09	6.25	6.41	6.57	6.74	6.91	7.07	7.24	7.42	7.59	7.76	7.94	8.12	8.30	8.47	8.66
28	9	345	5.47	5.63	5.78	5.94	6.09	6.25	6.42	6.58	6.74	6.91	7.08	7.25	7.42	7.59	7.77	7.94	8.12	8.30	8.48	8.66
28	8	344	5.48	5.63	5.79	5.94	6.10	6.26	6.42	6.59	6.75	6.92	7.09	7.26	7.43	7.60	7.77	7.95	8.13	8.30	8.48	8.67
28	7	343	5.49	5.64	5.79	5.95	6.11	6.27	6.43	6.59	6.76	6.92	7.09	7.26	7.43	7.60	7.78	7.95	8.13	8.31	8.49	8.67
28	6	342	5.50	5.65	5.80	5.96	6.11	6.27	6.44	6.60	6.76	6.93	7.10	7.27	7.44	7.61	7.78	7.96	8.14	8.31	8.49	8.67

AMORTIZATION TABLES (Continued)

MONTHLY INSTALLMENT PER THOUSAND DOLLARS INCLUDING INTEREST AT—

Term of Mortgage Years	Months	No. of Payments	5%	5¼%	5½%	5¾%	6%	6¼%	6½%	6¾%	7%	7¼%	7½%	7¾%	8%	8¼%	8½%	8¾%	9%	9¼%	9½%	9¾%
28	5	341	5.50	5.66	5.81	5.96	6.12	6.28	6.44	6.60	6.77	6.94	7.10	7.27	7.44	7.62	7.79	7.96	8.14	8.32	8.50	8.68
28	4	340	5.51	5.66	5.82	5.97	6.13	6.29	6.45	6.61	6.78	6.94	7.11	7.28	7.45	7.62	7.80	7.97	8.15	8.32	8.50	8.68
28	3	339	5.52	5.67	5.82	5.98	6.14	6.29	6.45	6.62	6.78	6.95	7.12	7.28	7.45	7.63	7.80	7.98	8.15	8.33	8.51	8.69
28	2	338	5.53	5.68	5.83	5.99	6.14	6.30	6.46	6.62	6.79	6.95	7.12	7.29	7.46	7.63	7.81	7.98	8.16	8.33	8.51	8.69
28	1	337	5.53	5.68	5.84	5.99	6.15	6.31	6.47	6.63	6.79	6.96	7.13	7.30	7.47	7.64	7.81	7.99	8.16	8.34	8.52	8.70
28	0	336	5.54	5.69	5.84	6.00	6.16	6.31	6.48	6.64	6.80	6.97	7.13	7.30	7.47	7.64	7.82	7.99	8.17	8.35	8.52	8.70
27	11	335	5.55	5.70	5.85	6.01	6.16	6.32	6.48	6.64	6.81	6.97	7.14	7.31	7.48	7.65	7.82	8.00	8.17	8.35	8.53	8.71
27	10	334	5.56	5.71	5.86	6.01	6.17	6.33	6.49	6.65	6.81	6.98	7.15	7.31	7.48	7.66	7.83	8.00	8.18	8.36	8.53	8.71
27	9	333	5.56	5.71	5.87	6.02	6.18	6.34	6.50	6.66	6.82	6.99	7.15	7.32	7.49	7.66	7.83	8.01	8.18	8.36	8.54	8.72
27	8	332	5.57	5.72	5.87	6.03	6.18	6.34	6.50	6.66	6.83	6.99	7.16	7.33	7.50	7.67	7.84	8.01	8.19	8.37	8.54	8.72
27	7	331	5.58	5.73	5.88	6.04	6.19	6.35	6.51	6.67	6.83	7.00	7.17	7.33	7.50	7.67	7.85	8.02	8.20	8.37	8.55	8.73
27	6	330	5.59	5.74	5.89	6.04	6.20	6.36	6.52	6.68	6.84	7.01	7.17	7.34	7.51	7.68	7.85	8.03	8.20	8.38	8.56	8.73
27	5	329	5.59	5.75	5.90	6.05	6.21	6.36	6.52	6.69	6.85	7.01	7.18	7.35	7.52	7.69	7.86	8.03	8.21	8.38	8.56	8.74
27	4	328	5.60	5.75	5.90	6.06	6.21	6.37	6.53	6.69	6.85	7.02	7.19	7.35	7.52	7.69	7.86	8.04	8.21	8.39	8.57	8.74
27	3	327	5.61	5.76	5.91	6.07	6.22	6.38	6.54	6.70	6.86	7.03	7.19	7.36	7.53	7.70	7.87	8.04	8.22	8.39	8.57	8.75
27	2	326	5.62	5.77	5.92	6.07	6.23	6.39	6.55	6.71	6.87	7.03	7.20	7.37	7.53	7.71	7.88	8.05	8.22	8.40	8.58	8.76
27	1	325	5.63	5.78	5.93	6.08	6.24	6.39	6.55	6.71	6.88	7.04	7.21	7.37	7.54	7.71	7.88	8.06	8.23	8.41	8.58	8.76
27	0	324	5.64	5.78	5.94	6.09	6.24	6.40	6.56	6.72	6.88	7.05	7.21	7.38	7.55	7.72	7.89	8.06	8.24	8.41	8.59	8.77
26	11	323	5.64	5.79	5.94	6.10	6.25	6.41	6.57	6.73	6.89	7.05	7.22	7.39	7.55	7.72	7.90	8.07	8.24	8.42	8.59	8.77
26	10	322	5.65	5.80	5.95	6.11	6.26	6.42	6.58	6.74	6.90	7.06	7.23	7.39	7.56	7.73	7.90	8.07	8.25	8.42	8.60	8.78
26	9	321	5.66	5.81	5.96	6.11	6.27	6.42	6.58	6.74	6.90	7.07	7.23	7.40	7.57	7.74	7.91	8.08	8.25	8.43	8.61	8.78
26	8	320	5.67	5.82	5.97	6.12	6.28	6.43	6.59	6.75	6.91	7.08	7.24	7.41	7.57	7.74	7.91	8.09	8.26	8.43	8.61	8.79
26	7	319	5.68	5.83	5.98	6.13	6.28	6.44	6.60	6.76	6.92	7.08	7.25	7.41	7.58	7.75	7.92	8.09	8.27	8.44	8.62	8.80
26	6	318	5.69	5.83	5.99	6.14	6.29	6.45	6.61	6.77	6.93	7.09	7.25	7.42	7.59	7.76	7.93	8.10	8.27	8.45	8.62	8.80
26	5	317	5.69	5.84	5.99	6.15	6.30	6.46	6.61	6.77	6.93	7.10	7.26	7.43	7.60	7.76	7.93	8.11	8.28	8.45	8.63	8.81
26	4	316	5.70	5.85	6.00	6.15	6.31	6.46	6.62	6.78	6.94	7.10	7.27	7.43	7.60	7.77	7.94	8.11	8.29	8.46	8.64	8.81
26	3	315	5.71	5.86	6.01	6.16	6.32	6.47	6.63	6.79	6.95	7.11	7.28	7.44	7.61	7.78	7.95	8.12	8.29	8.47	8.64	8.82
26	2	314	5.72	5.87	6.02	6.17	6.32	6.48	6.64	6.80	6.96	7.12	7.28	7.45	7.62	7.79	7.95	8.13	8.30	8.47	8.65	8.82
26	1	313	5.73	5.88	6.03	6.18	6.33	6.49	6.65	6.80	6.97	7.13	7.29	7.46	7.62	7.79	7.96	8.13	8.31	8.48	8.65	8.83
26	0	312	5.74	5.89	6.04	6.19	6.34	6.50	6.65	6.81	6.97	7.14	7.30	7.46	7.63	7.80	7.97	8.14	8.31	8.49	8.66	8.84
25	11	311	5.75	5.90	6.05	6.20	6.35	6.51	6.66	6.82	6.98	7.14	7.31	7.47	7.64	7.81	7.98	8.15	8.32	8.49	8.67	8.84

8.85	8.67	8.50	8.33	8.15	7.98	7.81	7.65	7.48	7.31	7.15	6.99	6.83	6.67	6.51	6.36	6.21	6.05	5.90	5.76	310	10	25
8.86	8.68	8.51	8.33	8.16	7.99	7.82	7.65	7.49	7.32	7.16	7.00	6.84	6.68	6.52	6.37	6.21	6.06	5.91	5.77	309	9	25
8.86	8.69	8.51	8.34	8.17	8.00	7.83	7.66	7.49	7.33	7.17	7.01	6.85	6.69	6.53	6.38	6.22	6.07	5.92	5.77	308	8	25
8.87	8.69	8.52	8.35	8.17	8.00	7.84	7.67	7.50	7.34	7.17	7.01	6.85	6.70	6.54	6.38	6.23	6.08	5.93	5.78	307	7	25
8.88	8.70	8.53	8.35	8.18	8.01	7.84	7.68	7.51	7.35	7.18	7.02	6.86	6.70	6.55	6.39	6.24	6.09	5.94	5.79	306	6	25
8.88	8.71	8.53	8.36	8.19	8.02	7.85	7.68	7.52	7.35	7.19	7.03	6.87	6.71	6.56	6.40	6.25	6.10	5.95	5.80	305	5	25
8.89	8.71	8.54	8.37	8.20	8.03	7.86	7.69	7.53	7.36	7.20	7.04	6.88	6.72	6.57	6.41	6.26	6.11	5.96	5.81	304	4	25
8.90	8.72	8.55	8.37	8.20	8.03	7.87	7.70	7.53	7.37	7.21	7.05	6.89	6.73	6.57	6.42	6.27	6.12	5.97	5.82	303	3	25
8.90	8.73	8.55	8.38	8.21	8.04	7.87	7.71	7.54	7.38	7.22	7.06	6.90	6.74	6.58	6.43	6.28	6.13	5.98	5.83	302	2	25
8.91	8.73	8.56	8.39	8.22	8.05	7.88	7.72	7.55	7.39	7.22	7.06	6.91	6.75	6.59	6.44	6.29	6.14	5.99	5.84	301	1	25
8.92	8.74	8.57	8.40	8.23	8.06	7.89	7.72	7.56	7.39	7.23	7.07	6.91	6.76	6.60	6.45	6.30	6.15	6.00	5.85	300	0	25
8.92	8.75	8.58	8.40	8.23	8.07	7.90	7.73	7.57	7.40	7.24	7.08	6.92	6.77	6.61	6.46	6.31	6.16	6.01	5.86	299	11	24
8.93	8.76	8.58	8.41	8.24	8.07	7.91	7.74	7.57	7.41	7.25	7.09	6.93	6.78	6.62	6.47	6.32	6.17	6.02	5.87	298	10	24
8.94	8.76	8.59	8.42	8.25	8.08	7.91	7.75	7.58	7.42	7.26	7.10	6.94	6.78	6.63	6.48	6.32	6.17	6.03	5.88	297	9	24
8.94	8.77	8.60	8.43	8.26	8.09	7.92	7.76	7.59	7.43	7.27	7.11	6.95	6.79	6.64	6.49	6.33	6.18	6.04	5.89	296	8	24
8.95	8.78	8.61	8.44	8.27	8.10	7.93	7.76	7.60	7.44	7.28	7.12	6.96	6.80	6.65	6.50	6.34	6.19	6.05	5.90	295	7	24
8.96	8.79	8.61	8.44	8.27	8.11	7.94	7.77	7.61	7.45	7.29	7.13	6.97	6.81	6.66	6.50	6.35	6.20	6.06	5.91	294	6	24
8.97	8.79	8.62	8.45	8.28	8.11	7.95	7.78	7.62	7.46	7.29	7.14	6.98	6.82	6.67	6.51	6.36	6.21	6.07	5.92	293	5	24
8.97	8.80	8.63	8.46	8.29	8.12	7.96	7.79	7.63	7.46	7.30	7.14	6.99	6.83	6.68	6.52	6.37	6.22	6.08	5.93	292	4	24
8.98	8.81	8.64	8.47	8.30	8.13	7.96	7.80	7.64	7.47	7.31	7.15	7.00	6.84	6.69	6.53	6.38	6.23	6.09	5.94	291	3	24
8.99	8.82	8.65	8.48	8.31	8.14	7.97	7.81	7.64	7.48	7.32	7.16	7.01	6.85	6.70	6.54	6.39	6.25	6.10	5.95	290	2	24
9.00	8.82	8.65	8.48	8.31	8.15	7.98	7.82	7.65	7.49	7.33	7.17	7.02	6.86	6.71	6.55	6.40	6.26	6.11	5.96	289	1	24
9.01	8.83	8.66	8.49	8.32	8.16	7.99	7.83	7.66	7.50	7.34	7.18	7.03	6.87	6.72	6.56	6.41	6.27	6.12	5.97	288	0	24
9.01	8.84	8.67	8.50	8.33	8.16	8.00	7.83	7.67	7.51	7.35	7.19	7.04	6.88	6.73	6.58	6.42	6.28	6.13	5.98	287	11	23
9.02	8.85	8.68	8.51	8.34	8.17	8.01	7.84	7.68	7.52	7.36	7.20	7.05	6.89	6.74	6.59	6.44	6.29	6.14	6.00	286	10	23
9.03	8.86	8.69	8.52	8.35	8.18	8.02	7.85	7.69	7.53	7.37	7.21	7.06	6.90	6.75	6.60	6.45	6.30	6.15	6.01	285	9	23
9.04	8.87	8.69	8.53	8.36	8.19	8.03	7.86	7.70	7.54	7.38	7.22	7.07	6.91	6.76	6.61	6.46	6.31	6.16	6.02	284	8	23
9.05	8.87	8.70	8.53	8.37	8.20	8.04	7.87	7.71	7.55	7.39	7.23	7.08	6.92	6.77	6.62	6.47	6.32	6.17	6.03	283	7	23
9.05	8.88	8.71	8.54	8.38	8.21	8.04	7.88	7.72	7.56	7.40	7.24	7.09	6.93	6.78	6.63	6.48	6.33	6.18	6.04	282	6	23
9.06	8.89	8.72	8.55	8.38	8.22	8.05	7.89	7.73	7.57	7.41	7.25	7.10	6.94	6.79	6.64	6.49	6.34	6.20	6.05	281	5	23
9.07	8.90	8.73	8.56	8.39	8.23	8.06	7.90	7.74	7.58	7.42	7.26	7.11	6.95	6.80	6.65	6.50	6.35	6.21	6.06	280	4	23
9.08	8.91	8.74	8.57	8.40	8.24	8.07	7.91	7.75	7.59	7.43	7.27	7.12	6.96	6.81	6.66	6.51	6.36	6.22	6.07	279	3	23
9.09	8.92	8.75	8.58	8.41	8.25	8.08	7.92	7.76	7.60	7.44	7.28	7.13	6.97	6.82	6.67	6.52	6.37	6.23	6.09	278	2	23
9.10	8.93	8.76	8.59	8.42	8.26	8.09	7.93	7.77	7.61	7.45	7.29	7.14	6.98	6.83	6.68	6.53	6.39	6.24	6.10	277	1	23
9.11	8.93	8.77	8.60	8.43	8.27	8.10	7.94	7.78	7.62	7.46	7.30	7.15	7.00	6.84	6.69	6.54	6.40	6.25	6.11	276	0	23
9.11	8.94	8.77	8.61	8.44	8.28	8.11	7.95	7.79	7.63	7.47	7.31	7.16	7.01	6.85	6.70	6.56	6.41	6.26	6.12	275	11	22
9.12	8.95	8.78	8.62	8.45	8.29	8.12	7.96	7.80	7.64	7.48	7.33	7.17	7.02	6.87	6.72	6.57	6.42	6.28	6.13	274	10	22
9.13	8.96	8.79	8.63	8.46	8.30	8.13	7.97	7.81	7.65	7.49	7.34	7.18	7.03	6.88	6.73	6.58	6.43	6.29	6.14	273	9	22

AMORTIZATION TABLES (Continued)

MONTHLY INSTALLMENT PER THOUSAND DOLLARS INCLUDING INTEREST AT—

Term of Mortgage Years	Months	No. of Payments	5%	5¼%	5½%	5¾%	6%	6¼%	6½%	6¾%	7%	7¼%	7½%	7¾%	8%	8¼%	8½%	8¾%	9%	9¼%	9½%	9¾%
22	8	272	6.16	6.30	6.44	6.59	6.74	6.89	7.04	7.19	7.35	7.50	7.66	7.82	7.98	8.14	8.31	8.47	8.61	8.80	8.97	9.14
22	7	271	6.17	6.31	6.46	6.60	6.75	6.90	7.05	7.20	7.36	7.51	7.67	7.83	7.99	8.15	8.32	8.48	8.65	8.81	8.98	9.15
22	6	270	6.18	6.32	6.47	6.62	6.76	6.91	7.06	7.22	7.37	7.53	7.68	7.84	8.00	8.16	8.33	8.49	8.66	8.82	8.99	9.16
22	5	269	6.19	6.34	6.48	6.63	6.77	6.97	7.07	7.23	7.38	7.54	7.69	7.85	8.01	8.17	8.34	8.50	8.67	8.83	9.00	9.17
22	4	268	6.21	6.35	6.49	6.64	6.79	6.94	7.09	7.24	7.39	7.55	7.70	7.86	8.02	8.18	8.35	8.51	8.68	8.84	9.01	9.18
22	3	267	6.22	6.36	6.51	6.65	6.80	6.95	7.10	7.25	7.40	7.56	7.72	7.87	8.03	8.19	8.36	8.52	8.65	8.85	9.02	9.19
22	2	266	6.23	6.37	6.52	6.66	6.81	6.96	7.11	7.26	7.42	7.57	7.73	7.89	8.04	8.21	8.37	8.53	8.70	8.86	9.03	9.20
22	1	265	6.24	6.39	6.53	6.68	6.82	6.97	7.12	7.27	7.43	7.58	7.74	7.90	8.06	8.22	8.38	8.54	8.71	8.87	9.04	9.21
21	0	264	6.26	6.40	6.54	6.69	6.84	6.98	7.13	7.29	7.44	7.59	7.75	7.91	8.07	8.23	8.39	8.55	8.72	8.88	9.05	9.22
21	11	263	6.27	6.41	6.56	6.70	6.85	7.00	7.15	7.30	7.45	7.61	7.76	7.92	8.08	8.24	8.40	8.56	8.73	8.89	9.06	9.23
21	10	262	6.28	6.43	6.57	6.71	6.86	7.01	7.16	7.31	7.46	7.62	7.77	7.93	8.09	8.25	8.41	8.57	8.74	8.90	9.07	9.24
21	9	261	6.30	6.44	6.58	6.73	6.87	7.02	7.17	7.32	7.48	7.63	7.79	7.94	8.10	8.26	8.42	8.58	8.75	8.91	9.08	9.25
21	8	260	6.31	6.45	6.60	6.74	6.89	7.03	7.18	7.34	7.49	7.64	7.80	7.95	8.11	8.27	8.43	8.60	8.76	8.92	9.09	9.26
21	7	259	6.32	6.47	6.61	6.75	6.90	7.05	7.20	7.35	7.50	7.65	7.81	7.97	8.12	8.28	8.44	8.61	8.77	8.94	9.10	9.27
21	6	258	6.34	6.48	6.62	6.77	6.91	7.06	7.21	7.36	7.51	7.67	7.82	7.98	8.14	8.30	8.46	8.62	8.78	8.95	9.11	9.28
21	5	257	6.35	6.49	6.64	6.78	6.93	7.07	7.22	7.37	7.53	7.68	7.83	7.99	8.15	8.31	8.47	8.63	8.79	8.96	9.12	9.29
21	4	256	6.37	6.51	6.65	6.79	6.94	7.09	7.24	7.39	7.54	7.69	7.85	8.00	8.16	8.32	8.48	8.64	8.80	8.97	9.13	9.30
21	3	255	6.38	6.52	6.66	6.81	6.95	7.10	7.25	7.40	7.55	7.70	7.86	8.01	8.17	8.33	8.49	8.65	8.82	8.98	9.15	9.31
21	2	254	6.39	6.53	6.68	6.82	6.97	7.11	7.26	7.41	7.56	7.72	7.87	8.03	8.18	8.34	8.50	8.66	8.83	8.99	9.16	9.32
21	1	253	6.41	6.55	6.69	6.83	6.98	7.13	7.28	7.43	7.58	7.73	7.88	8.04	8.20	8.36	8.52	8.68	8.84	9.00	9.17	9.33
21	0	252	6.42	6.56	6.70	6.85	6.99	7.14	7.29	7.44	7.59	7.74	7.90	8.05	8.21	8.37	8.53	8.69	8.85	9.01	9.18	9.35
20	11	251	6.44	6.58	6.72	6.86	7.01	7.15	7.30	7.45	7.60	7.76	7.91	8.07	8.22	8.38	8.54	8.70	8.86	9.03	9.19	9.36
20	10	250	6.45	6.59	6.73	6.88	7.02	7.17	7.32	7.47	7.62	7.77	7.92	8.08	8.23	8.39	8.55	8.71	8.87	9.04	9.20	9.37
20	9	249	6.47	6.61	6.75	6.89	7.04	7.18	7.33	7.48	7.63	7.78	7.94	8.09	8.25	8.41	8.56	8.73	8.89	9.05	9.21	9.38
20	8	248	6.48	6.62	6.76	6.91	7.05	7.20	7.34	7.49	7.64	7.80	7.95	8.10	8.26	8.42	8.58	8.74	8.90	9.06	9.23	9.39
20	7	247	6.50	6.64	6.78	6.92	7.06	7.21	7.36	7.51	7.66	7.81	7.96	8.12	8.27	8.43	8.59	8.75	8.91	9.07	9.24	9.40
20	6	246	6.51	6.65	6.79	6.93	7.08	7.22	7.37	7.52	7.67	7.82	7.98	8.13	8.29	8.44	8.60	8.76	8.92	9.09	9.25	9.42
20	5	245	6.53	6.67	6.81	6.95	7.09	7.24	7.39	7.54	7.69	7.84	7.99	8.14	8.30	8.46	8.62	8.78	8.94	9.10	9.26	9.43
20	4	244	6.54	6.68	6.82	6.96	7.11	7.25	7.40	7.55	7.70	7.85	8.00	8.16	8.31	8.47	8.63	8.79	8.95	9.11	9.28	9.44
20	3	243	6.56	6.70	6.84	6.98	7.12	7.27	7.42	7.56	7.71	7.87	8.02	8.17	8.33	8.48	8.64	8.80	8.96	9.12	9.29	9.45
20	2	242	6.57	6.71	6.85	6.99	7.14	7.28	7.43	7.58	7.73	7.88	8.03	8.19	8.34	8.50	8.66	8.82	8.98	9.14	9.30	9.46
20	1	241	6.59	6.73	6.87	7.01	7.15	7.30	7.45	7.59	7.74	7.89	8.05	8.20	8.36	8.51	8.67	8.83	8.99	9.15	9.31	9.48

Yr	Mo	Months																				
20	0	240	6.60	6.74	6.88	7.03	7.17	7.31	7.46	7.61	7.76	7.91	8.06	8.21	8.37	8.53	8.68	8.84	9.00	9.16	9.33	9.49
19	11	239	6.62	6.76	6.90	7.04	7.18	7.33	7.48	7.62	7.77	7.92	8.08	8.23	8.38	8.54	8.70	8.86	9.02	9.18	9.34	9.50
19	10	238	6.64	6.78	6.92	7.06	7.20	7.35	7.49	7.64	7.79	7.94	8.09	8.24	8.40	8.55	8.71	8.87	9.03	9.19	9.35	9.52
19	9	237	6.65	6.79	6.93	7.07	7.22	7.36	7.51	7.65	7.80	7.95	8.11	8.26	8.41	8.57	8.73	8.88	9.04	9.20	9.37	9.53
19	8	236	6.67	6.81	6.95	7.09	7.23	7.38	7.52	7.67	7.82	7.97	8.12	8.27	8.43	8.58	8.74	8.90	9.06	9.22	9.38	9.54
19	7	235	6.69	6.82	6.96	7.11	7.25	7.39	7.54	7.69	7.83	7.98	8.14	8.29	8.44	8.60	8.75	8.91	9.07	9.23	9.39	9.56
19	6	234	6.70	6.84	6.98	7.12	7.26	7.41	7.55	7.70	7.85	8.00	8.15	8.30	8.46	8.61	8.77	8.93	9.09	9.25	9.41	9.57
19	5	233	6.72	6.86	7.00	7.14	7.28	7.43	7.57	7.72	7.87	8.02	8.17	8.32	8.47	8.63	8.78	8.94	9.10	9.26	9.42	9.58
19	4	232	6.74	6.88	7.01	7.16	7.30	7.44	7.59	7.73	7.88	8.03	8.18	8.33	8.49	8.64	8.80	8.96	9.11	9.27	9.44	9.60
19	3	231	6.75	6.89	7.03	7.17	7.31	7.46	7.60	7.75	7.90	8.05	8.20	8.35	8.50	8.66	8.81	8.97	9.13	9.29	9.45	9.61
19	2	230	6.77	6.91	7.05	7.19	7.33	7.47	7.62	7.77	7.91	8.06	8.21	8.37	8.52	8.67	8.83	8.99	9.14	9.30	9.46	9.63
19	1	229	6.79	6.93	7.07	7.21	7.35	7.49	7.64	7.78	7.93	8.08	8.23	8.38	8.53	8.69	8.84	9.00	9.16	9.32	9.48	9.64
19	0	228	6.81	6.95	7.08	7.22	7.37	7.51	7.65	7.80	7.95	8.10	8.25	8.40	8.55	8.70	8.86	9.02	9.17	9.33	9.49	9.65
18	11	227	6.83	6.96	7.10	7.24	7.38	7.53	7.67	7.82	7.96	8.11	8.26	8.41	8.57	8.72	8.88	9.03	9.19	9.35	9.51	9.67
18	10	226	6.84	6.98	7.12	7.26	7.40	7.54	7.69	7.83	7.98	8.13	8.28	8.43	8.58	8.74	8.89	9.05	9.20	9.36	9.52	9.68
18	9	225	6.86	7.00	7.14	7.28	7.42	7.56	7.71	7.85	8.00	8.15	8.30	8.45	8.60	8.75	8.91	9.06	9.22	9.38	9.54	9.70
18	8	224	6.88	7.02	7.16	7.30	7.44	7.58	7.72	7.87	8.02	8.16	8.31	8.46	8.62	8.77	8.92	9.08	9.24	9.39	9.55	9.71
18	7	223	6.90	7.04	7.17	7.31	7.45	7.60	7.74	7.89	8.03	8.18	8.33	8.48	8.63	8.79	8.94	9.10	9.25	9.41	9.57	9.73
18	6	222	6.92	7.05	7.19	7.33	7.47	7.62	7.76	7.90	8.05	8.20	8.35	8.50	8.65	8.80	8.96	9.11	9.27	9.43	9.59	9.75
18	5	221	6.94	7.07	7.21	7.35	7.49	7.63	7.78	7.92	8.07	8.22	8.36	8.51	8.67	8.82	8.97	9.13	9.28	9.44	9.60	9.76
18	4	220	6.96	7.09	7.23	7.37	7.51	7.65	7.80	7.94	8.09	8.23	8.38	8.53	8.68	8.84	8.99	9.15	9.30	9.46	9.62	9.78
18	3	219	6.98	7.11	7.25	7.39	7.53	7.67	7.81	7.96	8.10	8.25	8.40	8.55	8.70	8.85	9.01	9.16	9.32	9.48	9.63	9.79
18	2	218	7.00	7.13	7.27	7.41	7.55	7.69	7.83	7.98	8.12	8.27	8.42	8.57	8.72	8.87	9.02	9.18	9.34	9.49	9.65	9.81
18	1	217	7.02	7.15	7.29	7.43	7.57	7.71	7.85	8.00	8.14	8.29	8.44	8.59	8.74	8.89	9.04	9.20	9.35	9.51	9.67	9.83
18	0	216	7.04	7.17	7.31	7.45	7.59	7.73	7.87	8.01	8.16	8.31	8.45	8.60	8.75	8.91	9.06	9.21	9.37	9.53	9.68	9.84
17	11	215	7.06	7.19	7.33	7.47	7.61	7.75	7.89	8.03	8.18	8.33	8.47	8.62	8.77	8.92	9.08	9.23	9.39	9.54	9.70	9.86
17	10	214	7.08	7.21	7.35	7.49	7.63	7.77	7.91	8.05	8.20	8.34	8.49	8.64	8.79	8.94	9.10	9.25	9.40	9.56	9.72	9.88
17	9	213	7.10	7.23	7.37	7.51	7.65	7.79	7.93	8.07	8.22	8.36	8.51	8.66	8.81	8.96	9.11	9.27	9.42	9.58	9.74	9.89
17	8	212	7.12	7.25	7.39	7.53	7.67	7.81	7.95	8.09	8.24	8.38	8.53	8.68	8.83	8.98	9.13	9.29	9.44	9.60	9.75	9.91
17	7	211	7.14	7.27	7.41	7.55	7.69	7.83	7.97	8.11	8.26	8.40	8.55	8.70	8.85	9.00	9.15	9.30	9.46	9.61	9.77	9.93
17	6	210	7.16	7.29	7.43	7.57	7.71	7.85	7.99	8.13	8.28	8.42	8.57	8.72	8.87	9.02	9.17	9.32	9.48	9.63	9.79	9.95
17	5	209	7.18	7.32	7.45	7.59	7.73	7.87	8.01	8.15	8.30	8.44	8.59	8.74	8.89	9.04	9.19	9.34	9.50	9.65	9.81	9.97
17	4	208	7.20	7.34	7.47	7.61	7.75	7.89	8.03	8.17	8.32	8.46	8.61	8.76	8.91	9.06	9.21	9.36	9.52	9.67	9.83	9.98
17	3	207	7.22	7.36	7.49	7.63	7.77	7.91	8.05	8.19	8.34	8.48	8.63	8.78	8.93	9.08	9.23	9.38	9.53	9.69	9.85	10.00
17	2	206	7.25	7.38	7.52	7.65	7.79	7.93	8.07	8.22	8.36	8.50	8.65	8.80	8.95	9.10	9.25	9.40	9.55	9.71	9.86	10.02
17	1	205	7.27	7.40	7.54	7.68	7.81	7.95	8.09	8.24	8.38	8.53	8.67	8.82	8.97	9.12	9.27	9.42	9.57	9.73	9.88	10.04
17	0	204	7.29	7.43	7.56	7.70	7.84	7.98	8.12	8.26	8.40	8.55	8.69	8.84	8.99	9.14	9.29	9.44	9.59	9.75	9.90	10.06
16	11	203	7.31	7.45	7.58	7.72	7.86	8.00	8.14	8.28	8.42	8.57	8.71	8.86	9.01	9.16	9.31	9.46	9.61	9.77	9.92	10.08

AMORTIZATION TABLES (Continued)

MONTHLY INSTALLMENT PER THOUSAND DOLLARS INCLUDING INTEREST AT—

Term of Mortgage Years	Months	No. of Payments	5%	5¼%	5½%	5¾%	6%	6¼%	6½%	6¾%	7%	7¼%	7½%	7¾%	8%	8¼%	8½%	8¾%	9%	9¼%	9½%	9¾%
16	10	202	7.34	7.47	7.61	7.74	7.88	8.02	8.16	8.30	8.45	8.59	8.73	8.88	9.03	9.18	9.33	9.48	9.63	9.79	9.94	10.10
16	9	201	7.36	7.49	7.63	7.77	7.90	8.04	8.18	8.32	8.47	8.61	8.76	8.90	9.05	9.20	9.35	9.50	9.65	9.81	9.96	10.12
16	8	200	7.38	7.52	7.65	7.79	7.93	8.07	8.21	8.35	8.49	8.63	8.78	8.92	9.07	9.22	9.37	9.52	9.67	9.83	9.98	10.14
16	7	199	7.41	7.54	7.68	7.81	7.95	8.09	8.23	8.37	8.51	8.66	8.80	8.95	9.09	9.24	9.39	9.54	9.70	9.85	10.00	10.16
16	6	198	7.43	7.57	7.70	7.84	7.97	8.11	8.25	8.39	8.53	8.68	8.82	8.97	9.12	9.26	9.41	9.57	9.72	9.87	10.02	10.18
16	5	197	7.46	7.59	7.72	7.86	8.00	8.14	8.27	8.42	8.56	8.70	8.85	8.99	9.14	9.29	9.44	9.59	9.74	9.89	10.05	10.20
16	4	196	7.48	7.61	7.75	7.88	8.02	8.16	8.30	8.44	8.58	8.72	8.87	9.01	9.16	9.31	9.46	9.61	9.76	9.91	10.07	10.22
16	3	195	7.51	7.64	7.77	7.91	8.05	8.18	8.32	8.46	8.60	8.75	8.89	9.04	9.18	9.33	9.48	9.63	9.78	9.93	10.09	10.24
16	2	194	7.53	7.66	7.80	7.93	8.07	8.21	8.35	8.49	8.63	8.77	8.92	9.06	9.21	9.35	9.50	9.65	9.80	9.96	10.11	10.26
16	1	193	7.56	7.69	7.82	7.96	8.09	8.23	8.37	8.51	8.65	8.80	8.94	9.08	9.23	9.38	9.53	9.68	9.83	9.98	10.13	10.29
16	0	192	7.58	7.71	7.85	7.98	8.12	8.26	8.40	8.54	8.68	8.82	8.96	9.11	9.25	9.40	9.55	9.70	9.85	10.00	10.15	10.31
15	11	191	7.61	7.74	7.87	8.01	8.14	8.28	8.42	8.56	8.70	8.84	8.99	9.13	9.28	9.43	9.57	9.72	9.87	10.02	10.18	10.33
15	10	190	7.63	7.77	7.90	8.03	8.17	8.31	8.45	8.59	8.73	8.87	9.01	9.16	9.30	9.45	9.60	9.75	9.90	10.05	10.20	10.35
15	9	189	7.66	7.79	7.93	8.06	8.20	8.33	8.47	8.61	8.75	8.89	9.04	9.18	9.33	9.47	9.62	9.77	9.92	10.07	10.22	10.38
15	8	188	7.69	7.82	7.95	8.09	8.22	8.36	8.50	8.64	8.78	8.92	9.06	9.21	9.35	9.50	9.65	9.79	9.94	10.10	10.25	10.40
15	7	187	7.71	7.85	7.98	8.11	8.25	8.39	8.52	8.66	8.80	8.95	9.09	9.23	9.38	9.52	9.67	9.82	9.97	10.12	10.27	10.42
15	6	186	7.74	7.87	8.01	8.14	8.28	8.41	8.55	8.69	8.83	8.97	9.11	9.26	9.40	9.55	9.70	9.84	9.99	10.14	10.30	10.45
15	5	185	7.77	7.90	8.03	8.17	8.30	8.44	8.58	8.72	8.86	9.00	9.14	9.28	9.43	9.57	9.72	9.87	10.02	10.17	10.32	10.47
15	4	184	7.80	7.93	8.06	8.20	8.33	8.47	8.60	8.74	8.88	9.02	9.17	9.31	9.45	9.60	9.75	9.89	10.04	10.19	10.34	10.50
15	3	183	7.83	7.96	8.09	8.22	8.36	8.49	8.63	8.77	8.91	9.05	9.19	9.34	9.48	9.63	9.77	9.92	10.07	10.22	10.37	10.52
15	2	182	7.85	7.99	8.12	8.25	8.39	8.52	8.66	8.80	8.94	9.08	9.22	9.36	9.51	9.65	9.80	9.95	10.09	10.24	10.40	10.55
15	1	181	7.88	8.01	8.15	8.28	8.41	8.55	8.69	8.83	8.97	9.11	9.25	9.39	9.53	9.68	9.83	9.97	10.12	10.27	10.42	10.57
15	0	180	7.91	8.04	8.18	8.31	8.44	8.58	8.72	8.85	8.99	9.13	9.28	9.42	9.56	9.71	9.85	10.00	10.15	10.30	10.45	10.60
14	11	179	7.94	8.07	8.21	8.34	8.47	8.61	8.74	8.88	9.02	9.16	9.30	9.45	9.59	9.73	9.88	10.03	10.17	10.32	10.47	10.62
14	10	178	7.97	8.10	8.24	8.37	8.50	8.64	8.77	8.91	9.05	9.19	9.33	9.47	9.62	9.76	9.91	10.05	10.20	10.35	10.50	10.65
14	9	177	8.00	8.13	8.27	8.40	8.53	8.67	8.80	8.94	9.08	9.22	9.36	9.50	9.65	9.79	9.94	10.08	10.23	10.38	10.53	10.68
14	8	176	8.03	8.16	8.30	8.43	8.56	8.70	8.83	8.97	9.11	9.25	9.39	9.53	9.67	9.82	9.96	10.11	10.26	10.41	10.56	10.71
14	7	175	8.06	8.20	8.33	8.46	8.59	8.73	8.86	9.00	9.14	9.28	9.42	9.56	9.70	9.85	9.99	10.14	10.29	10.43	10.58	10.73
14	6	174	8.10	8.23	8.36	8.49	8.62	8.76	8.89	9.03	9.17	9.31	9.45	9.59	9.73	9.88	10.02	10.17	10.31	10.46	10.61	10.76
14	5	173	8.13	8.26	8.39	8.52	8.65	8.79	8.93	9.06	9.20	9.34	9.48	9.62	9.76	9.91	10.05	10.20	10.34	10.49	10.64	10.79
14	4	172	8.16	8.29	8.42	8.55	8.69	8.82	8.96	9.09	9.23	9.37	9.51	9.65	9.79	9.94	10.08	10.23	10.37	10.52	10.67	10.82
14	3	171	8.19	8.32	8.45	8.59	8.72	8.85	8.99	9.12	9.26	9.40	9.54	9.68	9.82	9.97	10.11	10.26	10.40	10.55	10.70	10.85

Yr	Mo	Term																				
14	2	170	8.23	8.36	8.49	8.62	8.75	8.89	9.02	9.16	9.29	9.43	9.57	9.71	9.85	10.00	10.14	10.29	10.43	10.58	10.73	10.88
14	1	169	8.26	8.39	8.52	8.65	8.78	8.92	9.05	9.19	9.33	9.46	9.60	9.74	9.89	10.03	10.17	10.32	10.46	10.61	10.76	10.91
14	0	168	8.29	8.42	8.55	8.68	8.82	8.95	9.09	9.22	9.36	9.50	9.64	9.78	9.92	10.06	10.20	10.35	10.49	10.64	10.79	10.94
13	11	167	8.33	8.46	8.59	8.72	8.85	8.98	9.12	9.26	9.39	9.53	9.67	9.81	9.95	10.09	10.24	10.38	10.53	10.67	10.82	10.97
13	10	166	8.36	8.49	8.62	8.75	8.89	9.02	9.15	9.29	9.43	9.56	9.70	9.84	9.98	10.13	10.27	10.41	10.56	10.70	10.85	11.00
13	9	165	8.40	8.53	8.66	8.79	8.92	9.05	9.19	9.32	9.46	9.60	9.74	9.88	10.02	10.16	10.30	10.45	10.59	10.74	10.88	11.03
13	8	164	8.43	8.56	8.69	8.82	8.95	9.09	9.22	9.36	9.49	9.63	9.77	9.91	10.05	10.19	10.33	10.48	10.62	10.77	10.92	11.06
13	7	163	8.47	8.60	8.73	8.86	8.99	9.12	9.26	9.39	9.53	9.67	9.80	9.94	10.08	10.23	10.37	10.51	10.66	10.80	10.95	11.10
13	6	162	8.51	8.63	8.76	8.89	9.03	9.16	9.29	9.43	9.56	9.70	9.84	9.98	10.12	10.26	10.40	10.55	10.69	10.83	10.98	11.13
13	5	161	8.54	8.67	8.80	8.93	9.06	9.20	9.33	9.46	9.60	9.74	9.87	10.01	10.15	10.29	10.44	10.58	10.72	10.87	11.01	11.16
13	4	160	8.58	8.71	8.84	8.97	9.10	9.23	9.37	9.50	9.64	9.77	9.91	10.05	10.19	10.33	10.47	10.61	10.76	10.90	11.05	11.20
13	3	159	8.62	8.75	8.88	9.01	9.14	9.27	9.40	9.54	9.67	9.81	9.95	10.09	10.22	10.37	10.51	10.65	10.79	10.94	11.08	11.23
13	2	158	8.66	8.78	8.91	9.04	9.17	9.31	9.44	9.57	9.71	9.85	9.98	10.12	10.26	10.40	10.54	10.69	10.83	10.97	11.12	11.27
13	1	157	8.70	8.82	8.95	9.08	9.21	9.35	9.48	9.61	9.75	9.88	10.02	10.16	10.30	10.44	10.58	10.72	10.87	11.01	11.15	11.30
13	0	156	8.74	8.86	8.99	9.12	9.25	9.38	9.52	9.65	9.79	9.92	10.06	10.20	10.34	10.48	10.62	10.76	10.90	11.05	11.19	11.34
12	11	155	8.78	8.90	9.03	9.16	9.29	9.42	9.56	9.69	9.82	9.96	10.10	10.23	10.37	10.51	10.65	10.80	10.94	11.08	11.23	11.37
12	10	154	8.82	8.94	9.07	9.20	9.33	9.46	9.60	9.73	9.86	10.00	10.14	10.27	10.41	10.55	10.69	10.83	10.98	11.12	11.26	11.41
12	9	153	8.86	8.98	9.11	9.24	9.37	9.50	9.64	9.77	9.90	10.04	10.18	10.31	10.45	10.59	10.73	10.87	11.01	11.16	11.30	11.45
12	8	152	8.90	9.03	9.15	9.28	9.41	9.54	9.68	9.81	9.94	10.08	10.22	10.35	10.49	10.63	10.77	10.91	11.05	11.20	11.34	11.49
12	7	151	8.94	9.07	9.20	9.32	9.45	9.59	9.72	9.85	9.99	10.12	10.26	10.39	10.53	10.67	10.81	10.95	11.09	11.24	11.38	11.52
12	6	150	8.98	9.11	9.24	9.37	9.50	9.63	9.76	9.89	10.03	10.16	10.30	10.43	10.57	10.71	10.85	10.99	11.13	11.28	11.42	11.56
12	5	149	9.03	9.15	9.28	9.41	9.54	9.67	9.80	9.94	10.07	10.20	10.34	10.48	10.61	10.75	10.89	11.03	11.17	11.32	11.46	11.60
12	4	148	9.07	9.20	9.33	9.45	9.58	9.71	9.85	9.98	10.11	10.25	10.38	10.52	10.66	10.79	10.93	11.07	11.21	11.36	11.50	11.64
12	3	147	9.12	9.24	9.37	9.50	9.63	9.76	9.89	10.02	10.15	10.29	10.42	10.56	10.70	10.84	10.98	11.12	11.26	11.40	11.54	11.68
12	2	146	9.16	9.29	9.41	9.54	9.67	9.80	9.93	10.07	10.20	10.33	10.47	10.60	10.74	10.88	11.02	11.16	11.30	11.44	11.58	11.73
12	1	145	9.21	9.33	9.46	9.59	9.72	9.85	9.98	10.11	10.24	10.38	10.51	10.65	10.79	10.92	11.06	11.20	11.34	11.48	11.63	11.77
12	0	144	9.25	9.38	9.51	9.63	9.76	9.89	10.02	10.16	10.29	10.42	10.56	10.69	10.83	10.97	11.11	11.24	11.39	11.53	11.67	11.81
11	11	143	9.30	9.43	9.55	9.68	9.81	9.94	10.07	10.20	10.33	10.47	10.60	10.74	10.87	11.01	11.15	11.29	11.43	11.57	11.71	11.86
11	10	142	9.35	9.47	9.60	9.73	9.86	9.99	10.12	10.25	10.38	10.51	10.65	10.78	10.92	11.06	11.20	11.33	11.47	11.62	11.76	11.90
11	9	141	9.40	9.52	9.65	9.78	9.91	10.03	10.17	10.30	10.43	10.56	10.70	10.83	10.97	11.10	11.24	11.38	11.52	11.66	11.80	11.94
11	8	140	9.45	9.57	9.70	9.83	9.95	10.08	10.21	10.34	10.48	10.61	10.74	10.88	11.01	11.15	11.29	11.43	11.57	11.71	11.85	11.99
11	7	139	9.50	9.62	9.75	9.88	10.00	10.13	10.26	10.39	10.53	10.66	10.79	10.93	11.06	11.20	11.34	11.47	11.61	11.75	11.90	12.04
11	6	138	9.55	9.67	9.80	9.93	10.05	10.18	10.31	10.44	10.58	10.71	10.84	10.98	11.11	11.25	11.38	11.52	11.66	11.80	11.94	12.08
11	5	137	9.60	9.72	9.85	9.98	10.11	10.23	10.36	10.49	10.63	10.76	10.89	11.03	11.16	11.30	11.43	11.57	11.71	11.85	11.99	12.13
11	4	136	9.65	9.78	9.90	10.03	10.16	10.29	10.41	10.55	10.68	10.81	10.94	11.08	11.21	11.35	11.48	11.62	11.76	11.90	12.04	12.18
11	3	135	9.71	9.83	9.96	10.08	10.21	10.34	10.47	10.60	10.73	10.86	10.99	11.13	11.26	11.40	11.53	11.67	11.81	11.95	12.09	12.23
11	2	134	9.76	9.88	10.01	10.14	10.26	10.39	10.52	10.65	10.78	10.91	11.05	11.18	11.31	11.45	11.59	11.72	11.86	12.00	12.14	12.28
11	1	133	9.81	9.94	10.06	10.19	10.32	10.45	10.57	10.70	10.83	10.97	11.10	11.23	11.37	11.50	11.64	11.78	11.91	12.05	12.19	12.33

AMORTIZATION TABLES (Continued)

Term of Mortgage Years	Months	No. of Payments	MONTHLY INSTALLMENT PER THOUSAND DOLLARS INCLUDING INTEREST AT—																			
			5%	5¼%	5½%	5¾%	6%	6¼%	6½%	6¾%	7%	7¼%	7½%	7¾%	8%	8¼%	8½%	8¾%	9%	9¼%	9½%	9¾%
11	0	132	9.87	9.99	10.12	10.25	10.37	10.50	10.63	10.76	10.89	11.02	11.15	11.29	11.42	11.56	11.69	11.83	11.97	12.10	12.24	12.38
10	11	131	9.93	10.05	10.18	10.30	10.43	10.56	10.68	10.81	10.94	11.08	11.21	11.34	11.47	11.61	11.75	11.88	12.02	12.16	12.30	12.44
10	10	130	9.98	10.11	10.23	10.36	10.48	10.61	10.74	10.87	11.00	11.13	11.26	11.40	11.53	11.66	11.80	11.94	12.07	12.21	12.35	12.49
10	9	129	10.04	10.17	10.29	10.42	10.54	10.67	10.80	10.93	11.06	11.19	11.32	11.45	11.59	11.72	11.86	11.99	12.13	12.27	12.41	12.55
10	8	128	10.10	10.22	10.35	10.47	10.60	10.73	10.86	10.99	11.12	11.25	11.38	11.51	11.64	11.78	11.91	12.05	12.19	12.32	12.46	12.60
10	7	127	10.16	10.28	10.41	10.53	10.66	10.79	10.92	11.04	11.17	11.31	11.44	11.57	11.70	11.84	11.97	12.11	12.24	12.38	12.52	12.66
10	6	126	10.22	10.35	10.47	10.60	10.72	10.85	10.98	11.10	11.23	11.36	11.50	11.63	11.76	11.89	12.03	12.16	12.30	12.44	12.58	12.71
10	5	125	10.28	10.41	10.53	10.66	10.78	10.91	11.04	11.17	11.30	11.43	11.56	11.69	11.82	11.95	12.09	12.22	12.36	12.50	12.63	12.77
10	4	124	10.35	10.47	10.60	10.72	10.85	10.97	11.10	11.23	11.36	11.49	11.62	11.75	11.88	12.02	12.15	12.28	12.42	12.56	12.69	12.83
10	3	123	10.41	10.54	10.66	10.78	10.91	11.04	11.16	11.29	11.42	11.55	11.68	11.81	11.94	12.08	12.21	12.35	12.48	12.62	12.76	12.89
10	2	122	10.48	10.60	10.72	10.85	10.97	11.10	11.23	11.36	11.48	11.61	11.74	11.88	12.01	12.14	12.27	12.41	12.54	12.68	12.82	12.96
10	1	121	10.54	10.67	10.79	10.91	11.04	11.17	11.29	11.42	11.55	11.68	11.81	11.94	12.07	12.20	12.34	12.47	12.61	12.74	12.88	13.02
10	0	120	10.61	10.73	10.86	10.98	11.11	11.23	11.36	11.49	11.62	11.75	11.88	12.01	12.14	12.27	12.40	12.54	12.67	12.81	12.94	13.08

APPENDIX III*

SAMPLE COOPERATIVE DOCUMENTS

*Reprinted with permission of Church Management Corporation.

Apt. No.:
Shares:

Lessor,

TO

Lessee

PROPRIETARY LEASE

TABLE OF CONTENTS

(i)

(iii)

(iv)

PROPRIETARY LEASE

PROPRIETARY LEASE, made as of   , 19 , by and between   ., a New York corporation, having an office at   , N.Y., N.Y., hereinafter called the Lessor, and

hereinafter called the Lessee.

WHEREAS, the Lessor is the owner of the land and the building erected thereon in the City and State of New York known as and by the street number   , hereinafter called the "building"; and

WHEREAS, the Lessee is the owner of   shares of the Lessor, to which this lease is appurtenant and which have been allocated to Apartment   in the building;

Demised Premises; Term

Now, THEREFORE, in consideration of the premises, the Lessor hereby leases to the Lessee, and the Lessee hires from the Lessor, subject to the terms and conditions hereof, Apartment   in the building (hereinafter referred to as the apartment) for a term from   , 19 , until December 31, 2024 (unless sooner terminated as hereinafter provided). As used herein "the apartment" means the rooms in the building as partitioned on the date of the execution of this lease designated by the above-stated apartment number, together with their appurtenances and fixtures and any closets, terraces, balconies, roof, or portion thereof outside of said partitioned rooms, which are allocated exclusively to the occupant of the apartment.

Rent (Maintenance) How Fixed

1.(a) The rent (sometimes called maintenance) payable by the Lessee for each year, or portion of a year, during the term shall equal that proportion of the Lessor's cash requirements for such year, or

1

portion of a year, which the number of shares of Lessor allocated to the apartment bears to the total number of shares of the Lessor issued and outstanding on the date of the determination of such cash requirements. Such maintenance shall be payable in equal monthly installments in advance on the first day of each month, unless the Board of Directors of the Lessor (hereinafter called Directors) at the time of its determination of the cash requirements shall otherwise direct. The Lessee shall also pay such additional rent as may be provided for herein when due.

Accompanying Shares to Be Specified in Proprietary Leases

(b) In every proprietary lease heretofore executed by the Lessor there has been specified, and in every proprietary lease hereafter executed by it there will be specified, the number of shares of the Lessor issued to a lessee simultaneously therewith, which number, in relation to the total number of shares of the Lessor issued and outstanding, shall constitute the basis for fixing, as herein before provided, the proportionate share of the Lessor's cash requirements which shall be payable as rent by the Lessee.

Cash Requirements Defined

(c) "Cash requirements" whenever used herein shall mean the estimated amount in cash which the Directors shall from time to time in its judgment determine to be necessary or proper for (1) the operation, maintenance, care, alteration and improvement of the corporate property during the year or portion of the year for which such determination is made; (2) the creation of such reserve for contingencies as it may deem proper; and (3) the payment of any obligations, liabilities or expenses incurred or to be incurred, after giving consideration to (i) income expected to be received during such period (other than rent from proprietary lessees), and (ii) cash on hand which the Directors in its discretion may choose to apply. The Directors may from time to time modify its prior determination and increase or diminish the amount previously determined as cash requirements of the corporation for a year or portion thereof. No determination of cash requirements shall have any retroactive effect on the amount of the rent payable by the lessee for any period prior

2

to the date of such determination. All determinations of cash requirements shall be conclusive as to all lessees.

Authority Limited to Board of Directors

(d) Whenever in this paragraph or any other paragraph of this lease, a power or privilege is given to the Directors, the same may be exercised only by the Directors, and in no event may any such power or privilege be exercised by a creditor, receiver or trustee.

Issuance of Additional Shares

(e) If the Lessor shall hereafter issue shares (whether now or hereafter authorized) in addition to those issued on the date of the execution of this lease, the holders of the shares hereafter issued shall be obligated to pay rent at the same rate as the other proprietary lessees from and after the date of issuance. If any such shares be issued on a date other than the first or last day of the month, the rent for the month in which issued shall be apportioned. The cash requirements as last determined shall, upon the issuance of such shares, be deemed increased by an amount equal to such rent.

Paid-in Surplus

(f) The Directors may from time to time as may be proper determine how much of the maintenance and other receipts, when received, shall be credited on the corporate accounts to "Paid-in-Surplus" (but not more than such amount as represents payments on account of principal of mortgages on the property and other capital expenditures).

Failure to Fix Cash Requirements

(g) The failure of the Directors to determine the Lessor's cash requirements for any year or portion thereof shall not be deemed a waiver or modification in any respect of the covenants and provisions hereof, or a release of the Lessee from the obligation to pay the maintenance or any installment thereof, but the maintenance computed on the basis of the cash requirements as last determined for any year or portion thereof shall thereafter continue to be the maintenance until a new determination of cash requirements shall be made.

3

LESSOR'S REPAIRS

2. The Lessor shall at its expense keep in good repair all of the building including all of the apartments, the sidewalks and courts surrounding the same, and its equipment and apparatus except those portions the maintenance and repair of which are expressly stated to be the responsibility of the Lessee pursuant to Paragraph 18 hereof.

SERVICES BY LESSOR

3. The Lessor shall maintain and manage the building as a first-class apartment building, and shall keep the elevators and the public halls, cellars and stairways clean and properly lighted and heated, and shall provide the number of attendants requisite, in the judgment of the Directors, for the proper care and service of the building, and shall provide the apartment with a proper and sufficient supply of hot and cold water and of heat, and if there be central air-conditioning equipment supplied by the Lessor, air conditioning when deemed appropriate by the Directors. The covenants by the Lessor herein contained are subject, however, to the discretionary power of the Directors to determine from time to time what services and what attendants shall be proper and the manner of maintaining and operating the building, and also what existing services shall be increased, reduced, changed, modified or terminated.

Damage to Apartment or Building

4. (a) If the apartment or the means of access thereto or the building shall be damaged by fire or other cause covered by multiperil policies commonly carried by cooperative corporations in New York City (any other damage to be repaired by Lessor or Lessee pursuant to Paragraphs 2 and 18, as the case may be), the Lessor shall at its own cost and expense, with reasonable dispatch after receipt of notice of said damage, repair or replace or cause to be repaired or replaced, with materials of a kind and quality then customary in buildings of the type of the building, the building, the apartment, and the means of access thereto, including the walls, floors, ceilings, pipes, wiring and conduits in the apartment. Anything in this Paragraph or Paragraph

4

2 to the contrary notwithstanding, Lessor shall not be required to repair or replace, or cause to be repaired or replaced, equipment, fixtures, furniture, furnishings or decorations installed by the Lessee or any of his predecessors in title nor shall the Lessor be obligated to repaint or replace wallpaper or other decorations in the apartment or to refinish floors located therein.

Rent Abatement

(b) In case the damage resulting from fire or other cause shall be so extensive as to render the apartment partly or wholly untenantable, or if the means of access thereto shall be destroyed, the rent hereunder shall proportionately abate until the apartment shall again be rendered wholly tenantable or the means of access restored; but if said damage shall be caused by the act or negligence of the Lessee or the agents, employees, guests or members of the family of the Lessee or any occupant of the apartment, such rental shall abate only to the extent of the rental value insurance, if any, collected by Lessor with respect to the apartment.

Expiration of Lease Due to Damage

(c) If the Directors shall determine that (i) the building is totally destroyed by fire or other cause, or (ii) the building is so damaged that it cannot be repaired within a reasonable time after the loss shall have been adjusted with the insurance carriers, or (iii) the destruction or damage was caused by hazards which are not covered under the Lessor's insurance policies then in effect, and if in any such case the record holders of at least two-thirds of the issued shares at a shareholders' meeting duly called for that purpose held within 120 days after the determination by the Directors, shall vote not to repair, restore or rebuild, then upon the giving of notice pursuant to Paragraph 31 hereof, this Lease and all other proprietary leases and all right, title and interest of the parties thereunder and the tenancies thereby created, shall thereupon wholly cease and expire and rent shall be paid to the date of such destruction or damage. The Lessee hereby waives any and all rights under Section 227 of the Real Property Law and in no event shall the Lessee have any option or right to terminate this Lease. except as provided herein.

5

Waiver of Subrogation.

(d) Lessor agrees to use its best efforts to obtain a provision in all insurance policies carried by it waiving the right of subrogation against the Lessee; and, to the extent that any loss or damage is covered by the Lessor by any insurance policies which contain such waiver of subrogation, the Lessor releases the Lessee from any liability with respect to such loss or damage. In the event that Lessee suffers loss or damage for which Lessor would be liable, and Lessee carries insurance which covers such loss or damage and such insurance policy or policies contain a waiver of subrogation against the Landlord, then in such event Lessee releases Lessor from any liability with respect to such loss or damage.

INSPECTION OF BOOKS OF ACCOUNT ANNUAL REPORT

5. The Lessor shall keep full and correct books of account at its principal office or at such other place as the Directors may from time to time determine, and the same shall be open during all reasonable hours to inspection by the Lessee or a representative of the Lessee. The Lessor shall deliver to the Lessee within a reasonable time after the end of each fiscal year an annual report of corporate financial affairs, including a balance sheet and a statement of income and expenses, certified by an independent certified public accountant.

CHANGES IN TERMS AND CONDITIONS OF PROPRIETY LEASES

6. Each proprietary lease shall be in the form of this lease, unless a variation of any lease is authorized by lessees owning at least two-thirds of the Lessor's shares then issued and executed by the Lessor and lessee affected. The form and provisions of all the proprietary leases then in effect and thereafter to be executed may be changed by the approval of lessees owning at least 75% of the Lessor's shares then issued, and such changes shall be binding on all lessees even if they did not vote for such changes except that the proportionate share of rent or cash requirements payable by any lessee may not be increased nor may his right to cancel the lease under the conditions set forth in Paragraph 35 be eliminated or impaired without his express consent. Approval by lessees as provided for herein shall be evidenced by writ-

6

ten consent or by affirmative vote taken at a meeting called for such purpose. Notwithstanding the foregoing, in no event shall any change in the form of proprietary lease and any of the provisions thereof be made which shall adversely affect certain rights granted to (i) purchasers of Unsold Shares (pursuant to Paragraph 38 hereof), (ii) the Secured Party (its successors or assigns) as set forth in Paragraph 17(b) below or (iii) individuals repurchasing shares and proprietary leases (as provided under Paragraph 16(g) hereof), unless all such purchasers of Unsold Shares, the Secured Party and individuals effecting such repurchase affected thereby shall have unanimously agreed to each such change.

Penthouses, Terraces and Balconies

7. If the apartment includes a terrace, balcony, or a portion of the roof adjoining a penthouse, the Lessee shall have and enjoy the exclusive use of the terrace or balcony or that portion of the roof appurtenant to the penthouse, subject to the applicable provisions of this lease and to the use of the terrace, balcony or roof by the Lessor to the extent herein permitted. The Lessee's use thereof shall be subject to such regulations as may, from time to time, be prescribed by the Directors. The Lessor shall have the right to erect equipment on the roof, including radio and television aerials and antennas, for its use and the use of the lessees in the building and shall have the right of access thereto for such installations and for the repair thereof. The Lessee shall keep the terrace, balcony, or portion of the roof appurtenant to his apartment clean and free from snow, ice, leaves and other debris and shall maintain all screens and drain boxes in good condition. No planting, fences, structures or lattices shall be erected or installed on the terraces, balconies, or roof of the building without the prior written approval of the Lessor. No cooking shall be permitted on any terraces, balconies or the roof of the building, nor shall the walls thereof be painted by the Lessee without the prior written approval of the Lessor. Any planting or other structures erected by the Lessee or his predecessor in interest may be removed and restored by the Lessor at the expense of the Lessee for the purpose of repairs, unkeep or maintenance of the building.

7

ASSIGNMENT OF LESSOR'S RIGHTS AGAINST OCCUPANT

8. If at the date of the commencement of this lease, any third party shall be in possession or have the right to possession of the apartment, then the Lessor hereby assigns to the Lessee all of the Lessor's rights against said third party from and after the date of the commencement of the term hereof, and the Lessee by the execution hereof assumes all of the Lessor's obligations to said third party from said date. The Lessor agrees to cooperate with the Lessee, but at the Lessee's expense, in the enforcment of the Lessee's rights against said third party.

CANCELLATION OF PRIOR AGREEMENTS

9. If at the date of the commencement of this lease, the Lessee has the right to possession of the apartment under any agreement or statutory tenancy, this lease shall supersede such agreement or statutory tenancy which shall be of no further effect after the date of commencement of this lease, except for claims theretofore arising thereunder.

QUIET ENJOYMENT

10. The Lessee, upon paying the rent and performing the covenants and complying with the conditions on the part of the Lessee to be performed as herein set forth, shall, at all times during the term hereby granted, quietly have, hold and enjoy the apartment without any let, suit, trouble or hindrance from the Lessor, subject, however, to the rights of present tenants or occupants of the apartment, and subject to any and all mortgages and underlying leases of the land and building, as provided in Paragraph 22 below.

INDEMNITY

11. The Lessee agrees to save the Lessor harmless from all liability, loss, damage and expense arising from injury to person or property occasioned by the failure of the Lessee to comply with any provision hereof, or due wholly or in part to any act, default or omission of the Lessee or of any person dwelling or visiting in the apartment, or by the Lessor, its agents, servants or contractors when

8

acting as agent for the Lessee as in this lease provided. This paragraph shall not apply to any loss or damage when Lessor is covered by insurance which provides for waiver of subrogation against the Lessee.

PAYMENT OF RENT

12. The Lessee will pay the rent to the Lessor upon the terms and at the times herein provided, without any deduction on account of any set-off or claim which the Lessee may have against the Lessor, and if the Lessee shall fail to pay any installment of rent promptly, the Lessee shall pay interest thereon at the maximum legal rate from the date when such installment shall have become due to the date of the payment thereof, and such interest shall be deemed additional rent hereunder.

HOUSE RULES

13. The Lessor has adopted House Rules which are appended hereto, and the Directors may alter, amend or repeal such House Rules and adopt new House Rules. This lease shall be in all respects subject to such House Rules which, when a copy thereof has been furnished to the Lessee, shall be taken to be part hereof, and the Lessee hereby covenants to comply with all such House Rules and see that they are faithfully observed by the family, guests, employees and subtenants of the Lessee. Breach of a House Rule shall be a default under this lease. The Lessor shall not be responsible to the Lessee for the non-observance or violation of House Rules by any other lessee or person.

USE OF PREMISES

14. The Lessee shall not, without the written consent of the Lessor on such conditions as Lessor may prescribe, occupy or use the apartment or permit the same or any part thereof to be occupied or used for any purpose other than as a private dwelling for the Lessee and Lessee's spouse, their children, grandchildren, parents, grandparents, brothers and sisters and domestic employees, and in no event shall more than one married couple occupy the apartment without the written consent of the Lessor. In addition to the foregoing, the apartment may be occupied from time to time by guests of the Lessee for

9

a period of time not exceeding one month, unless a longer period is approved in writing by the Lessor, but no guests may occupy the apartment unless one or more of the permitted adult residents are then in occupancy or unless consented to in writing by the Lessor.

SUBLETTING

15. Except as provided in Paragraphs 17(b) and 38 of this lease, the Lessee shall not sublet the whole or any part of the apartment or renew or extend any previously authorized sublease, unless consent thereto shall have been duly authorized by a resolution of the Directors, or given in writing by a majority of the Directors or, if the Directors shall have failed or refused to give such consent, then by lessees owning at least 65% of the then issued shares of the Lessor. Consent by lessees as provided for herein shall be evidenced by written consent or by affirmative vote taken at a meeting called for such purpose. Any consent to subletting may be subject to such conditions as the Directors or lessees, as the case may be, may impose. There shall be no limitation on the right of Directors or lessees to grant or withhold consent, for any reason or for no reason, to a subletting. No consent to a subletting shall operate to release the Lessee from any obligation hereunder.

ASSIGNMENT

16.(a) The Lessee shall not assign this lease or transfer the shares to which it is appurtenant or any interest therein, and no such assignment or transfer shall take effect as against the Lessor for any purpose, until

(i) An instrument of assignment in form approved by Lessor executed and acknowledged by the assignor shall be delivered to the Lessor; and

(ii) An agreement executed and acknowledged by the assignee in form approved by Lessor assuming and agreeing to be bound by all the covenants and conditions of this lease to be performed or complied with by the Lessee on and after the effective date of said assignment shall have been delivered to the

10

Lessor, or, at the request of the Lessor, the assignee shall have surrendered the assigned lease and entered into a new lease in the same form for the remainder of the term, in which case the Lessee's lease shall be deemed cancelled as of the effective date of said assignment; and

(iii) All shares of the Lessor to which this lease is appurtenant shall have been transferred to the assignee, with proper transfer taxes paid and stamps affixed; and

(iv) All sums due from the Lessee shall have been paid to the Lessor, together with a sum to be fixed by the Directors to cover reasonable legal and other expenses of the Lessor and its managing agent in connection with such assignment and transfer of shares (subject to Paragraphs 17(b) and 38 hereof); and

(v) A search or certification from a title or abstract company as the Directors may require shall be delivered to Lessor; and

(vi) Except in the case of an assignment, transfer or bequest of the shares and this lease to the Lessee's spouse or adult siblings or parents, and except as otherwise provided in Paragraphs 16(g), 17(b) and 38 of this lease, consent to such assignment shall have been authorized by resolution of the Directors, or given in writing by a majority of the Directors; or, if the Directors shall have failed or refused to give such consent within 30 days after submission of references to them or Lessor's agent, then by lessees owning of record at least 65% of the then issued shares of the Lessor. Consent by lessees as provided for herein shall be evidenced by written consent or by affirmative vote taken at a meeting called for such purpose in the manner as provided in the by-laws.

Consents: On Death of Lessee

(b) If the Lessee shall die, consent shall not be unreasonably withheld to an assignment of the lease and shares to a financially responsible member of the Lessee's family (other than the Lessee's spouse, adult siblings, or parents as to whom no consent is required).

11

Consents Generally: Stockholders' and
Directors' Obligations to Consent

(c) There shall be no limitation, except as above specifically provided, on the right of Directors or lessees to grant or withhold consent, for any reason or for no reason, to an assignment.

Release of Lessee Upon Assignment

(d) If the lease shall be assigned in compliance herewith, the Lessee-assignor shall have no further liability on any of the covenants of this lease to be thereafter performed.

Further Assignment or Subletting

(e) Regardless of any prior consent theretofore given, neither the Lessee nor his executor, nor administrator, nor any trustee or receiver of the property of the Lessee, nor anyone to whom the interests of the Lessee shall pass by law, shall be entitled further to assign this lease, or to sublet the apartment, or any part thereof, except upon compliance with the requirements of this lease.

Statement by Lessor

(f) If this lease is then in force and effect, Lessor will, upon request of Lessee, deliver to the assignee a written statement that this lease remains on the date thereof in force and effect; but no such statement shall be deemed an admission that there is no default under the lease.

Resales Pursuant to Plan

(g) Notwithstanding the foregoing provisions of this Paragraph 16 or of Paragraph 15 above, in the event the Lessee exercises his right (the "Right of Repurchase") to cause this proprietary lease and appurtenant shares of Lessor to be repurchased by an individual or individuals (the "Repurchaser") supplied in the manner provided in the Offering Plan (the "Plan") to convert the building to cooperative ownership (pursuant to which Plan, Lessor acquired title to the building), then (i) no consent to the assignment of the shares and this lease shall be required to be obtained from the Directors or shareholders

12

of Lessor for either the repurchase by the Repurchaser or the subsequent resale thereof by the Repurchaser, except that in the latter event, a resale must first be approved in writing by the then managing agent of the building (which consent shall not be unreasonably withheld or delayed and shall be granted if resold to a financially responsible individual or individuals); (ii) no sums of whatsoever nature (other than stock transfer stamps) shall be charged to the Lessee, or the Repurchaser or the individual or individuals to whom the Repurchaser has resold this lease and accompanying shares, in connection with said repurchase or subsequent resale (including, without limitation, legal or other expenses of Lessor or its managing agent as provided in subparagraph (a)(iv) of this Paragraph); (iii) the provisions of subparagraph (a)(i), (ii), and (iii) of this Paragraph shall be the only requirements to be complied with by Lessee and the Repurchaser in connection with such repurchase or subsequent resale (Lessor agreeing that whenever its approval as to the form of an instrument is required pursuant to subparagraph (a)(i) or (a)(ii) above, Lessor shall not unreasonably withhold its approval); and (iv) the Repurchaser shall have the absolute right to sublet the apartment from time to time, without obtaining the consent of the Directors or shareholders of Lessor and without payment of any charge of whatsoever nature in connection therewith, subject, however, only to obtaining the prior written consent of the then managing agent of the building as to the proposed sublessee, which consent shall not be unreasonably withheld or delayed (and shall be granted in the event a subletting to a financially responsible individual or to a reputable person).

Pledge of Shares and Lease

17.(a) A pledge of this lease and the shares to which it is appurtenant shall not be a violation of this lease; but, except as otherwise provided elsewhere herein, neither the pledgee nor any transferee of the pledged security shall be entitled to have the shares transferred of record on the books of the Lessor, nor to vote such shares, nor to occupy or permit the occupancy by others of the apartment, nor to sell such shares or this lease, without first obtaining the consent of the Lessor in accordance with and after complying with all of the provisions of Paragraphs 14, 15 or 16, as the case may be. The acceptance by Lessor of payments by the pledgee or any transferee of the pledged

13

security on account of rent or additional rent shall not constitute a waiver of the aforesaid provisions.

Secured Party

(b) Notwithstanding the provisions of subparagraph (a) of this Paragraph 17 or any other provision of this lease to the contrary, the following provisions of this Paragraph shall govern and be binding.

(i) The Lessor agrees that it shall give to any holder of a security interest in the shares of the Lessor specified in the recitals of this lease or mortgagee of this lease who so requests (any such holder, including, without limitation, Associates (the "Sponsor-Seller" under the aforesaid Plan) being hereinafter referred to collectively as a "Secured Party"), a copy of any notice of default which the Lessor gives to the Lessee pursuant to the terms of this lease, and if the Lessee shall fail to cure the default specified in such notice within the time and in the manner provided for in this lease, then the Secured Party shall have an additional period of time, equal to the time originally given to the Lessee, to cure said default for the account of the Lessee or to cause same to be cured, and the Lessor will not act upon said default unless and until the time in which the Secured Party may cure said default or cause same to be cured as aforesaid, shall have elapsed, and the default shall not have been cured.

(ii) If this lease is terminated by the Lessor as provided in Paragraphs 31 or 36 of this lease, (1) the Lessor promptly shall give notice of such termination to the Secured Party and (2) upon request of the Secured Party made within thirty (30) days of the giving of such notice the Lessor (i) shall commence and prosecute a summary dispossess proceeding to obtain possession of the apartment, and (ii) shall, within sixty (60) days of its receipt of the aforesaid request by the Secured Party, re-issue the aforementioned shares to, and (with respect to any termination other than under Paragraph 36 below) shall enter into a new proprietary lease for the apartment with, any individual designated by the Secured Party, or the individual nominee of the individual so designated by the Secured Party, all

14

without the consent of the Directors or the shareholders to which reference is made in Paragraphs 16(a)(vi) and 32(c) but with the consent only of the Lessor's then managing agent which shall not be unreasonably withheld or delayed, provided, however, that the Lessor shall have received payment, on behalf of the Lessee, of all rent, additional rent and other sums owed by the Lessee to the Lessor under this lease for the period ending on the date of reissuance of the aforementioned shares of the Lessor including, without limitation, sums owed under Paragraphs 32 (a) and (c) of this lease; the individual designated by the Secured Party (if and as long as such individual (by himself or a member of his family) does not actually occupy the apartment) shall have all of the rights provided for in Paragraphs 15, 16, 21 and 38 of this lease as if he were a holder of Unsold Shares; and, accordingly, no surplus shall be payable by the Lessor to the Lessee as otherwise provided in Paragraph 32(c).

(iii) If the purchase by the Lessee of the shares allocated to the apartment was financed by (A) Sponsor-Seller or (B) a loan made by a bank, savings bank or savings and loan association and a default or an event of default shall have occurred under the terms of the security agreement-leasehold mortgage or either of them entered into between the Lessee and the Secured Party, and if (1) notice of said default or event of default shall have been given to the Lessor, (2) an individual designated by the Secured Party, or the individual nominee of the individual so designated by the Secured Party, shall be entitled to become the owner of the shares and the Lessee under this lease pursuant to the terms of said security agreement-leasehold mortgage, or either of them, (3) not less than five days' written notice of an intended transfer of the shares and this lease shall have been given to the Lessor and the Lessee, (4) there has been paid, on behalf of the Lessee, all rent, additional rent and other sums owed by the Lessee to the Lessor under this lease for the period ending on the date of transfer of the aforementioned shares as hereinafter provided, and (5) the Lessor shall be furnished with such affidavits, certificates, and opinions of counsel, in form and substance reasonably satisfactory to the Lessor, indicating that the foregoing conditions (1) through (4) have been met, then (a) a transfer of the shares

15

and the proprietary lease shall be made to such individual, upon request, and without the payment of any fees, charges or expenses of Lessor or its managing agent referred to in Paragraph 16(a)(iv) and without the consent of the Directors or the shareholders to which reference is made in Paragraph 16(a)(vi), but with the consent only of the Lessor's then managing agent which shall not be unreasonably withheld or delayed, and (b) the individual to whom such transfer is made (if and as long as such individual (by himself or a member of his family) does not actually occupy the apartment) shall have all of the rights provided for in Paragraphs 15, 16, 21 and 38 of this lease as if he were a holder of Unsold Shares.

(iv) Without the prior written consent of any Secured Party who has requested a copy of any notice of default as hereinbefore provided in subparagraph (b)(i) of this Paragraph 17, (a) the Lessor and the Lessee will not enter into any agreement modifying or cancelling this lease, (b) no change in the form, terms or conditions of this lease, as permitted by Paragraph 6, shall eliminate or modify any rights, privileges or obligations of a Secured Party as set forth in this Paragraph 17(b), (c) the Lessor will not terminate or accept a surrender of this lease, except as provided in Paragraphs 31 or 36 of this lease, (d) the Lessee will not assign or surrender (pursuant to Paragraph 35 hereof) this lease or sublet the apartment, (e) any modification, cancellation, surrender, termination or assignment of this lease or any sublease of the apartment not made in accordance with the provisions hereof shall be void and of no effect, (f) the Lessor will not consent to any further mortgage on this lease or security interest created in the shares, (g) the Lessee will not make any further mortgage or create any further security interest in the shares or this lease, and (h) any such further mortgage or security interest shall be void and of no effect.

(v) Any designee of a Secured Party to whom a transfer of this lease shall have been made pursuant to the terms of subparagraphs (b) (ii) or (iii) hereof may cancel this lease under the terms of Paragraph 35 hereof; except that such des-

16

ignee may cancel this lease at any time after the designee acquires this lease and the shares appurtenant hereto due to foreclosure of the security agreement-leasehold mortgage, provided not less than thirty (30) days' prior written notice of its intention to cancel is given (such notice may be sent at any time during the calendar year).

(vi) A Secured Party claiming or exercising any of the rights and privileges granted it pursuant to the provisions of this subparagraph (b) shall be deemed to have agreed to indemnify Lessor for all loss, liability and expense (including reasonable attorneys' fees) arising out of claims by Lessee, or his successors or assigns, against Lessor or the Secured Party, or their respective successors or assigns, for acts or omissions to act on the part of either Lessor or Secured Party, or their respective successors or assigns, pursuant to this subparagraph (b). Lessor will give the Secured Party written notice with reasonable promptness of any such claim against Lessor and the Secured Party may contest such claim in the name and on behalf of Lessor with counsel selected by the Secured Party at the Secured Party's sole expense. Lessor shall execute such papers and do such things as are reasonably necessary to implement the provisions of this subpart (vi).

(vii) Upon Lessee's final payment under the loan given by the Secured Party, or upon prepayment of said loan, Secured Party will give Lessor notice of such final payment or prepayment (as the case may be).

(viii) Upon request of the holder of Unsold Shares (referred to in Paragraph 38 below) or Repurchaser, Lessor shall enter into an agreement (commonly known as a "Recognition Agreement") with a Secured Party pursuant to which Lessor will acknowledge and agree that the foregoing provisions of this subparagraph (b) shall enure to the benefit of, and apply to, the Secured Party. The Recognition Agreement may contain such additional or different provisions as the Secured Party may request and Lessor shall execute and deliver same to Lender provided only that such additional or different provisions are approved by counsel to Lessor (which approval may not be un-

17

reasonably withheld or delayed and shall be given or deemed given if same are of substantially similar tenor to the provisions of this subparagraph (b)). All costs and expenses incurred by Lessor in connection with such Recognition Agreement (including legal fees) shall be borne entirely by Lessor, and no charge therefor may be assessed to said holder of Unsold Shares or Repurchaser, or their respective successors or assigns, or an individual acquiring this lease and the appurtenant shares from the holder of Unsold Shares or Repurchaser (whether as the result of foreclosure, resale or otherwise), except that said individual acquiring this lease and appurtenant shares from the holder of Unsold Shares or Repurchaser will be required to pay the legal and other expenses of Lessor and its managing agent pursuant to Paragraph 16(a)(iv) hereof on the resale or transfer of the same. The provisions of this subpart (viii) shall not apply to a lessee who is not a holder of Unsold Shares or a Repurchaser.

(ix) Subject to the provisions of subpart (viii) above, a Recognition Agreement between a Lender and Lessor may contain such additional or different provisions as the Lessor and said Lender may agree to.

REPAIRS BY THE LESSEE

18. (a) The Lessee shall take possession of the apartment and its appurtenances and fixtures "as is" as of the commencement of the term hereof. Subject to the provisions of Paragraph 4 above, the Lessee shall keep the interior of the apartment (including interior walls, floors and ceilings, but excluding windows, window panes, window frames, sashes, sills, entrance and terrace doors, frames and saddles) in good repair, shall do all of the painting and decorating required for his apartment, including the interior of window frames, sashes and sills, and shall be solely responsible for the maintenance, repair, and replacement of plumbing, gas and heating fixtures and equipment and such refrigerators, dishwashers, removable and through-the-wall air conditioners, washing machines, ranges and other appliances, as may be in the apartment. Plumbing, gas and heating fixtures as used herein shall include exposed gas, steam and water

18

pipes attached to fixtures, appliances and equipment and the fixtures, appliances and equipment to which they are attached, and any special pipes or equipment which the Lessee may install within the wall or ceiling, or under the floor, but shall not include gas, steam, water or other pipes or conduits within the walls, ceilings or floors or air conditioning or heating equipment which is part of the standard building equipment. The Lessee shall be solely responsible for the maintenance, repair and replacement of all lighting and electrical fixtures, appliances, and equipment, and all meters, fuse boxes or circuit breakers and electrical wiring and conduits from the junction box at the riser into and through the Lessee's apartment. Any ventilator or air conditioning device which shall be visible from the outside of the building shall at all times be painted by the Lessee in a standard color which the Lessor may select for the building.

Odors and Noises

(b) The Lessee shall not permit unreasonable cooking or other odors to escape into the building. The Lessee shall not permit or suffer any unreasonable noises or anything which will interfere with the rights of other lessees or unreasonably annoy them or obstruct the public halls or stairways.

Equipment and Appliances

(c) If, in the Lessor's sole judgment, any of the Lessee's equipment or appliances shall result in damage to the building or poor quality or interruption of service to other portions of the building, or overloading of, or damage to facilities maintained by the Lessor for the supplying of water, gas, electricity or air conditioning to the building, or if any such appliances visible from the outside of the building shall become rusty or discolored, the Lessee shall promptly, on notice from the Lessor, remedy the condition and, pending such remedy, shall cease using any appliance or equipment which may be creating the objectionable condition.

Rules and Regulations and Requirements of Mortgage

(d) The Lessee will comply with all the requirements of the Board of Fire Underwriters, insurance authorities and all governmental

19

authorities and with all laws, ordinances, rules and regulations with respect to the occupancy or use of the apartment. If any mortgage affecting the land or the building shall contain any provisions pertaining to the right of the Lessee to make changes or alterations in the apartment, or to remove any of the fixtures, appliances, equipment or installations, the Lessee herein shall comply with the requirements of such mortgage or mortgages relating thereto. Upon the Lessee's written request, Lessor will furnish Lessee with copies of applicable provisions of each and every such mortgage.

Lessor's Right to Remedy Lessee's Defaults

19. If the Lessee shall fail for 30 days after notice to make repairs to any part of the apartment, its fixtures or equipment as herein required, or shall fail to remedy a condition which has become objectionable to the Lessor for reasons above set forth, or if the Lessee or any person dwelling in the apartment shall request the Lessor, its agents or servants to perform any act not hereby required to be performed by the Lessor, the Lessor may make such repairs, or arrange for others to do the same, or remove such objectionable condition or equipment, or perform such act, without liability on the Lessor; provided that, if the condition requires prompt action, notice of less than 30 days may be given or, in case of emergency, no notice need be given. In all such cases the Lessor, its agents, servants and contractors shall, as between the Lessor and Lessee, be conclusively deemed to be acting as agents of the Lessee and all contracts therefor made by the Lessor shall be so construed whether or not made in the name of the Lessee. If Lessee shall fail to perform or comply with any of the other covenants or provisions of this lease within the time required by a notice from Lessor (not less than 5 days), then Lessor may, but shall not be obligated, to comply therewith, and for such purpose may enter upon the apartment of Lessee. The Lessor shall be entitled to recover from the Lessee all expenses incurred or for which it has contracted hereunder, such expenses to be payable by the Lessee on demand as additional rent.

Increase in Rate of Fire Insurance

20. The Lessee shall not permit or suffer anything to be done or kept in the apartment which will increase the rate of fire insurance

on the building or the contents thereof. If, by reason of the occupancy or use of the apartment by the Lessee, the rate of fire insurance on the building or an apartment or the contents of either shall be increased, the Lessee shall (if such occupancy or use continues for more than 30 days after written notice from the Lessor specifying the objectionable occupancy or use) become personally liable for the additional insurance premiums incurred by Lessor or any lessee or lessees of apartments in the building on all policies so affected, and the Lessor shall have the right to collect the same for its benefit or the benefit of any such lessees as additional rent for the apartment due on the first day of the calendar month following written demand therefor by the Lessor.

ALTERATIONS

21. (a) The Lessee shall not, without first obtaining the written consent of the Lessor, which consent shall not be unreasonably withheld or delayed, make in the apartment or building, or on any roof, penthouse, terrace or balcony appurtenant thereto, any alteration, enclosure or addition or any alteration of or addition to the water, gas, or steam risers or pipes, heating or air conditiong system or units, electrical conduits, wiring or outlets, plumbing fixtures, intercommunication or alarm system, or any other installation or facility in the apartment or building. The performance by Lessee of any work in the apartment shall be in accordance with any applicable rules and regulations of the Lessor and governmental agencies having jurisdiction thereof. The Lessee shall not in any case install any appliances which will overload the existing wires or equipment in the buiding. Anything herein or in subparagraph (b) below to the contrary notwithstanding, the consent of the Lessor shall not be required for any of the foregoing alterations, enclosures, or additions made by, or the removal of any additions, improvements or fixtures from the apartment by, a holder of Unsold Shares or Repurchaser, but the consent only of the Lessor's then managing agent will be sufficient, which consent shall not be unreasonably withheld or delayed.

Removal of Fixtures

(b) Without Lessor's written consent, the Lessee shall not remove any fixtures, appliances, additions or improvements from the apart-

21

ment except as hereinafter provided. If the Lessee, or a prior lessee, shall have heretofore placed, or the Lessee shall hereafter place in the apartment, at the Lessee's own expense, any additions, improvements, appliances or fixtures, including but not limited to fireplace mantels, lighting fixtures, refrigerators, air conditioners, dishwashers, washing machines, ranges, woodwork, wall paneling, ceilings, special doors or decorations, special cabinet work, special stair railings or other built-in ornamental items, which can be removed without structural alterations or permanent damage to the apartment, then title thereto shall remain in the Lessee and the Lessee shall have the right, prior to the termination of this lease, to remove the same at the Lessee's own expense, provided: (i) that the Lessee at the time of such removal shall not be in default in the payment of rent or in the performance or observance of any other covenants or conditions of this lease; (ii) that the Lessee shall, at the Lessee's own expense, prior to the termination of this lease, repair all damage to the apartment which shall have been caused by either the installation or removal of any of such additions, improvements, appliances or fixtures; (iii) that if the Lessee shall have removed from the apartment any articles or materials owned by the Lessor or its predecessor in title, or any fixtures or equipment necessary for the use of the apartment, the Lessee shall either restore such articles and materials and fixtures and equipment and repair any damage resulting from their removal and restoration, or replace them with others of a kind and quality customary in comparable buildings and satisfactory to the Lessor; (iv) that if any mortgagee had acquired a lien on any such property prior to the execution of this lease, Lessor shall first procure from such mortgagee its written consent to such removal, and any cost and expense incurred by the Lessor in respect thereof shall have been paid by the Lessee; and (v) that prior to any such removal, the Lessee shall give written notice thereof to the Lessor.

Surrender on Expiration of Term

(c) On the expiration or termination of this lease, the Lessee shall surrender to the Lessor possession of the apartment with all additions, improvements, appliances and fixtures then included therein, except as hereinabove provided. Any additions, improvements, fixtures or appliances not removed by the Lessee on or before such expiration

22

or termination of this lease shall, at the option of the Lessor, be deemed abandoned and shall become the property of the Lessor and may be disposed of by the Lessor without liability or accountability to the Lessee. Any other personal property not removed by the Lessee at or prior to the termination of this lease may be removed by the Lessor to any place of storage and stored for the account of the Lessee without the Lessor in any way being liable for trespass, conversion or negligence by reason of any acts of the Lessor or of the Lessor's agents, or of any carrier employed in transporting such property to the place of storage, or by reason of the negligence of any person in caring for such property while in storage.

Lease Subordinate to Mortgages and Ground Leases

22. This lease is and shall be subject and subordinate to all present and future ground or underlying leases and to any mortgages now or hereafter liens upon such leases or on the land and building, or buildings, and to any and all extensions, modifications, consolidations, renewals and replacements thereof. This clause shall be self-operative and no further instrument of subordination shall be required by any such mortgagee or ground or underlying lessee. In confirmation of such subordination the Lessee shall at any time, and from time to time, on demand, execute any instruments that may be required by any mortgagee, or by the Lessor, for the purpose of more formally subjecting this lease to the lien of any such mortgage or mortgages or ground or underlying leases, and the duly elected officers, for the time being, of the Lessor are and each of them is hereby irrevocably appointed the attorney-in-fact and agent of the Lessee to execute the same upon such demand, and the Lessee hereby ratifies any such instrument hereafter executed by virtue of the power of attorney hereby given.

In the event that a ground or underlying lease is executed and delivered to the holder of a mortgage or mortgages on such ground or underlying lease or to a nominee or designee of or a corporation formed by or for the benefit of such holder, the Lessee hereunder will attorn to such mortgagee or the nominee or designee of such mortgagee or to any corporation formed by or for the benefit of such mortgagee.

23

Mechanic's Lien

23. In case a notice of mechanic's lien against the building shall be filed purporting to be for labor or material furnished or delivered at the building or the apartment to or for the Lessee, or anyone claiming under the Lessee, the Lessee shall forthwith cause such lien to be discharged by payment, bonding or otherwise; and if the Lessee shall fail to do so within ten days after notice from the Lessor, then the Lessor may cause such lien to be discharged by payment, bonding or otherwise, without investigation as to the validity thereof or of any offsets or defenses thereto, and shall have the right to collect, as additional rent, all amounts so paid and all costs and expenses paid or incurred in connection therewith, including reasonable attorneys' fees and disbursements, together with interest thereon from the time or times of payment.

Cooperation

24. The Lessee shall always in good faith endeavor to observe and promote the cooperative purposes for the accomplishment of which the Lessor is incorporated.

Right of Entry; Key

25. The Lessor and its agents and their authorized workmen shall be permitted to visit, examine, or enter the apartment and any storage space assigned to Lessee at any reasonable hour of the day upon notice, or at any time and without notice in case of emergency, to make or facilitate repairs in any part of the building or to cure any default by the Lessee and to remove such portions of the walls, floors and ceilings of the apartment and storage space as may be required for any such purpose, but the Lessor shall thereafter restore the apartment and storage space to its proper and usual condition at Lessor's expense if such repairs are the obligation of Lessor, or at Lessee's expense if such repairs are the obligation of Lessee or are caused by the act or omission of the Lessee or any of the Lessee's family, guests, agents, employees or subtenants. In order that the Lessor shall at all times have access to the apartment or storage rooms for the purposes provided for in this lease, the Lessee shall provide the Lessor with a key to each lock providing access to the apartment or the storage rooms,

24

and if any lock shall be altered or new lock installed, the Lessee shall provide the Lessor with a key thereto immediately upon installation. If the Lessee shall not be personally present to open and permit an entry at any time when an entry therein shall be necessary or permissible hereunder and shall not have furnished a key to Lessor, the Lessor or the Lessor's agents (but, except in an emergency, only when specifically authorized by an officer of the Lessor or an officer of the managing agent of Lessor) may forcibly enter the apartment or storage space without liability for damages by reason thereof (if during such entry the Lessor shall accord reasonable care to the Lessee's property), and without in any manner affecting the obligations and covenants of this lease. The right and authority hereby reserved do not impose, nor does the Lessor assume by reason thereof, any responsibility or liability for the care or supervision of the apartment, or any of the pipes, fixtures, appliances or appurtenancies therein contained, except as herein specifically provided.

WAIVERS

26. The failure of the Lessor to insist, in any one or more instances, upon a strict performance of any of the provisions of this lease, or to exercise any right or option herein contained, or to serve any notice, or to institute any action or proceeding, shall not be construed as a waiver, or a relinquishment for the future, of any such provisions, options or rights, but such provision, option or right shall continue and remain in full force and effect. The receipt by the Lessor of rent, with knowledge of the breach of any covenant hereof, shall not be deemed a waiver of such breach, and no waiver by the Lessor of any provision hereof shall be deemed to have been made unless in a writing expressly approved by the Directors.

NOTICES

27. Any notice by or demand from either party to the other shall be duly given only if in writing and sent by certified or registered mail return receipt requested: if by the Lessee, addressed to the Lessor at the building with a copy sent by regular mail to the Lessor's managing agent; if to the Lessee, addressed to the building. Either party may by notice served in accordance herewith designate a different address

25

for service of such notice or demand. Notices or demands shall be deemed given on the date when mailed, except notices of change of address shall be deemed served when received.

REIMBURSEMENT OF LESSOR'S EXPENSES

28. If the Lessee shall at any time be in default hereunder and the Lessor shall incur any expense (whether paid or not) in performing acts which the Lessee is required to perform, or in instituting any action or proceeding based on such default, or defending, or asserting a counterclaim in, any action or proceeding brought by the Lessee, the expense thereof to the Lessor, including reasonable attorneys' fees and disbursements, shall be paid by the Lessee to the Lessor, on demand, as additional rent.

LESSOR'S IMMUNITIES

29. (a) The Lessor shall not be liable, except by reason of Lessor's negligence, for any failure or insufficiency of heat, or of air conditioning (where air conditioning is supplied or air conditioning equipment is maintained by the Lessor), water supply, electric current, gas, telephone, or elevator service or other service to be supplied by the Lessor hereunder, or for interference with light, air, view or other interests of the Lessee. No abatement of rent or other compensation or claim of eviction shall be made or allowed because of the making or failure to make or delay in making any repairs, alterations or decorations to the building, or any fixtures or appurtenances therein, or for space taken to comply with any law, ordinance or governmental regulation, or for interruption or curtailment of any service agreed to be furnished by the Lessor, due to accidents, alterations or repairs, or to difficulty or delay in securing supplies or labor or other cause beyond Lessor's control, unless due to Lessor's negligence.

Storage Space and Laundry

(b) If the Lessor shall furnish to the Lessee any storage bins or space, the use of the laundry, or any facility outside the apartment, including but not limited to a television antenna, the same shall be deemed to have been furnished gratuitously by the Lessor under a revocable license. The Lessee shall not use such storage space for the

26

storage of valuable or perishable property and any such storage space assigned to Lessee shall be kept by Lessee clean and free of combustibles. If washing machines or other equipment are made available to the Lessee, the Lessee shall use the same on the understanding that such machines or equipment may or may not be in good order and repair and that the Lessor is not responsible for such equipment, nor for any damage caused to the property of the Lessee resulting from the Lessee's use thereof, and that any use that Lessee may make of such equipment shall be at his own cost, risk and expense.

Automobiles and Other Property

(c) The Lessor shall not be responsible for any damage to any automobile or other vehicle left in the care of any employee of the Lessor by the Lessee, and the Lessee hereby agrees to hold the Lessor harmless from any liability arising from any injury to person or property caused by or with such automobile or other vehicle while in the care of such employee. The Lessor shall not be responsible for any property left with or entrusted to any employee of the Lessor, or for the loss of or damage to any property within or without the apartment by theft or otherwise.

WINDOW CLEANING

30. The Lessee will not require, permit, suffer or allow the cleaning of any window in the premises from the outside (within the meaning of Section 202 of the New York Labor Law) unless the equipment and safety devices required by law, ordinance, rules and regulations, including, without limitation, Section 202 of the New York Labor Law, are provided and used, and unless the industrial code of the State of New York is fully complied with; and the Lessee hereby agrees to indemnify the Lessor and its employees, other lessees, and the managing agent, for all losses, damages or fines suffered by them as a result of the Lessee's requiring, permitting, suffering or allowing any window in the premises to be cleaned from the outside in violation of the requirements of the aforesaid laws, ordinances, regulations and rules.

TERMINATION OF LEASE BY LESSOR

31. If upon, or at any time after, the happening of any of the events mentioned in subdivisions (a) to (j) inclusive of this Paragraph

27

31, the Lessor shall give to the Lessee a notice stating that the term hereof will expire on a date at least five days thereafter, the term of this lease shall expire on the date so fixed in such notice as fully and completely as if it were the date herein definitely fixed for the expiration of the term, and all right, title and interest of the Lessee hereunder shall thereupon wholly cease and expire, and the Lessee shall thereupon quit and surrender the apartment to the Lessor, it being the intention of the parties hereto to create hereby a conditional limitation, and thereupon the Lessor shall have the right to re-enter the apartment and to remove all persons and personal property therefrom, either by summary dispossess proceedings, or by any suitable action or proceeding at law or in equity, or by force or otherwise, and to repossess the apartment in its former estate as if this lease had not been made, and no liability whatsoever shall attach to the Lessor by reason of the exercise of the right of re-entry, re-possession and removal herein granted and reserved:

Lessee Ceasing to Own Accompanying Shares

(a) If the Lessee shall cease to be the owner of the shares to which this lease is appurtenant, or if this lease shall pass or be assigned to anyone who is not then the owner of all of said shares;

Lessee Becoming a Bankrupt

(b) If at any time during the term of this lease (i) the then holder hereof shall be adjudicated a bankrupt under the laws of the United States; or (ii) a receiver of all of the property of such holder or of this lease shall be appointed under any provision of the laws of the State of New York, or under any statute of the United States, or any statute of any state of the United States and the order appointing such receiver shall not be vacated within thirty days; or (iii) such holder shall make a general assignment for the benefit of creditors; or (iv) any of the shares owned by such holder to which this lease is appurtenant shall be duly levied upon under the process of any court whatever unless such levy shall be discharged within thirty days; or (v) this lease or any of the shares to which it is appurtenant shall pass by operation of law or otherwise to anyone other than the Lessee

28

herein named or a person to whom such Lessee has assigned this lease in the manner herein permitted, but this subsection (v) shall not be applicable if this lease shall devolve upon the executors or administrators of the Lessee and provided that within eight (8) months (which period may be extended by the Directors) after the death said lease and shares shall have been transferred to any assignee in accordance with Paragraph 16 hereof; or (vi) this lease or any of the shares to which it is appurtenant shall pass to anyone other than the Lessee herein named by reason of a default by the Lessee under a pledge or security agreement or a leasehold mortgage made by the Lessee (except as otherwise permitted in Paragraph 17(b) above);

Assignment, Subletting or Unauthorized Occupancy

(c) If there be an assignment of this lease, or any subletting hereunder, without full compliance with the requirements of Paragraphs 15 or 16 hereof; or if any person not authorized by Paragraph 14 shall be permitted to use or occupy the apartment, and the Lessee shall fail to cause such unauthorized person to vacate the apartment within ten days after written notice from the Lessor;

Default in Rent

(d) If the Lessee shall be in default for a period of one month in the payment of any rent or additional rent or of any installment thereof and shall fail to cure such default within ten days after written notice from the Lessor;

Default in Other Covenants

(e) If the Lessee shall be in default in the performance of any covenant or provision hereof, other than the covenant to pay rent, and such default shall continue for thirty days after written notice from the Lessor; provided, however, that if said default consists of the failure to perform any act the performance of which requires any substantial period of time, then if within said period of thirty days such performance is commenced and thereafter diligently prosecuted to conclusion with-

29

out delay and interruption, the Lessee shall be deemed to have cured said default;

Lessee's Objectionable Conduct

(f) If at any time the Lessor shall determine, upon the affirmative vote of two-thirds of its then Board of Directors, at a meeting duly called for that purpose, that because of objectionable conduct on the part of the Lessee, or of a person dwelling or visiting in the apartment, repeated after written notice from Lessor, the tenancy of the Lessee is undesirable (it being understood, without limiting the generality of the foregoing, that repeatedly to violate or disregard the House Rules hereto attached or hereafter established in accordance with the provisions of this lease, or to permit or tolerate a person of dissolute, loose or immoral character to enter or remain in the building or the apartment, shall be deemed to be objectionable conduct);

Termination of All Proprietary Leases

(g) If at any time the Lessor shall determine, upon the affirmative vote of two-thirds of its then Board of Directors at a meeting of such directors duly called for that purpose, and the affirmative vote of the record holders of at least 80% in amount of its then issued shares, at a shareholders' meeting duly called for that purpose, to terminate all proprietary leases;

Destruction of Building

(h) If the building shall be destroyed or damaged and the shareholders shall decide not to repair or rebuild as provided in Paragraph 4;

Condemnation

(i) If at any time the building or a substantial portion thereof shall be taken by condemnation proceedings;

Lessee's Default Under Security Agreement

(j) If Lessee shall default in the payment or performance of any of Lessee's obligations under any pledge, leasehold mort-

30

gage or other security agreement (the "Security Agreement") given a Secured Party (who has complied with the provisions of said Paragraph 17 (b)), and written notice of such default is given to Lessor by the Secured Party, or its counsel.

LESSOR'S RIGHTS AFTER LESSEE'S DEFAULT

32. (a) In the event the Lessor resumes possession of the apartment, either by summary proceedings, action of ejectment or otherwise, because of default by the Lessee in the payment of any rent or additional rent due hereunder, or on the expiration of the term pursuant to a notice given as provided in Paragraph 31 hereof upon the happening of any event specified in subsections (a) to (f) inclusive or (j) of Paragraph 31, Lessee shall continue to remain liable for payment of a sum equal to the rent which would have become due hereunder and shall pay the same in installments at the time such rent would be due hereunder. No suit brought to recover any installment of such rent or additional rent shall prejudice the right of the Lessor to recover any subsequent installment. After resuming possession, the Lessor may, at its option, from time to time (i) relet the apartment for its own account, or (ii) relet the apartment as the agent of the Lessee, in the name of the Lessee or in its own name, for a term or terms which may be less than or greater than the period which would otherwise have constituted the balance of the term of this lease, and may grant concessions or free rent, in its discretion. Any reletting of the apartment shall be deemed for the account of the Lessee, unless within ten days after such reletting the Lessor shall notify the Lessee that the premises have been relet for the Lessor's own account. The fact that the Lessor may have relet the apartment as agent for the Lessee shall not prevent the Lessor from thereafter notifying the Lessee that it proposes to relet the apartment for its own account. If the Lessor relets the apartment as agent for the Lessee, it shall, after reimbursing itself for its expenses in connection therewith, including leasing commissions and a reasonable amount for attorneys' fees and expenses, and decorations, alterations and repairs in and to the apartment, apply the remaining avails of such reletting against the Lessee's continuing obligations hereunder. There shall be a final accounting between the Lessor and the Lessee upon the earliest of the four following dates: (A) the date of expiration of the term of this lease as stated on page 1 hereof; (B) the date as of

31

which a new proprietary lease covering the apartment shall have become effective; (C) the date the Lessor gives written notice to the Lessee that it has relet the apartment for its own account; (D) the date upon which all proprietary leases of the Lessor terminate. From and after the date upon which the Lessor becomes obligated to account to the Lessee, as above provided, the Lessor shall have no further duty to account to the Lessee for any avails of reletting and the Lessee shall have no further liability for sums thereafter accruing hereunder, but such termination of the Lessee's liability shall not affect any liabilities theretofore accrued.

Collection of Rent from Subtenants

(b) If the Lessee shall at any time sublet the apartment and shall default in the payment of any rent or additional rent, the Lessor may, at its option, so long as such default shall continue, demand and receive from the subtenant the rent due or becoming due from such subtenant to the Lessee, and apply the amount to pay sums due and to become due from the Lessee to the Lessor. Any payment by a subtenant to the Lessor shall constitute a discharge of the obligation of such subtenant to the Lessee, to the extent of the amount so paid. The acceptance of rent from any subtenant shall not be deemed a consent to or approval of any subletting or assignment by the Lessee, or a release or discharge of any of the obligations of the Lessee hereunder.

Sale of Shares

(c) Upon the termination of this lease under the provisions of subdivisions (a) to (f) inclusive or (j) of Paragraph 31, the Lessee shall surrender to the corporation the certificate for the shares of the corporation owned by the Lessee to which this lease is appurtenant. Whether or not said certificate is surrendered, the Lessor may issue a new proprietary lease for the apartment and issue a new certificate for the shares of the Lessor owned by the Lessee and allocated to the apartment when a purchaser therefor is obtained, provided that with respect to a termination pursuant to said subdivisions (a) to (f) inclusive the issuance of such shares and such lease to such purchaser is authorized by a resolution of the Directors, or by a writing signed by a majority of the Directors or by lessees owning, of record, at least

32

a majority of the shares of the Lessor accompanying proprietary leases then in force. Upon such issuance the certificate owned or held by the Lessee shall be automatically cancelled and rendered null and void. The Lessor shall apply the proceeds received for the issuance of such shares first, towards the payment of Lessee's indebtedness hereunder (including interest, attorneys' fees and other expenses incurred by the Lessor), second, if said termination shall result pursuant to subdivision (j) of Paragraph 31 by reason of a default under the Security Agreement, towards the payment of Lessee's indebtedness under the Security Agreement (including all costs, expenses and charges payable by Lessee thereunder), and third, if the proceeds are sufficient to pay the same, the Lessor shall pay over any surplus to the Lessee, but, if insufficient, the Lessee shall remain liable for the balance of the indebtedness due hereunder or (if applicable) under said Security Agreement. Upon the issuance of any such new proprietary lease and certificate, the Lessee's liability hereunder shall cease and the Lessee shall only be liable for rent and expenses accrued to that time. The Lessor shall not, however, be obligated to sell such shares and appurtenant lease or otherwise make any attempt to mitigate damages.

WAIVER OF RIGHT OF REDEMPTION

33. The Lessee hereby expressly waives any and all right of redemption in case the Lessee shall be dispossessed by judgment or warrant of any court or judge. The words "enter", "re-enter" and "re-entry" as used in this lease are not restricted to their technical legal meaning.

SURRENDER OF POSSESSION

34. Upon the termination of this lease under the provisions of subdivisions (a) to (f) inclusive or (j) of Paragraph 31, the Lessee shall remain liable as provided in Paragraph 32 of this lease. Upon the termination of this lease under any other of its provisions, the Lessee shall be and remain liable to pay all rent, additional rent and other charges due or accrued and to perform all covenants and agreements of the Lessee up to the date of such termination. On or before any such termination the Lessee shall vacate the apartment and surrender possession thereof to the Lessor or its assigns, and upon demand of the Lessor or its assigns, shall execute, acknowledge and deliver to the

33

Lessor or its assigns any instrument which may reasonably be required to evidence the surrendering of all estate and interest of the Lessee in the apartment, or in the building of which it is a part.

LESSEE'S OPTION TO CANCEL

35. (a) This lease may be cancelled by the Lessee on any September 30th after the third anniversary of the consummation of the Plan of cooperative organization pursuant to which proprietary leases were originally issued, upon complying with all the provisions hereinafter set forth. Irrevocable written notice of intention to cancel must be given by the Lessee to the Lessor on or before April 1 in the calendar year in which such cancellation is to occur. At the time of the giving of such notice of intention to cancel there must be deposited with the Lessor by the Lessee:

Deposits Required

(i) the Lessee's counterpart of this lease with a written assignment in form required by the Lessor, in blank, effective as of August 31 of the year of cancellation, free from all sub-leases, tenancies, liens, encumbrances, pledges, security interests and other charges whatsoever (except rights of occupancy of third parties existing on the date the Lessor acquired title to the Building);

(ii) the Lessee's certificate for his shares of the Lessor, endorsed in blank for transfer and with all necessary transfer tax stamps affixed and with payment of any transfer taxes due thereon;

(iii) a written statement setting forth in detail those additions, improvements, fixtures or equipment which the Lessee has, under the terms of this lease, the right to and intends to remove.

Removal of Fixtures; Possession

(b) All additions, improvements, appliances and fixtures which are removable under the terms of this lease and which are enumerated in the statement made as provided in subdivision (iii) above shall be removed by the Lessee prior to August 31st of the year of cancellation,

34

and on or before said August 31st the Lessee shall deliver possession of the apartment to the Lessor in good condition with all required equipment, fixtures and appliances installed and in proper operating condition and free from all subleases and tenancies, liens, encumbrances, pledges, security interest and other charges and pay to the Lessor all rent, additional rent and other charges which shall be payable under this lease up to and including the following September 30th.

Permission to Show and Occupy Premises

(c) The Lessor and its agents may show the apartment to prospective lessees, contractors and architects at reasonable times after notice of the Lessee's intention to cancel. After August 31st or the earlier vacating of the apartment, the Lessor and its agents, employees and lessees may enter the apartment, occupy the same and make such alterations and additions therein as the Lessor may deem necessary or desirable without diminution or abatement of the rent due hereunder.

Effective Date of Cancellation

(d) If the Lessee is not otherwise in default hereunder and if the Lessee shall have timely complied with all of the provisions of subdivisions (a) and (b) hereof, then this lease shall be cancelled and all rights, duties and obligations of the parties hereunder shall cease as of the September 30th fixed in said notice, and the shares of Lessor shall become the absolute property of the Lessor, provided, however, that the Lessee shall not be released from any indebtedness owing to the Lessor on said last mentioned date.

Rights on Lessee Default

(e) If the Lessee shall give the notice but fail to comply with any of the other provisions of this paragraph, the Lessor shall have the option at any time prior to September 30th (i) of returning to the Lessee this lease, the certificate for shares and other documents deposited, and thereupon the Lessee shall be deemed to have withdrawn the notice of intention to cancel this lease, or (ii) of treating this lease as cancelled as of the September 30th named in the notice of intention to cancel as the date for the cancellation of such lease, and bringing

35

such proceedings and actions as it may deem best to enforce the covenants of the Lessee hereinabove contained and to collect from the Lessee the payments which the Lessee is required to make hereunder, togther with reasonable attorneys' fees and expenses.

EXTENSION OF OPTION TO CANCEL

36. (a) If on April 1st in any year the total number of shares owned by lessees holding proprietary leases, who have given notice pursuant to Paragraph 35 of intention to cancel such proprietary leases on September 30th of said year, shall aggregate ten percent (10%) or more of the Lessor's outstanding shares, exclusive of treasury shares, then the Lessor shall, prior to April 30th in such year, give a written notice to the holders of all issued shares of the Lessor, stating the total number of shares then outstanding and in its treasury and the total number of shares owned by lessees holding proprietary leases who have given notice of intention to cancel. In such case the proprietary lessees to whom such notice shall have been given shall have the right to cancel their leases in compliance with the provisions of Paragraph 35 hereof, provided only that written notice of the intention to cancel such leases shall be given on or before July 1st instead of April 1st.

Right of Lessees to Cancel

(b) If lessees owning at least 80% of the then issued and outstanding shares of the Lessor shall exercise the option to cancel their leases in one year, then this and all other proprietary leases shall thereupon terminate on the September 30th of the year in which such options shall have been exercised, as though every lessee had exercised such option. In such event none of the lessees shall be required to surrender his shares to the Lessor and all certificates for shares delivered to the Lessor by those who had, during that year, served notice of intention to cancel their leases under the provisions hereof, shall be returned to such lessees.

CONTINUANCE OF COOPERATIVE MANAGEMENT OF BUILDING AFTER ALL LEASES TERMINATED

37. No later than thirty days after the termination of all proprietary leases, whether by expiration of their terms or otherwise,

36

a special meeting of shareholders of the Lessor shall take place to determine whether (a) to continue to operate the building as a residential apartment building, (b) to alter, demolish or rebuild the building or any part thereof, or (c) to sell the building and liquidate the assets of the Lessor, and the Directors shall carry out the determination made at said meeting of shareholders of the Lessor, and all of the holders of the then issued and outstanding shares of the Lessor shall have such rights as enure to shareholders of corporations having title to real estate.

Unsold Shares

38. (a) The term "Unsold Shares" means and has exclusive reference to the shares of the Lessor which were (i) issued to the Lessor's grantor(s) or individuals produced by the Lessor's grantor(s) pursuant to the Plan of cooperative organization of Lessor or Contract of Sale under which the Lessor acquired title to the building or to a nominee of such grantor(s) or individual(s) or (ii) repurchased by the Repurchaser; and, all shares which are Unsold Shares retain their character as such (regardless of transfer) until (1) such shares become the property of a purchaser for bona fide occupancy (by himself or a member of his family) of the apartment to which such shares are allocated, or (2) the holder of such shares (or a member of his family) becomes a bona fide occupant of the apartment. This Paragraph 38 shall become inoperative as to this lease upon the occurrence of either of said events with respect to the Unsold Shares held by the Lessee named herein or his assignee. The term "holder of Unsold Shares" wherever used herein shall include a "purchaser of Unsold Shares", such terms being used interchangeably in this lease.

Subletting Apartment and Sale of Shares

(b) Neither the subletting of the apartment nor the assignment of this lease, by the Lessee who is the holder of the block of Unsold Shares allocated thereto, shall require the consents of the Directors or shareholders, as provided in Paragraphs 15 and 16, but the consent only of the Lessor's then managing agent, provided the same shall not be unreasonably withheld or delayed, shall be sufficient for approval and the taking effect of such subletting or assignment and of the transfer of such shares in the case of an assignment.

37

Change in Form of Lease

(c) Without the consent of the Lessee, no change in the form, terms or conditions of this proprietary lease, as permitted by Paragraph 6, shall (1) affect the rights of the Lessee who is the holder of the Unsold Shares accompanying this lease to sublet the apartment or to assign this lease, as provided in this paragraph, or (2) eliminate or modify any rights, privileges or obligations of such Lessee.

FORECLOSURE—RECEIVER OF RENTS

39. Notwithstanding anything contained in this lease, if any action shall be instituted to foreclose any mortgage on the land or the building or the leasehold of the land or building, the Lessee shall, on demand, pay to the receiver of the rents appointed in such action rent, if any, owing hereunder on the date of such appointment and shall pay thereafter to such receiver in advance, on the first day of each month during the pendency of such action, as rent hereunder, the rent for the apartment as last determined and established by the Directors prior to the commencement of said action, and such rent shall be paid during the period of such receivership, whether or not the Directors shall have determined and established the rent payable hereunder for any part of the period during which such receivership may continue. The provisions of this Paragraph are intended for the benefit of present and future mortgagees of the land or the building or the leasehold of the land or building and may not be modified or annulled without the prior written consent of any such mortgage holder.

TO WHOM COVENANTS APPLY

40. The references herein to the Lessor shall be deemed to include its successors and assigns, and the references herein to the Lessee or to a shareholder of the Lessor shall be deemed to include the executors, administrators, legal representatives, legatees, distributees and assigns of the Lessee or of such shareholder; and the covenants herein contained shall apply to, bind and enure to the benefit of the Lessor and its successors and assigns, and the Lessee and the executors and administrators, legal representatives, legatees, distributees and assigns of the Lessee, except as hereinabove stated. The covenants and provisions of this Lease which relate to the Secured Party or Repurchaser shall

38

enure to the benefit of said Secured Party or Repurchaser and their respective heirs, legal representatives, legatees, distributees, successors and assigns.

WAIVER OF TRIAL BY JURY

41. To the extent permitted by law, the respective parties hereto shall and they hereby do waive trial by jury in any action, proceeding or counterclaim brought by either of the parties hereto against the other on any matters whatsoever arising out of or in any way connected with this lease, the Lessee's use or occupancy of the apartment, or any claim of damage resulting from any act or omission of the parties in any way connected with this lease or the apartment.

LESSOR'S ADDITIONAL REMEDIES

42. In the event of a breach or threatened breach by Lessee of any provision hereof, the Lessee shall have the right of injunction and the right to invoke any remedy at law or in equity, as if re-entry, summary proceedings and other remedies were not herein provided for, and the election of one or more remedies shall not preclude the Lessor from any other remedy.

LESSEE MORE THAN ONE PERSON

43. If more than one person is named as Lessee hereunder, the Lessor may require the signatures of all such persons in connection with any notice to be given or action to be taken by the Lessee hereunder, including, without limiting the generality of the foregoing, the surrender or assignment of this lease, or any request for consent to assignment or subletting. Each person named as Lessee shall be jointly and severally liable for all of the Lessee's obligations hereunder. Any notice by the Lessor to any person named as Lessee shall be sufficient, and shall have the same force and effect, as though given to all persons named as Lessee.

EFFECT OF PARTIAL INVALIDITY

44. If any clause or provision herein contained shall be adjudged invalid, the same shall not affect the validity of any other clause or

39

provision of this lease, or constitute any cause of action in favor of either party as against the other.

NOTICE TO LESSOR OF DEFAULT

45. The Lessee may not institute an action or proceeding against the Lessor or defend, or make a counterclaim in any action by the Lessor related to the Lessee's failure to pay rent, if such action, defense or counterclaim is based upon the Lessor's failure to comply with its obligations under this lease or any law, ordinance or governmental regulation unless such failure shall have continued for thirty days after the giving of written notice thereof by the Lessee to the Lessor.

UNITY OF SHARES AND LEASE

46. The shares of the Lessor held by the Lessee and allocated to the apartment have been acquired and are owned subject to the following conditions agreed upon with the Lessor and with each of the other proprietary lessees for their mutual benefit:

(a) the shares represented by each certificate are transferable only as an entirety and only in connection with a simultaneous transfer of this lease, unless transferred pursuant to Article V, Section 4 of the By-laws of the Lessor in connection with the re-grouping of space in one or more apartments.

(b) the shares shall not be sold except to the Lessor or to an assignee of this lease after compliance with all of the provisions of Paragraph 16 of this lease relating to assignments.

CHARGES FOR GAS AND ELECTRICITY

47. If at any time or times during the term of this lease the consumption of gas or electricity, or both, in the apartment is measured by a meter which also measures consumption outside the apartment, the Lessor may determine from time to time by resolution of the Board of Directors thereof, the charges, if any, to be paid by the Lessee on account of such consumption of gas or electricity, or both, and any such charges shall be payable monthly in advance or in such payments

40

or installments as shall be required by the Directors, and at such times as shall be provided in such resolution.

No Discrimination

48. The Lessor will not discriminate against any person because of his race, creed, religion, color, national origin or ancestry when exercising any right reserved to it in this lease.

Marginal Headings

49. The marginal headings of the several paragraphs of this lease shall not be deemed a part of this lease.

Changes to Be in Writing

50. The provisions of this lease cannot be changed orally.

In Witness Whereof, the parties have executed this lease.

Lessor: 75 East End Owners Inc.

(Seal)

By ....
President
Secretary

Lessee:

.... (L.S.)

.... (L.S.)

41

STATE OF NEW YORK } ss.:
COUNTY OF

    On the   day of   , in the year 19 , before me personally appeared   , to me known, who being by me duly sworn, did depose and say that he resides at   ; that he is the   of 75 EAST END OWNERS INC.; the corporation described in and which executed the foregoing instrument; that he knows the seal of said corporation; that the seal affixed to said instrument is such corporate seal; that it was so affixed by order of the Board of Directors of said corporation, and that he signed h name thereto by like order.

STATE OF NEW YORK } ss.:
COUNTY OF

    On the   day of   , in the year 19 , before me personally appeared   , to me personally known and known to me to be the individual described in and who executed the foregoing instrument, and duly acknowledged to me that he executed the same.

42

HOUSE RULES

(1) The public halls and stairways of the building shall not be obstructed or used for any purpose other than ingress to and egress from the apartments in the building, and the fire towers shall not be obstructed in any way.

(2) No patient of any doctor who has offices in the building shall be permitted to wait in the lobby.

(3) Children shall not play in the public halls, courts, stairways, fire towers or elevators and shall not be permitted on the roof unless accompanied by a responsible adult.

(4) No public hall above the ground floor of the building shall be decorated or furnished by any Lessee in any manner without the prior consent of all of the Lessees to whose apartments such hall serves as a means of ingress and egress; in the event of disagreement among such Lessees, the Board of Directors shall decide.

(5) No Lessee shall make or permit any disturbing noises in the building or do or permit anything to be done therein which will interfere with the rights, comfort or convenience of other Lessees. No Lessee shall play upon or suffer to be played upon any musical instrument or permit to be operated a phonograph or a radio or television loud speaker in such Lessee's apartment between the hours of eleven o'clock p.m. and the following eight o'clock a.m. if the same shall disturb or annoy other occupants of the building. No construction or repair work or other installation involving noise shall be conducted in any apartment except on weekdays (not including legal holidays) and only between the hours of 8:30 a.m. and 5:00 p.m.

(6) No article shall be placed in the halls or on the staircase landings or fire towers, nor shall anything be hung or shaken from the doors, windows, terraces or balconies or placed upon the window sills of the building.

(7) No awnings, window air-conditioning units or ventilators shall be used in or about the building except such as shall have been expressly approved by the Lessor or the managing agent, nor shall anything be projected out of any window of the building without similar approval.

43

(8) No sign, notice, advertisement or illumination shall be inscribed or exposed on or at any window or other part of the building, except such as shall have been approved in writing by the Lessor or the managing agent.

(9) No velocipedes, bicycles, scooters or similar vehicles shall be allowed in a passenger elevator and baby carriages and the abovementioned vehicles shall not be allowed to stand in the public halls, passageways, areas or courts of the building.

(10) Messengers and tradespeople shall use such means of ingress and egress as shall be designated by the Lessor.

(11) Kitchen supplies, market goods and packages of every kind are to be delivered only at the service entrance of the building and through the service elevator to the apartments when such elevator is in operation.

(12) Trunks and heavy baggage shall be taken in or out of the building through the service entrance.

(13) Garbage and refuse from the apartments shall be disposed of only at such times and in such manner as the superintendent or the managing agent of the building may direct.

(14) Water closets and other water apparatus in the building shall not be used for any purposes other than those for which they were constructed, nor shall any sweepings, rubbish, rags or any other article be thrown into the water closets. The cost of repairing any damage resulting from misuse of any water closets or other apparatus shall be paid for by the Lessee in whose apartment it shall have been caused.

(15) No Lessee shall send any employee of the Lessor out of the building on any private business of a Lessee.

(16) No bird or animal shall be kept or harbored in the building unless the same in each instance be expressly permitted in writing by the Lessor; such permission shall be revocable by the Lessor. In no event shall dogs be permitted on elevators or in any of the public portions of the building unless carried or on leash. No pigeons or other birds or animals shall be fed from the window sills, terraces, balconies or in the yard, court spaces or other public portions of the building, or on the sidewalks or street adjacent to the building.

(17) No radio or television aerial shall be attached to or hung from the exterior of the building without the prior written approval of the Lessor or the managing agent.

(18) No vehicle belonging to a Lessee or to a member of the family or guest, subtenant or employee of a Lessee shall be parked in such manner as to impede or prevent ready access to any entrance of the building by another vehicle.

(19) The Lessee shall use the available laundry facilities only upon such days and during such hours as may be designated by the Lessor or the managing agent.

(20) The Lessor shall have the right from time to time to curtail or relocate any space devoted to storage or laundry purposes.

(21) Unless expressly authorized by the Board of Directors in each case, the floors of each apartment must be covered with rugs or carpeting or equally effective noice-reducing material, to the extent of at least 80% of the floor area of each room excepting only kitchens, pantries, bathrooms, maid's rooms, closets, and foyer.

(22) No group tour or exhibition of any apartment or its contents shall be conducted, nor shall any auction sale be held in any apartment without the consent of the Lessor or its managing agent.

(23) The Lessee shall keep the windows of the apartment clean. In case of refusal or neglect of the Lessee during 10 days after notice in writing from the Lessor or the managing agent to clean the windows, such cleaning may be done by the Lessor, which shall have the right, by its officers or authorized agents, to enter the apartment for the purpose and to charge the cost of such cleaning to the Lessee.

(24) The passenger and service elevators, unless of automatic type and intended for operation by a passenger, shall be operated only by employees of the Lessor, and there shall be no interference whatever with the same by Lessees or members of their families or their guests, employees or subtenants.

(25) Complaints regarding the service of the building shall be made in writing to the managing agent of the Lessor.

(26) Any consent or approval given under these House Rules by the Lessor shall be revocable at any time.

45

(27) If there be a garage in the building, the Lessee will abide by all arrangements made by the Lessor with the garage operator with regard to the garage and the driveways thereto.

(28) The following rules shall be observed with respect to incinerator equipment:

(i) All wet debris is to be securely wrapped or bagged in small package size to fit easily into the hopper panel.

(ii) Debris should be completely drip-free before it leaves the apartment and carried to the incinerator closet in a careful manner and in a drip-proof container; then placed into the flue hopper so it will drop into the flue for disposal.

(iii) No bottles or cans shall be dropped down the flue before 10:00 a.m. or after 5:00 p.m., but shall be left in a neat manner in service elevator area, if such items must be disposed of before 10:00 a.m. or after 5:00 p.m.

(iv) Cartons, boxes, crates, sticks of wood or other solid matter shall not be stuffed into hopper opening. Small items of this nature may be left in a neat manner on the incinerator closet floor. Bulky items should be left at service elevator area between 10:00 a.m. and 6:00 p.m. and service employee summoned to dispose of them by way of the service elevator.

(v) Under no circumstances should carpet sweepings containing naphthalene, camphor balls or flakes, floor scrapings, plastic wrappings or covers, oil soaked rags, empty paint or aerosol cans or any other inflammable, explosive, highly combusible substances or lighted cigarettes or cigar stubs be thrown into the incinerator flue.

(vi) Vacuum cleaner bags must never be emptied into the flue. Such dust, dirt, etc. should be wrapped in a securely tied bag or package and then be placed through hopper door panel into flue.

(vii) The superintendent shall be notified of any drippings, or moist refuse, appearing on incinerator closet floor and corridors.

(29) No Lessee shall install any plantings on the terrace, balcony or roof without the prior written approval of the Lessor. Plantings

46

shall be contained in boxes of wood lined with metal or other material impervious to dampness and standing on supports at least two inches from the terrace, balcony or roof surface, and if adjoining a wall, at least three inches from such wall. Suitable weep holes shall be provided in the boxes to draw off water. In special locations, such as a corner abutting a parapet wall, plantings may be contained in masonry or hollow tile walls which shall be at least three inches from the parapet and flashing, with the floor of drainage tiles and suitable weep holes at the sides to draw off water. It shall be the responsibility of the Lessee to maintain the containers in good condition, and the drainage tiles and weep holes in operating condition.

(30) The agents of the Lessor, and any contractor or workman authorized by the Lessor, may enter any apartment at any reasonable hour of the day for the purpose of inspecting such apartment to ascertain whether measures are necessary or desirable to control or exterminate any vermin, insects or other pests and for the purpose of taking such measures as may be necessary to control or exterminate any such vermin, insects or other pests. If the Lessor takes measures to control or exterminate carpet beetles, the cost thereof shall be payable by the Lessee, as additional rent.

(31) These House Rules may be added to, amended or repealed at any time by resolution of the Board of Directors of the Lessor.

47

75 EAST END OWNERS INC.

BY-LAWS

TABLE OF CONTENTS

(ii)

(iii)

BY-LAWS

OF

75 EAST END OWNERS INC.

ARTICLE I

MEETING OF SHAREHOLDERS

SECTION 1. *Annual Meeting.* The annual meeting of the share-holders of the corporation, for the election of directors and for such other business as may properly come before such meeting, shall be held in the Borough of Manhattan, City of New York, at such hour and place as may be designated in the notice of meeting, on the second Tuesday in May of each and every year, unless a legal holiday, in which event such meeting shall be held on the first day thereafter not a legal holiday. The notice of meeting shall be in writing and signed by the president or a vice president or the secretary or an assistant secretary. Such notice shall state the time when and the place within the city where such meeting is to be held, and a copy thereof shall be served, either personally or by mail, upon each shareholder of record entitled to vote at such meeting, not less than ten nor more than fifty days before the meeting.

SECTION 2. *Special Meetings.* Special meetings of shareholders other than those regulated by statute, may be called at any time by any officer of the corporation or by a majority of the board of directors, and it shall also be the duty of the secretary to call such a meeting whenever requested in writing so to do by shareholders of record of at least one-quarter of the outstanding capital stock. A notice of each special meeting, stating the time, place and purpose thereof and the officer or other person or persons by whom the meeting is called, shall be served, either personally or by mail, on each shareholder of record, not less than ten nor more than fifty days before the date of the meeting. No business other than that stated in the notice shall be transacted at any special meeting unless the shareholders of record of all out-standing shares of the corporation are present thereat in person or by proxy.

1

SECTION 3. *Waiver of Mailing of Notice.* The notice provided for in the two foregoing sections is not indispensable, and any shareholders' meeting whatever shall be valid for all purposes if the shareholders of record of all outstanding shares of the corporation are present thereat in person or by proxy, or if a quorum is present as provided in the next succeeding section and notice of the time, place and purpose of such meeting has been duly waived in writing by all shareholders not so present. The attendance of any shareholder at a meeting, in person or by proxy, without protesting prior to the conclusion of the meeting the lack of notice of such meeting, shall constitute a waiver of notice by him. Any notice to be served upon a shareholder by mail shall be directed to the shareholder at his address as it appears on the stock book unless the shareholder shall have filed with the secretary of the corporation, prior to the giving of a notice, a written request that notices intended for him be mailed to such other address, in which case it shall be mailed to the address designated in such request.

SECTION 4. *Quorum.* At all meetings of shareholders in order to constitute a quorum and to permit the transaction of any business except to adjourn a meeting, there shall be present either in person or by proxy the holders of not less than a majority of the shares entitled to vote thereat. A majority of the shareholders present may adjourn a meeting to a subsequent day despite the absence of a quorum.

SECTION 5. *Voting.* Each shareholder of record shall be entitled at each shareholders' meeting to one vote, in person or by proxy, for each share standing in his name on the stock book at the time of the meeting. All proxies shall be in writing but need not be acknowledged or witnessed, and shall be filed with the secretary at or previous to the time of the meeting. The person named as proxy need not himself be a shareholder of the corporation. All voting shall be viva voce, except that any qualified voter may demand a ballot vote, in which case the voting shall be by ballot, and each ballot shall state the name of the shareholder voting and the number of shares owned by him, and in addition, the name of the proxy, if such ballot is cast by a proxy. All elections shall be determined by a plurality vote and unless otherwise specified in these by-laws or the Certificate of Incorporation, the affirmative vote of a majority represented cast at any meeting of

2

shareholders shall be necessary for the transaction of any item of business and shall constitute the act of the shareholders.

SECTION 6. *Inspectors of Election.* At any election of directors where more candidates are nominated than there are positions to be filled, the election shall be conducted by two inspectors of election to be appointed by the president. No director or candidate for director shall be eligible to appointment as inspector. Before entering upon the discharge of their duties, the inspectors appointed to act at any meeting of the shareholders shall be sworn faithfully to execute the duties of inspectors at such meeting with strict impartiality, and according to the best of their ability, and the oath so taken shall be subscribed by them and immediately filed with the secretary of the corporation with a certificate of the result of the vote taken at such meeting. If there are not two inspectors present, ready and willing to act, the required number of temporary inspectors to make up such number shall be appointed by the chairman of the meeting.

SECTION 7. *Consent of Shareholders.* Whenever the shareholders are required or permitted to take any action by vote, such action may be taken without a meeting on written consent, setting forth the action so taken and signed by the holders of all outstanding shares entitled to vote thereon.

SECTION 8. *Order of Business.* At each meeting of shareholders, the president, or in his absence a vice president, shall act as chairman of the meeting. The secretary, or in his absence such person as may be appointed by the chairman, shall act as secretary of the meeting. So far as is consistent with the purposes of the meeting, the order of business shall be as follows:

1. Call to order.

2. Presentation of proofs of due calling of the meeting.

3. Roll call and presentation and examination of proxies.

4. Reading of minutes of previous meeting or meetings.

5. Reports of officers and committees.

3

6. If the annual meeting, the appointment of inspectors of election, if any.

7. If the annual meeting, the election of directors.

8. Unfinished business.

9. New business.

10. Adjournment.

ARTICLE II

DIRECTORS

SECTION 1. *Qualification and Number.* At least one director shall be a resident of the State of New York. All directors shall be at least 21 years of age.

The number of directors shall not be less than three and not more than seven. Prior to the election of directors by shareholders, the board shall consist of three (3) members. The first board elected at the first annual shareholders' meeting shall consist of seven (7) members. The number of directors shall be determined by the shareholders from time to time at any annual or any special meeting of shareholders called for that purpose, and the number so determined shall be the number of directors of the corporation until changed by further action of the shareholders, provided, however, that the number of directors shall not be decreased to a number less than the number of directors then in office, except at an annual meeting of shareholders. Reference is made to Section 7 of this Article for the power of the board to fix the number of directors.

SECTION 2. *Election and Term.* The directors constituting the first Board of Directors shall be elected by the incorporator at the organization meeting of the incorporator. Directors, other than those constituting the first Board, shall be elected at the annual meeting of shareholders, or at a special meeting called for that purpose as provided by law, by a plurality of the votes cast at such election. The entire number of directors to be elected shall be balloted for at one and the same time and not separately.

4

Directors elected by the incorporator shall serve until the election and qualification of directors elected at the first annual meeting of shareholders. Directors elected at the first annual meeting of shareholders and at meetings subsequent thereto shall serve until the date herein fixed for the next annual meeting of shareholders and until the election and qualification of their respective successors.

SECTION 3. *Vacancies*. When any vacancy exists or occurs among the directors by death, resignation or otherwise, the same shall be filled for the remainder of the term by a majority of votes cast at a special meeting of the remaining directors duly called for the purpose or at any regular meeting of the directors, even though a quorum shall not be present at such special or regular meeting. If the number of the directors is increased, the additional directors shall be elected by a plurality of the votes cast at a meeting of shareholders duly called for the purpose and shall serve for the term above prescribed. If all the directors die or resign, any shareholder may call a special meeting of the shareholders as provided herein and directors for the unexpired term may be elected at such special meeting in the manner provided for their election at the annual meeting.

SECTION 4. *Resignation and Removal*. Any director may resign at any time by written notice delivered or sent by registered mail, return receipt requested, to the president or secretary of the corporation. Such resignation shall take effect at the time specified therein, and, unless specifically requested, acceptance of such resignation shall not be necessary to make it effective.

Any director may be removed from office at any time with or without cause and at the pleasure of the shareholders, upon affirmative vote of the shareholders of record taken at a shareholders' meeting duly called for the purpose; provided, however, that the directors elected by the holders of "Unsold Shares" (as such term is defined in the corporation's proprietary lease referred to in Article V below) can be removed only by such holders of Unsold Shares who alone will have the right to designate a replacement.

Except for directors elected by the holders of Unsold Shares, a director who ceases to be a shareholder or whose spouse ceases to be

5

a shareholder, as the case may be, shall be deemed to have resigned as a director.

SECTION 5. *Meetings.* Meetings of the Board of Directors, regular or special, shall be held at such place within the City of New York as shall be specified in the notice calling the meeting. The first meeting of each newly elected Board of Directors shall be held immediately after the annual meeting of the shareholders and no notice of such meeting shall be necessary to the newly elected directors in order legally to constitute the meeting, provided a quorum shall be present, or it may convene at such place and time as shall be fixed by the consent in writing of all the directors. Regular meetings of the Board of Directors shall be held not less than once every eight weeks and may be held upon such notice, or without notice, and at such time and at such place in the City of New York as shall from time to time be determined by the Board. Special meetings of the Board of Directors may be called by the president on two days' notice to each director, either personally or by mail or by telegram; special meetings shall be called by the president or secretary in like manner and on like notice on the written request of a majority of the number of directors fixed by Section 1 of this Article II, except in the case of a special meeting called to fill vacancies in the Board of Directors, in which case a majority of the then acting directors shall suffice. Notice of a meeting need not be given to any director who submits a signed waiver of notice whether before or after the meeting, or who attends the meeting without protesting prior thereto or at its commencement, the lack of notice. Neither the business to be transacted at, nor the purpose of, any regular or special meeting of the Board of Directors need be specified in the notice or waiver of notice of such meeting, except where otherwise required by law or by these by-laws. A majority of the number of directors fixed by Section 1 of this Article II shall constitute a quorum for the transaction of business unless a greater or lesser number is required by law or by the certificate of incorporation or elsewhere by these by-laws. The act of a majority of the directors present at any meeting at which a quorum is present shall be the act of the Board of Directors, unless the act of a greater number is required by law or by the certificate of incorporation or elsewhere in these by-laws. If a quorum shall not be present at any meeting of directors, the directors present may adjourn the meeting from time to

6

time, without notice other than announcement at the meeting, until a quorum shall be present. At all meetings of the Board of Directors, each director shall be entitled to one vote.

SECTION 6. *Annual Budget.* In furtherance of the definitions and provisions of the proprietary leases entered into or to be entered into by the corporation with its shareholders, the board of directors shall determine the cash requirements as defined therein, for each particular year of the term of such proprietary lease, by resolution or resolutions adopted during the particular year in question or the preceding year, and shall likewise fix the terms and times of payment of the rent due from shareholders who are lessees under such proprietary leases to meet such cash requirements. Immediately after the adoption of any such resolution as above provided, the secretary shall mail or cause to be mailed, or deliver or cause to be delivered, to each shareholder who is such a lessee a statement of the amount of the cash requirements so determined or a copy of the resolution of the board concerning the same. The board of directors shall have discretionary power to prescribe the manner of maintaining and operating the apartment building of the corporation, and any other premises acquired by the corporation by purchase or otherwise, and to determine the aforesaid cash requirements. Every such determination by the board shall be final and conclusive as to all shareholders who are lessees under proprietary leases and any expenditures made by the corporation's officers or agents under the direction or with the approval of the board shall, as against such shareholders, be deemed necessarily and properly made for such purposes. The operating year of the corporation shall be the calendar year.

SECTION 7. *Duties and Powers.* The affairs and business of this corporation shall be managed by its board of directors except with respect to the powers which are herein delegated to the officers. The directors shall at all times act as a board, regularly convened, and they may adopt such rules and regulations for the conduct of their meetings, the execution of their resolutions and the management of the affairs of the corporation as they may deem proper, provided same are not inconsistent with the laws of the State of New York, the certificate of incorporation or these by-laws. Furthermore, the board, from time to time, may fix the number of directors of the corporation, provided, the number of directors shall be not less than three (3), nor more than

7

seven (7) or such higher number as the shareholders shall have determined pursuant to Article II, Section 1. The power of the Board to determine the number of directors as herein provided is subordinate to the power of the shareholders to make such determination under said Article II, Section 1, so that if the board after having fixed a new number of directors shall be overruled by the shareholders, the determination of the shareholders shall govern.

SECTION 8. *House Rules.* The board of directors shall have power to make and change reasonable house rules applicable to the apartment building owned or leased by the corporation whenever the board deems it advisable so to do. All house rules shall be binding upon all tenants and occupants of the apartment building. Copies of changes in house rules shall be furnished to each shareholder and shall be binding upon the delivery thereof in the manner provided in the proprietary lease.

SECTION 9. *Executive Committee.* The board of directors may by resolution appoint an executive committee to consist of three or more directors of the corporation. Such committee shall have and may exercise all of the powers of the board in the management of the business and affairs of the corporation during the intervals between the meetings of the board, so far as may be permitted by law, except that the executive committee shall not have power to determine the cash requirements defined in the proprietary leases, or to fix the rent to be paid under the proprietary leases, or to vary the terms of payment thereof as fixed by the board. Vacancies in membership on the Executive Committee shall be filled by the board of directors at a regular or special meeting.

SECTION 10. *Admissions Committee.* In furtherance of the cooperative purposes of the corporation and to assure, so far as possible, that the occupants of all apartments therein shall be congenial and that all proprietary leases shall be reputable and financially responsible, the board may by resolution create an Admissions Committee of two or more persons to interview and consider the qualifications of proposed assignees and subtenants. Once such committee has been created, no consent to transfer of stock or assignment of lease or subletting of apartments shall thereafter be given by any member of the board of directors until the Admissions Committee shall have approved

8

same, or until there shall have been a meeting of the board of directors to act on an unfavorable report of the Admissions Committee or any member thereof. All information received and reports by the Admissions Committee or any member of the board of directors (whether or not an Admissions Committee has been created) concerning a proposed assignee or subtenant, and the deliberations of the Committee and the board thereon shall be deemed confidential and disclosed to no one except other directors of the corporation. On all applications for consent to assignment or subletting, the only action of the board shall be to "approve" or "disapprove" without comment. No member of the Admissions Committee or the board of directors shall be required to explain to any shareholder or any other person the reasons for his determination.

SECTION 11. *Other Committees.* The board of directors shall also have the power to appoint such other committees, in accordance with Section 712 of the Business Corporation Law as it deems appropriate.

SECTION 12. *Contracts and Transactions of the Corporation.* No contract or other transaction between the corporation and any one or more of its directors or any other corporation, firm, association or other entity in which one or more of its directors are directors or officers, or are financially interested, shall be void or voidable for this reason alone or by reason alone that such director or directors are present at the meeting of the board, or of a Committee thereof, which approves such contract or transaction, or that he or their votes are counted for such purpose, provided that the provisions of Section 713 of the Business Corporation Law are complied with.

SECTION 13. *Compensation.* No director, by virtue of his office as such, nor for any other reason, at any time, shall receive any salary or compensation for his services as such director, or otherwise, unless and until the same shall have been duly authorized in writing, or by affirmative vote taken at a duly held stockholders' meeting, by the record holders of at least two-thirds (2/3) of the then outstanding shares of the stock of the corporation.

SECTION 14. *Distributions.* No tenant-shareholder shall be entitled, either conditionally or unconditionally, except upon a complete

9

or partial liquidation of the corporation, to receive any distribution not out of earnings and profits of the corporation.

ARTICLE III

OFFICERS

SECTION 1. *Election and Removal.* The board of directors at its first meeting after these by-laws become effective, and at each annual meeting, shall elect by a majority vote, a president and one or more vic-presidents, a secretary and a treasurer, and may also at any time appoint or elect one or more assistant secretaries or assistant treasurers and accord to such assistant officers such powers as the board deems proper. Any person otherwise qualified may hold any two offices, except the offices of president and secretary. Each of the officers shall serve until the next annual meeting of the board and until the election or appointment of his respective successor; but any officer may be removed from office at any time, and a successor chosen, at the pleasure of the board, upon affirmative vote, taken at any meeting, by a majority of the then total authorized number of directors.

SECTION 2. *Qualification and Vacancies.* The president shall be a member of the board, but none of the other officers need be a member of the board.

Vacancies occurring in any office may be filled by the board at any time, upon affirmative vote taken at any meeting, by a majority of the then total authorized number of directors. An officer who ceases to be a shareholder or whose spouse ceases to be a shareholder, as the case may be, shall be deemed to have resigned as an officer.

SECTION 3. *President and Vice President.* The president shall preside at meetings of shareholders and of the board of directors. He shall, subject to the control of the board, have general management of the affairs of the corporation and shall perform all the duties incidental to his office or prescribed for him by these by-laws or by the board, and shall make and sign in the name of the corporation all contracts, leases and other instruments which are authorized from time to time by the board. In the absence or inability of the president, the vice president shall have the powers and perform the duties of the presi-

10

dent. The vice president shall at all times have power to make and sign proprietary leases in the name of the corporation.

SECTION 4. *Secretary.* The secretary shall keep and record in proper books provided for the purpose, the minutes of meetings of the board of directors and of the shareholders. He shall record all transfers of shares and cancel and preserve certificates of shares transferred, and he shall keep such other records as the board shall require. He shall attend to the giving and serving of notices of the corporation, he shall have custody of the corporate seal and affix the same to certificates of shares and to written instruments required by law, by these by-laws or by the board. He shall keep a book, to be known as the stock book, containing the names, alphabetically arranged, of all persons who are shareholders of the corporation, showing their places of residence, the number of shares of stock held by them respectively, the time when they respectively became the owners thereof, the amount paid thereon, and the denomination and amount of all stock transfer stamps affixed thereto, and such books shall be open daily during at least three business hours, for inspection by any judgment creditor of the corporation, or by any person who shall have been a shareholder of record for at least six months immediately preceding his demand, or by any person holding, or thereunto in writing authorized by the holders of, at least five per cent of all the outstanding shares. Persons so entitled to inspect the stock book may make extracts therefrom. In the absence or inability of the secretary, the assistant secretary shall have all of the powers and perform all of the duties of the secretary.

SECTION 5. *Treasurer.* The treasurer shall, subject to the control of the board, have the care and custody of, and be responsible for, all funds and securities of the corporation and shall keep the same in its name in such banks, trust companies or safe deposit companies as the board shall designate, and shall perform all other duties incidental to his office, or prescribed for him by these by-laws or by the board. If so required by the board, he shall, before receiving any such funds or securities, furnish to the corporation a bond with a surety company as surety, in such form and amount as the board from time to time shall determine. The premium upon such bond shall be paid by the corporation. Within a reasonable time after the close of each year ending December 31st but in no event later than April 1st of the year following

11

said December 31st, the treasurer shall furnish to each shareholder who is a lessee under a proprietary lease then in force a statement of the income, expenses and paid-in surplus of the corporation during such year. In addition, no later than March 15th of the year following the close of each year ending December 31st, the treasurer shall send to each shareholder who is a lessee under a proprietary lease in force during said prior year a statement on which there shall be indicated the portions of the rent paid by such shareholder under his proprietary lease during such year which have been used by the corporation for the payment of taxes on real estate and interest on its mortgage or other indebtedness and such other information as may be necessary to permit him to compute his income tax liability or income tax benefits that may accrue to him in respect thereof. In the absence or inability of the treasurer, the assistant treasurer shall have all of the powers and perform all of the duties of the treasurer.

SECTION 6. *Salaries.* No salary or other compensation for service shall be paid to any officer of the corporation for services rendered as such officer unless and until the same shall have been authorized in writing, or by affirmative vote taken at a meeting of shareholders called for that purpose, by the shareholders of record of at least two-thirds of the then outstanding capital stock.

ARTICLE IV

INDEMNIFICATION OF DIRECTORS AND OFFICERS

SECTION 1. (a) *In Actions by or in the Right of Corporation.* Any person made a party to an action by or in the right of the corporation to procure a judgment in its favor by reason of the fact that he, his testator or intestate, is or was a director or officer of the corporation, shall be indemnified by this corporation against the reasonable expenses, including attorneys' fee, actually and necessarily incurred by him, in connection with the defense of such action, or in connection with an appeal therein, except in relation to matters as to which such director or officer is adjudged to have breached his duty to the corporation under Section 717 of the Business Corporation Law and except with respect to those amounts and expenses referred to in Paragraph (b) of Section 722 of the Business Corporation Law.

12

(b) *In Other Actions or Proceedings.* Any person made, a party to an action or proceeding other than one by or in the right of the corporation to procure a judgment in its favor, whether civil or criminal, brought to impose a liability or penalty on such person for an act alleged to have been committed by such person, his testator or intestate, as a director or officer of the corporation, or of any other corporation which he served as such at the request of the corporation, shall be indemnified by this corporation against judgments, fines, amounts paid in settlement and reasonable expenses, including attorneys' fees, actually and necessarily incurred as a result of such action or proceeding, or any appeal therein, if such director or officer acted in good faith, for a purpose which he reasonably believed to be in the best interest of the corporation and, in criminal actions or proceedings, in addition, had no reasonable cause to believe that his conduct was unlawful.

The termination of any such civil or criminal action or proceeding by judgment, settlement, conviction or upon a plea of nolo contendere, or its equivalent, shall not in itself create a presumption that any such director or officer did not act in good faith for a purpose which he reasonably believed to be in the best interests of the corporation or that he had reasonable cause to believe that his conduct was unlawful.

(c) *Payment.* A person who has been wholly successful, on the merits or otherwise, in the defense of a civil or criminal action or proceeding of the character described in Sections 722 or 723 of the Business Corporation Law shall be entitled to indemnification as authorized in said Sections.

Except as provided in Paragraph (a) of Section 724 of the Business Corporation Law, any indemnification under Section 722 or 723 of that law, unless ordered by a court under Section 725 thereof, shall be made by the corporation only if authorized in the specific case in accordance with the provisions of Paragraph (a) of said Section 724.

Expenses incurred in defending a civil or criminal action or proceeding may be paid by the corporation in advance of the final disposition of such action or proceeding if authorized under Paragraph (b) of said Section 724.

(d) *Other Provisions.* Indemnification of directors or officers shall be subject to the other provisions affecting the same as set forth in Section 726 of the Business Corporation Law.

13

ARTICLE V

Proprietary Leases

Section 1. *Form.* The board of directors shall adopt a form of proprietary lease to be issued by the corporation for the leasing of all apartments, professional offices, extra servants' rooms and other space in the apartment building, if any, to be leased to shareholders under proprietary leases. Such proprietary leases shall be for such terms, with or without provisions for renewals, and shall contain such restrictions, limitations and provisions in respect to the assignment thereof, the subletting of the premises demised thereby, and the sale or transfer of the shares of stock of the corporation accompanying the same, and such other terms, provisions, conditions and covenants, as the board deems advisable. After a proprietary lease in the form so adopted by the board has been executed and delivered by the corporation, all proprietary leases subsequently executed and delivered shall be in the same form (except with respect to commencement of the lease term and the statement as to the number of shares owned by the lessee), and shall not be changed in form or substance unless varied in accordance with the terms thereof.

Section 2. *Assignment.* Proprietary leases shall be assigned or transferred only in compliance with, and shall never be assigned or transferred in violation of, the terms, conditions or provisions, of such proprietary leases. A duplicate original of each proprietary lease shall always be kept on file in the office of the corporation or with the managing agent of the apartment building.

Section 3. *Accompanying Shares.* The board of directors shall allocate to each apartment to be leased under a proprietary lease the number of shares of the corporation which must be owned by the proprietary lessee thereof. The board shall adopt the allocation of shares set forth in the Offering Plan pursuant to which the corporation was organized. The allocation or any re-allocation of shares to an apartment shall bear a reasonable relationship to the portion of the fair market value of the corporation's equity in the building and the land on which it stands which is attributable to the apartment. In the event of any dispute between the board of directors and a shareholder as to whether such "reasonable relationship" test has been met on a proposed reallocation of shares, such dispute shall be resolved by the then managing agent of the building, whose determination shall be final and conclusive.

14

SECTION 4. *Re-grouping of Space.* The board of directors, upon the written request of the owner or owners of one or more proprietary leases covering one or more apartments in the apartment building and of the shares issued to accompany the same, may in its discretion at any time, permit such owner or owners, at his or their own expense: A: (1) to subdivide any apartment into two or more apartments; (2) to combine all or any portions of any such apartments into one or any desired number of apartments; and (3) to reallocate the shares issued to accompany the proprietary lease or leases so affected in such proportions as the said owners request, provided only that (a) the allotment of shares is based upon the fair market value of the equity in the property (including the building) attributable to the subdivided or combined apartments, and (b) in any case, the total number of the shares so reallocated remains the same, and (c) the proprietary lease or leases so affected and the accompanying certificate(s) of shares are surrendered, and that there are executed and delivered in place thereof, respectively, a new proprietary lease for each such separate apartment, extra servant's room or suite of extra servant's rooms so created and a new certificate of shares for the number of shares so reallocated to each such new proprietary lease; or B: to incorporate one or more servant's rooms, or other space in the building, not covered by any proprietary lease, into one or more apartments covered by a proprietary lease, whether in connection with any regrouping of space pursuant to subparagraph A of this Section 4 or otherwise, and in allocating shares to any such resulting apartment or apartments, the board shall determine the number of shares from its treasury shares to be issued and allocated in connection with the incorporation of such additional space (such allocation to be based on the fair market value of the equity in the property (including the building) attributable to such resulting apartment or apartments), provided such incorporation shall be conditioned upon the surrender by the owner making such request of his proprietary lease and share certificate and provided further such owner shall execute a new proprietary lease covering such resulting apartment or apartments. A new certificate of shares for the number of shares so re-allocated to the new proprietary lease will be issued to the owner surrendering said share certificate.

Anything hereinabove contained to the contrary notwithstanding, the purchasers of Unsold Shares shall have the absolute right, without payment of any fee or charge of whatsoever nature, to change the size and layout of any apartment owned by them, including the right

15

to subdivide any apartment owned by them, or any of them, into two or more apartments or to combine all or any portion of any such apartments into one or any desired number of apartments, subject only to obtaining the prior consent of the then managing agent of the building with respect to any reallocation of shares issued and accompanying proprietary lease or leases so affected by such subdivision or combination (as the case may be). The reallocation of shares shall be based upon the fair market value of the equity in the property (including the building) attributable to the subdivided or combined apartments, but in any event, the total number of shares so reallocated shall remain the same. Upon the surrender of the share certificate or certificates and proprietary lease or leases affected by such subdivision or combination, the board of directors shall issue a new share certificate or certificates and accompanying proprietary lease or leases covering the subdivided or combined apartments (as the case may be) in accordance with the foregoing.

Any dispute under this Section 4 concerning the number of shares to be reallocated, shall be resolved by the then managing agent of the building, whose determination shall be final and conclusive.

SECTION 5. *Allocation of Shares to Additional Space.* The Board of Directors may, in its discretion, authorize the conversion of space in the building not covered by a proprietary lease into space suitable for the primary purposes of the corporation, as set forth in the certificate of incorporation, allocate theretofore unissued shares to such space, and authorize the execution of a proprietary lease or leases covering such space.

SECTION 6. *Fees on Assignment.* Subject to the provisions of the form of proprietary adopted by the board of directors (and the rights of holders of Unsold Shares as herein or in the proprietary lease set forth), the board of directors shall have authority to fix by resolution and to collect, before any assignment of a proprietary lease or any reallocation of shares takes effect as against the corporation as lessor, reasonable fees to cover the corporation's expenses and attorneys' fees in connection with such proposed assignment, or reallocation, or both, as the case may be. However, no such fees may be charged to the purchasers of Unsold Shares in connection with the sale or transfer of such Unsold Shares and appurtenant proprietary leases, or a reallocation of shares.

16

SECTION 7. *Lost Proprietary Leases.* In the event that any proprietary lease in full force and effect is lost, stolen, destroyed or mutilated, the board of directors may authorize the issuance of a new proprietary lease in lieu thereof, in the same form and with the same terms, provisions, conditions and limitations. The board may, in its discretion, before the issuance of such new proprietary lease, require the owner of the lost, stolen, destroyed or mutilated proprietary lease, or the legal representative of the owner, (i) to pay to the corporation a reasonable fee for the time and expense incurred in preparing the same; (ii) to make an affidavit or affirmation setting forth such facts as to the loss, theft, destruction or mutilation as it deems necessary and (iii) to give the corporation a bond in such sum as it directs, not exceeding double the value of the shares accompanying such proprietary lease, to indemnify the corporation.

ARTICLE VI

CAPITAL SHARES

SECTION 1. Shares of stock of the corporation shall be issued only in connection with the execution and delivery by the purchaser and the corporation of a proprietary lease of an apartment in the building owned by the corporation, and the ownership of the said shares so issued shall entitle the holder thereof to occupy for dwelling purposes the apartment specified in the proprietary lease so executed and delivered in connection with the issuance of said shares, subject to the covenants and agreements contained in such proprietary lease. Shares of stock of the corporation hereafter acquired and subsequently reissued, and unissued but authorized shares of the corporation hereafter issued, shall only be so reissued or issued, as the case may be, in conjunction with the execution of a proprietary lease of an apartment in the building.

SECTION 2. *Certificates and Issuance.* Certificates of the shares of the corporation shall be in the form prepared by the board of directors, and shall be signed by the president or a vice-president and the secretary or an assistant secretary or the treasurer or an assistant treasurer, and sealed with the seal of the corporation, and shall be numbered in the order in which issued. Certificates shall be bound in a book and issued in consecutive order therefrom, and in the margin or stub thereof shall be entered the name of the person holding the shares therein represented, the number of shares and the date of issue.

17

Each certificate exchanged or returned to the corporation shall be cancelled, and the date of cancellation shall be indicated thereon, by the secretary and such certificate shall be immediately pasted in the certificate book opposite the memorandum of its issue.

SECTION 3. *Transfer*. Transfers of shares shall be made only upon the books of the corporation by the holder in person or by power of attorney, duly executed and witnessed (or with such signature guaranty as the board may request) and filed with the secretary, and on the surrender of the certificate of such shares, except that shares sold by the corporation to satisfy any lien which it holds thereon, or shares required to be (but which are not) surrendered under the proprietary lease, may be transferred without the surrender of such certificate. No transfer of shares shall be valid as against the corporation, its shareholders and creditors, for any purpose, except to render the transferee liable for the debts of the corporation to the extent provided for in the Business Corporation Law, until it shall have been entered in the stock book as required by the Business Corporation Law or any other applicable law by an entry from whom and to whom transferred. No such transfer shall be valid or effected until all the requirements with respect thereto set forth in the proprietary shall have been satisfied and complied with.

SECTION 4. *Units of Issuance*. Shares issued to accompany each proprietary lease shall be issued in the amount allocated by the board of directors to the apartment or other space described in such proprietary lease. Unless and until all proprietary leases which shall have been executed by the corporation shall have been terminated, the shares of stock which accompany each proprietary lease shall be represented by a single certificate and shall not be sold or transferred except to the corporation or as an entirety to a person who has acquired such proprietary lease, or a new one in place thereof, after complying with and satisfying the requirements of such proprietary lease in respect to the assignment thereof.

SECTION 5. *Fees on Transfer*. Subject to the provisions of Section 6 of Article V hereof and subject further to the provisions of the proprietary lease, the board of directors shall have authority to fix by resolution and to collect, before the transfer of any shares, reasonable fees to cover the corporation's expenses and attorneys' fees in connection with such proposed transfer.

18

SECTION 6. *Corporation's Lien.* The corporation shall at all times
have a first lien upon the shares of each shareholder to secure the payment by such shareholder of all rent to become payable by such shareholder under the provisions of any proprietary lease issued by the
corporation and at any time held by such shareholder and for all other
indebtedness from such shareholder to the corporation and to secure
the performance by the shareholder of all the covenants and conditions
of said proprietary lease to be performed or complied with by the
shareholder. Unless and until such shareholder as lessee makes default in the payment of any of such rent or other indebtedness or in
the performance of any of such covenants or conditions, said shares
shall continue to stand in the name of the shareholder upon the books
of the corporation and the shareholder shall be entitled to exercise
the right to vote thereon as though said lien did not exist. The board
may refuse to consent to the transfer of such shares until any indebtedness of the shareholder to the corporation is paid. The corporation
shall have the right to issue to any purchaser of such shares upon the
enforcement by the corporation of such lien, or to the nominee of
such purchaser, a certificate for the shares so purchased substantially
of the tenor of the certificate issued to such defaulting shareholder,
and thereupon the certificate for such shares issued to such defaulting
shareholder shall become void and such defaulting shareholder shall
surrender the same to the corporation on demand. The failure of such
defaulting shareholder to so surrender such certificate shall not affect
the validity of the certifictae issued in replacement thereof.

SECTION 7. *Lost Certificates.* In the event that any certificate
of shares is lost, stolen, destroyed or mutilated, the board of directors
may authorize the issuance of a new certificate of the same tenor and
for the same number of shares in lieu thereof. The board may in its
discretion, before the issuance of such new certificate, require the
owner of the lost, stolen, destroyed or mutilated certificate, or the legal
representative of the owner to make an affidavit or affirmation setting
forth such facts as to the loss, theft, destruction or mutilation as it
deems necessary, and to give the corporation a bond in such reasonable sum as it directs, not exceeding double the appraised value of the
shares, to indemnify the corporation.

SECTION 8. *Legend on Shares Certificate.* Certificates representing shares of the corporation shall bear a legend reading as follows:

19

"The rights of any holder of the shares evidenced by this certificate are subject to the provisions of the Certificate of Incorporation and the by-laws of the Corporation and to all the terms, covenants, conditions and provisions of a certain proprietary lease made between the Corporation, as Lessor, and the person in whose name this certificate is issued, as Lessee, for an apartment in the apartment house which is owned by the Corporation and operated as a "co-operative", which proprietary lease limits and restricts the title and rights of any transferee of this certificate.

The shares represented by this certificate are transferable only as an entirety and only to an assignee of such proprietary lease approved in writing in accordance which the provisions of the proprietary lease. The directors of this Corporation may refuse to consent to the transfer of the shares represented by this certificate until any indebtedness of the shareholder to the Corporation is paid.

Copies of the Certificate of Incorporation, proprietary lease and by-laws are on file and available for inspection at the office of the managing agent of the building.

Pursuant to the Certificate of Incorporation, certain actions of the Board of Directors and of the shareholders require a greater quorum and/or a greater vote than would otherwise be required by law.

Pursuant to Article VI Section 6 of the by-laws, the Corporation shall at all times have a first lien upon the shares of each shareholder to secure the payment by such shareholder of all rent to become payable by such shareholder under the provisions of any proprietary lease issued by the Corporation and at any time held by such shareholder and for all other indebtedness from such shareholder to the corporation and to secure the performance by the shareholder of all the covenants and conditions of said proprietary lease to be performed or complied with by the shareholder. The Corporation shall have the right to issue to any purchaser of such shares upon the enforcement by the Corporation of such lien, or to the nominee of such purchaser, a certificate for the shares so purchased substantially of the tenor of the certificate issued to such defaulting shareholder, and thereupon the certificate for such shares issued to such defaulting shareholder shall become void

20

and such defaulting shareholder shall surrender the same to the Corporation on demand. The failure of such defaulting shareholder to so surrender such certificate shall not affect the validity of the certificate issued in replacement thereof."

SECTION 9. *No Preemptive Right.* Ownership of shares of the corporation shall not entitle the holders thereof to any preemptive right under Section 622 of the Business Corporation Law, or otherwise, it being the purpose and intent hereof that the board of directors, as in its discretion it may deem advisable, shall have the full right, power and authority to offer for subscription or sale, or to make any other disposition of any or all unissued shares of the corporation, or of any or all shares issued and thereafter acquired by the corporation.

ARTICLE VII

SEAL

SECTION 1. *Form.* The seal of the corporation shall be in the form of a circle and shall bear the name of the corporation, the year of its incorporation and the words "Corporate Seal, N. Y."

ARTICLE VIII

CHECKS, NOTES, ETC.

SECTION 1. *Signatures on Checks.* All checks, drafts, orders for payment of money and negotiable instruments shall be signed by such officer or officers, or employee or employees as shall be designated from time to time by the board of directors, by resolution or special order, for that purpose.

SECTION 2. *Signatures on Notes and Bonds.* Promissory notes and bonds of the corporation shall be signed by any two officers who, from time to time, shall be designated by the board of directors for that purpose.

SECTION 3. *Safe Deposit Boxes.* Any officer or officers who, from time to time, shall be designated by the board of directors for that purpose shall have access to any safe deposit box of the corporation in the vault of any safe deposit company.

SECTION 4. *Securities.* Any officer or officers who, from time to time, shall be designated by the board of directors for that purpose

21

shall have the power to control and direct the disposition of any bonds or other securities or property of the corporation deposited in the custody of any bank, trust company or other custodian.

ARTICLE IX

SALE, LEASE, DEMOLITION OR DISPOSITION OF PROPERTY

SECTION 1. No decision to demolish or reconstruct any building standing on the land owned or leased by the corporation, or to sell or exchange the corporation's fee simple interest therein, or to lease any such building in its entirety or substantially in its entirety, shall be made except upon the affirmative vote of the holders of two-thirds of the shares of the corporation then issued and outstanding. Notwithstanding the foregoing, the sale, exchange, lease or other disposition of the property owned by the corporation after the termination of all the proprietary leases which are made by the corporation shall be determined by the affirmative vote of the holders of a majority of the shares of the corporation then issued and outstanding.

ARTICLE X

AMENDMENTS

SECTION 1. *By the Shareholders.* These by-laws may be amended, altered, repealed or added to at any shareholders' meeting by vote of shareholders of record, present in person or by proxy, of at least two-thirds of the then outstanding capital shares, provided that the proposed amendment or the substance thereof has been inserted in the notice of meeting or that all of the shareholders are present in person or by proxy.

SECTION 2. *By the Directors.* The board of directors may, by a vote of two-thirds ($\frac{2}{3}$) of the then authorized total number of directors at any meeting (regular or special) of the board, make, alter, amend, repeal these by-laws, other than Article I Section 5, Article II Sections 6, 13 and 14, Article III Section 6, Article V Sections 1 and 4, Article VI Sections 1 and 4; provided, however, that the proposed amendment or the substance thereof shall have been contained in the notice of said meeting or that all directors shall be present in person and, provided further, that the board may not repeal or modify an amendment to these by-laws adopted by the shareholders pursuant to Section 1 of this Article IX.

22

SECTION 3. *General.* Anything herein contained to the contrary notwithstanding, these by-laws and any provision hereof may not be altered, amended or repealed in such a manner as would adversely affect the rights or interests of the Sponsor-Seller under said Offering Plan (or its successors and assigns) in any shares and accompanying proprietary leases that may have been pledged with the Sponsor-Seller in connection with financing the purchase of apartments in the building. Anything herein contained to the contrary notwithstanding, so long as any shares of the corporation are held by a purchaser or purchasers of Unsold Shares these By-Laws may not be altered, amended, repealed or added to without the unanimous consent of all such purchasers of Unsold Shares.

ARTICLE XI
FISCAL YEAR

1. *Fiscal Year.* The fiscal year of the corporation shall be the calendar year unless otherwise determined by resolution of the board of directors.

XII
REPORTS

1. *Annual Reports.* The corporation shall, on or before April 1st, following close of a fiscal year, send to each shareholder then listed on the books of the corporation for the prior fiscal year of operations, a financial statement including a balance sheet (as of the end of said prior fiscal year) and a profit and loss statement (for the entire prior fiscal year), prepared and certified by an independent certified public accountant.

2. *Tax Deduction Statement.* The corporation shall, on or before March 15th following the close of a fiscal year, send to each shareholder listed on the books of the corporation for the prior fiscal year, a statement setting forth the amount per share of that portion of the rent paid by such shareholder under his proprietary lease during such year which has been used by the corporation for payment of real estate taxes and interest on mortgage or other indebtedness paid by the corporation with respect to property owned by it.

23

APPENDIX IV*

SAMPLE CONDOMINIUM DOCUMENTS

*Reprinted with permission of Church Management Corporation.

OFFERING PLAN
PART II

Condominium Documents

TABLE OF CONTENTS

DOCUMENT NO. I

DECLARATION OF CONDOMINIUM OWNERSHIP

FOR

ONE BRATENAHL PLACE CONDOMINIUM

DECLARATION OF CONDOMINIUM OWNERSHIP

FOR

ONE BRATENAHL PLACE CONDOMINIUM

DECLARATION made and entered into this _____ day of _____, 1976, by BA ASSOCIATES LIMITED, an Ohio limited partnership (herein referred to as "BA").

W I T N E S S E T H, That,

WHEREAS, BA is the owner in fee simple of a parcel of land upon which there has been constructed a multi-story building for residential use, which parcel and building are more particularly described below (herein referred to as Parcel I); and

WHEREAS, BA desires to submit Parcel I including the building and all other improvements thereon and all easements, rights and appurtenances belonging or appertaining to Parcel I to the provisions of Chapter 5311 of the Ohio Revised Code; and

WHEREAS, the building and other improvements to Parcel I, and a building and improvements located on an adjacent parcel known as Parcel II (hereinafter defined) were constructed pursuant to and in accordance with a "Second Amended Final Plan of Development Area" which was approved by the Planning Commission of the Village of Bratenahl on April 10, 1967 (herein referred to as the "Development Plan"); and

WHEREAS, adjacent to Parcel II is a parcel of land known as Parcel III which has not as yet been developed or improved, but which the Development Plan contemplates may be developed in the future; and

WHEREAS, the Development Plan provides a comprehensive plan for the development of Parcel I, Parcel II and Parcel III with the parcels having and sharing certain combined site and utility improvements as shown in and contemplated by the Plan; and

WHEREAS, pursuant to the Development Plan, a Deed of Easements providing certain easements for the construction, maintenance and utilization of the combined site and utility improvements, and certain covenants with respect thereto has been recorded in Volume 12114, Page 19 of the Deed Records of Cuyahoga County; and

WHEREAS, in addition to its desire to submit Parcel I to the provisions of Chapter 5311 of the Ohio Revised Code, BA desires all owners, mortgagees, occupants and other persons hereafter acquiring any interest in Parcel I shall at all times enjoy the benefits of, and shall hold their interests subject to the obligations imposed by, the easements and covenants established in the Deed of Easements;

NOW, THEREFORE, BA, as the owner of Parcel I, for the purposes above set forth, declares as follows:

ARTICLE I
Definitions

The terms defined in this Article I (except as herein otherwise expressly provided or unless the context otherwise requires) for all purposes of this Declaration and of any amendment hereto shall have the respective meanings specified in this Article.

Association: One Bratenahl Place Condominium Association, the organization of all the Unit Owners which administers the Condominium Property and more specifically described in Article IX hereof and its successors in interest.

Board: The Board of Managers of the Association as the same may be constituted, from time to time.

Building: The Building constituting a part of the Condominium Property and more specifically described in Article V hereof.

Bylaws: The Bylaws adopted for the governance of the Association and referred to in Article IX hereof and attached as Exhibit F hereto.

Chapter 5311:   Chapter 5311 of the Ohio Revised Code, as the same may be from time to time amended or supplemented.

Commercial Space: The portion of the Common Areas and Facilities comprising the restaurant, and the related bar, kitchen and gourmet shop, the beauty shop and other commercial facilities and referred to in Article VII hereof.

Common Areas and Facilities: All parts of the Condominium Property except the Units and designated as Common Areas and Facilities in Article VII hereof.

Common Expenses: Those expenses designated as Common Expenses in Chapter 5311, in this Declaration or in the Bylaws and the following:

      (a)   all sums lawfully assessed against the Unit Owners by the Association;

      (b)   expenses of administration, maintenance, repair and replacement of the Common Areas and Facilities;

      (c)   expenses incurred pursuant to the Deed of Easements (hereinafter defined); and

      (d)   expenses determined from time to time to be Common Expenses by the Association.

– 2 –

Condominium Property: Parcel I, together with the Building and all other improvements and structures thereon, all easements, rights, and appurtenances belonging thereto, and all articles of personal property owned by the Association for the common use of the Unit Owners.

Declaration: This instrument, including all of the Exhibits hereto, and if amended as herein provided, as so amended.

Deed of Easements: The Deed of Easements dated April 30, 1967, filed for record May 1, 1967 and recorded in Volume 12114, Page 19, of Cuyahoga County Records.

Drawings: The drawings prepared and certified by W. W. Paine, Registered Architect and Robert Hill, Registered Surveyor, relating to the Condominium Property which drawings are attached as Exhibit D hereto.

Exclusive Use Areas: Those parts of the Common Areas and Facilities, other than Limited Common Areas and Facilities, reserved for use of a certain Unit or Units to the exclusion of other Units and designated as Exclusive Use Areas in Article VIII hereof.

Limited Common Areas and Facilities: Those parts of the Common Areas and Facilities reserved for use of a certain Unit to the exclusion of all other Units and designated as Limited Common Areas and Facilities in Article VIII hereof.

Occupant: The person or persons, natural or artificial, other than the Unit Owner, in possession of any Unit.

Ownership Interest: A Unit and the undivided interest in the Common Areas and Facilities appertaining thereto.

Parcel I: The entire tract of land described in Exhibit A hereto.

Parcel II: The entire tract of land described in Exhibit B hereto.

Parcel III: The entire tract of land described in Exhibit C hereto.

Rules: The rules and regulations governing the operation and use of the Condominium Property or any portion thereof from time to time adopted by the Association or the Board as provided in the Bylaws.

Unit: A part of the Condominium Property consisting of one or more rooms on one or more floors of the Building or any portion thereof and more specifically described in Article VI hereof.

Unit Owner: A person or persons, natural or artificial, owning the fee simple estate in a Unit.

ARTICLE II

ESTABLISHMENT OF CONDOMINIUM
AND DIVISION OF CONDOMINIUM PROPERTY

BA is the owner of Parcel I which is hereby submitted to the provisions of Chapter 5311 of the Ohio Revised Code.

ARTICLE III

NAME

The name by which the Condominium Property shall be known is ONE BRATENAHL PLACE CONDOMINIUM.

ARTICLE IV

PURPOSES AND RESTRICTIONS ON THE USE
OF CONDOMINIUM PROPERTY

1. **Purposes.**   The purposes of the Condominium Property are to provide housing and recreational facilities for the Unit Owners and their respective families, tenants, guests and servants in accordance with the provisions of Chapter 5311 and to provide certain commercial services for the convenience of such Unit Owners and their respective families, tenants, guests and servants.

2. **Restrictions on Use.**   The Units and the Common Areas and Facilities shall be used and occupied as follows:

(a)   No part of the Condominium Property shall be used for other than housing and the related common purposes for which the Condominium Property was designed. Each Unit shall be used and occupied as a residence for a single family and for no other purpose and in accordance with the Land Planning and Zoning Code and Zone Map of the Village of Bratenahl. No portion of any Unit, other than the entire Unit shall be leased to any person by the Unit Owner, and any lease shall be subject to the restrictions of this Declaration.

(b)   There shall be no obstruction of the Common Areas and Facilities nor shall anything be stored in the Common Areas and Facilities without the prior written consent of the Association except as expressly provided herein.

(c)   Without the prior written consent of the Association, nothing shall be done or kept in any Unit or in the Common Areas and Facilities which will

– 4 –

increase the rates of insurance for the Building or contents thereof, applicable for residential use. No Unit Owner shall permit anything to be done or kept in his Unit or in the Common Areas and Facilities which will result in the cancellation of insurance on the Building or contents thereof, or which would be in violation of any law or regulation of any governmental authority. No waste shall be committed in the Common Areas and Facilities.

(d)   Without the prior written consent of the Association, no Unit Owner shall cause or permit anything to be hung or displayed on the outside of windows or placed on the outside walls of the Building and no sign, awning, canopy, shutter, radio or television antenna shall be affixed to or placed upon the exterior walls or roof or any part thereof.

(e)   No animals or birds of any kind shall be raised, bred or kept in any Unit or in the Common Areas and Facilities, except that dogs, cats and other household pets may be kept in Units subject to Rules adopted by the Board, provided that they are not kept, bred, or maintained for any commercial purpose; and provided further that any pet causing or creating a nuisance or disturbance shall be permanently removed from the Condominium Property upon three (3) days' written notice from the Association.

(f)   No noxious or offensive activity shall be carried on in any Unit or in the Common Areas and Facilities, nor shall anything be done therein, either willfully or negligently, which may be or become an annoyance or nuisance to the other Unit Owners or Occupants.

(g)   Nothing shall be done in any Unit or in, on or to the Common Areas and Facilities which will impair the structural integrity of the Building or structurally change the Building except as otherwise provided herein.

(h)   No clothes, sheets, blankets, laundry of any kind or other articles shall be hung out or exposed on any part of the Common Areas and Facilities. The Common Areas and Facilities shall be kept free and clear of rubbish, debris and other unsightly materials.

(i)   Except in areas specifically designed and intended for such purpose, there shall be no playing, lounging or parking or placing of baby carriages, playpens, bicycles, wagons, toys, vehicles, benches or chairs in or on any part of the Common Areas and Facilities.

– 5 –

(j)   No industry, business, trade, occupation or profession of any kind, whether for commercial, religious, educational, charitable or other purposes shall be conducted, maintained, or permitted on any part of the Condominium Property except as may be permitted by the Association and subject to the Rules, nor shall any "For Sale" or "For Rent" signs or other window displays or advertising be maintained or permitted by any Unit Owner on any part of the Condominium Property or in any Unit therein, except that (i) BA or its agent may place "For Sale" or "For Rent" signs on any unsold or unoccupied Units and may place such other signs on the Condominium Property as they may deem necessary or desirable to facilitate the sale or leasing of unsold Units and (ii) the Association or its agent may place "For Sale" or "For Rent" signs on any Unit or on the Condominium Property for the purpose of facilitating the disposal of Units by any Unit Owner, mortgagee, or the Association.

(k)   Nothing shall be altered or constructed in or removed from the Common Areas and Facilities, except with the written consent of the Association.

(l)   During the period in which sales of Units by BA are in process, BA may occupy or grant permission to any person or entity to occupy, with or without rental, as determined by BA, one or more Units for business or promotional purposes, including clerical activities, sales offices and model Units for display and the like, provided that the activities in the Units so occupied do not unreasonably interfere with the quiet enjoyment of any Unit Owner or Occupant.

(m)   Unit Owners shall also abide by and be subject to the Rules.

ARTICLE V
GENERAL DESCRIPTION OF BUILDING

A general description of the Building constituting a part of the Condominium Property is as follows:

The Building, consisting of 16 stories and a basement and underground parking garage and containing 180 units, constructed of a concrete frame with exposed and textured columns and spandrel beams and poured concrete floors, the exterior surfaces being primarily of precast concrete panels and glass on the ground floor and precast concrete panels on the floors above, all as more fully set forth in the Drawings.

ARTICLE VI

UNITS

1. **Designation of Units.** Each Unit shall consist of the space bounded by the horizontal and vertical planes formed by the undecorated interior surfaces of its perimeter walls, windows, doors, floors and ceilings, projected, where appropriate, through any windows, doorways, pipes, ducts, wires or conduits or structural divisions such as interior walls or partitions which intervene, all as shown in the Drawings relating thereto, provided, however, that in the event the Drawings shall, with regard to any Unit, be inconsistent with the foregoing description of any Unit in any respect (which description is intended to describe each Unit as built), said Unit shall consist of the space so described and not as shown on the Drawings. Without limiting the generality of the foregoing, each Unit shall include (a) any finishing material applied or affixed to the interior surfaces of the perimeter walls, floors or ceilings, including, without limiting the generality of the foregoing, paint, lacquer, varnish, wallpaper, tile and paneling, (b) the receptable and switch plates or covers within the bounds of the Unit, and (c) the space occupied by any Common Areas and Facilities located within the bounds of the Unit, but shall not include any Common Areas and Facilities located within the bounds of such Unit. Subject to the rights of BA under Article XIX paragraph 1 of this Declaration, the Units forming a part of the Condominium are more particularly described in the Drawings and are designated as follows:

Designation	Location	No. Rooms & Baths
101	First Floor–North	5 – 2
102	First Floor–South	5 – 2
103	First Floor–North	6 – 2½
104	First Floor–South	5 – 2
105	First Floor–North	4 – 1
106	First Floor–South	6 – 2½
107	First Floor–North	6 – 2½
108	First Floor–South	4 – 1
109	First Floor–North	5 – 2
110	First Floor–South	6 – 2½

Designation	Location	No. Rooms & Baths
111	First Floor—North	5 — 2
112	First Floor—South	5 — 2
201	Second Floor—North	5 — 2
202	Second Floor—South	5 — 2
203	Second Floor—North	6 — 2½
204	Second Floor—South	5 — 2
205	Second Floor—North	5 — 2
206	Second Floor—South	5 — 2
207	Second Floor—North	5 — 2
208	Second Floor—South	5 — 2
209	Second Floor—North	5 — 2
210	Second Floor—South	6 — 2½
211	Second Floor—North	5 — 2
212	Second Floor—South	5 — 2
301	Third Floor—North	5 — 2
302	Third Floor—South	5 — 2
303	Third Floor—North	6 — 2½
304	Third Floor—South	5 — 2
305	Third Floor—North	4 — 1
306	Third Floor—South	6 — 2½
307	Third Floor—North	6 — 2½
308	Third Floor—South	4 — 1
309	Third Floor—North	5 — 2
310	Third Floor—South	6 — 2½
311	Third Floor—North	5 — 2
312	Third Floor—South	5 — 2
401	Fourth Floor—North	5 — 2
402	Fourth Floor—South	5 — 2
403	Fourth Floor—North	6 — 2½
404	Fourth Floor—South	5 — 2
405	Fourth Floor—North	5 — 2
406	Fourth Floor—South	5 — 2
407	Fourth Floor—North	5 — 2

Designation	Location	No. Rooms & Baths
408	Fourth Floor—South	5 – 2
409	Fourth Floor—North	5 – 2
410	Fourth Floor—South	6 – 2½
411	Fourth Floor—North	5 – 2
412	Fourth Floor—South	5 – 2
501	Fifth Floor—North	5 – 2
502	Fifth Floor—South	5 – 2
503	Fifth Floor—North	6 – 2½
504	Fifth Floor—South	5 – 2
505	Fifth Floor—North	4 – 1
506	Fifth Floor—South	6 – 2½
507	Fifth Floor—North	6 – 2½
508	Fifth Floor—South	4 – 1
509	Fifth Floor—North	5 – 2
510	Fifth Floor—South	6 – 2½
511	Fifth Floor—North	5 – 2
512	Fifth Floor—South	5 – 2
601	Sixth Floor—North	5 – 2
602	Sixth Floor—South	5 – 2
603	Sixth Floor—North	6 – 2½
604	Sixth Floor—South	5 – 2
605	Sixth Floor—North	5 – 2
606	Sixth Floor—South	5 – 2
607	Sixth Floor—North	5 – 2
608	Sixth Floor—South	5 – 2
609	Sixth Floor—North	5 – 2
610	Sixth Floor—South	6 – 2½
611	Sixth Floor—North	5 – 2
612	Sixth Floor—South	5 – 2
701	Seventh Floor—North	5 – 2
702	Seventh Floor—South	5 – 2

– 9 –

Designation	Location	No. Rooms & Baths
703	Seventh Floor—North	6 − 2½
704	Seventh Floor—South	5 − 2
705	Seventh Floor—North	4 − 1
706	Seventh Floor—South	6 − 2½
707	Seventh Floor—North	6 − 2½
708	Seventh Floor—South	4 − 1
709	Seventh Floor—North	5 − 2
710	Seventh Floor—South	6 − 2½
711	Seventh Floor—North	5 − 2
712	Seventh Floor—South	5 − 2
801	Eighth Floor—North	5 − 2
802	Eighth Floor—South	5 − 2
803	Eighth Floor—North	6 − 2
804	Eighth Floor—South	5 − 2
805	Eighth Floor—North	5 − 2
806	Eighth Floor—South	5 − 2
807	Eighth Floor—North	5 − 2
808	Eighth Floor—South	5 − 2
809	Eighth Floor—North	5 − 2
810	Eighth Floor—South	6 − 2½
811	Eighth Floor—North	5 − 2
812	Eighth Floor—South	5 − 2
901	Ninth Floor—North	5 − 2
902	Ninth Floor—South	5 − 2
903	Ninth Floor—North	6 − 2½
904	Ninth Floor—South	5 − 2
905	Ninth Floor—North	4 − 1
906	Ninth Floor—South	6 − 2½
907	Ninth Floor—North	6 − 2½
908	Ninth Floor—South	4 − 1
909	Ninth Floor—North	5 − 2

− 10 −

Designation	Location	No. Rooms & Baths
910	Ninth Floor—South	6 – 2½
911	Ninth Floor—North	5 – 2
912	Ninth Floor—South	5 – 2
1001	Tenth Floor—North	5 – 2
1002	Tenth Floor—South	5 – 2
1003	Tenth Floor—North	6 – 2½
1004	Tenth Floor—South	5 – 2
1005	Tenth Floor—North	5 – 2
1006	Tenth Floor—South	5 – 2
1007	Tenth Floor—North	5 – 2
1008	Tenth Floor—South	5 – 2
1009	Tenth Floor—North	5 – 2
1010	Tenth Floor—South	6 – 2½
1011	Tenth Floor—North	5 – 2
1012	Tenth Floor—South	5 – 2
1101	Eleventh Floor—North	5 – 2
1102	Eleventh Floor—South	5 – 2
1103	Eleventh Floor—North	6 – 2½
1104	Eleventh Floor—South	5 – 2
1105	Eleventh Floor—North	4 – 1
1106	Eleventh Floor—South	6 – 2½
1107	Eleventh Floor—North	6 – 2½
1108	Eleventh Floor—South	4 – 1
1109	Eleventh Floor—North	5 – 2
1110	Eleventh Floor—South	6 – 2½
1111	Eleventh Floor—North	5 – 2
1112	Eleventh Floor—South	5 – 2
1201	Twelfth Floor—North	5 – 2
1202	Twelfth Floor—South	5 – 2
1203	Twelfth Floor—North	6 – 2½
1204	Twelfth Floor—South	5 – 2

– 11 –

Designation	Location	No. Rooms & Baths
1205	Twelfth Floor—North	5 – 2
1206	Twelfth Floor—South	5 – 2
1207	Twelfth Floor—North	5 – 2
1208	Twelfth Floor—South	5 – 2
1209	Twelfth Floor—North	5 – 2
1210	Twelfth Floor—South	6 – 2½
1211	Twelfth Floor—North	5 – 2
1212	Twelfth Floor—South	5 – 2
1301	Thirteenth Floor—North	5 – 2
1302	Thirteenth Floor—South	5 – 2
1303	Thirteenth Floor—North	6 – 2½
1304	Thirteenth Floor—South	5 – 2
1305	Thirteenth Floor—North	4 – 1
1306	Thirteenth Floor—South	6 – 2½
1307	Thirteenth Floor—North	6 – 2½
1308	Thirteenth Floor—South	4 – 1
1309	Thirteenth Floor—North	5 – 2
1310	Thirteenth Floor—South	6 – 2½
1311	Thirteenth Floor—North	5 – 2
1312	Thirteenth Floor—South	5 – 2
1401	Fourteenth Floor—North	5 – 2
1402	Fourteenth Floor—South	5 – 2
1403	Fourteenth Floor—North	6 – 2½
1404	Fourteenth Floor—South	5 – 2
1405	Fourteenth Floor—North	5 – 2
1406	Fourteenth Floor—South	5 – 2
1407	Fourteenth Floor—North	5 – 2
1408	Fourteenth Floor—South	5 – 2
1409	Fourteenth Floor—North	5 – 2
1410	Fourteenth Floor—South	6 – 2½
1411	Fourteenth Floor—North	5 – 2

Designation	Location	No. Rooms & Baths
1412	Fourteenth Floor—South	5 – 2
1501	Fifteenth Floor—North	5 – 2
1502	Fifteenth Floor—South	5 – 2
1503	Fifteenth Floor—North	6 – 2½
1504	Fifteenth Floor—South	5 – 2
1505	Fifteenth Floor—North	4 – 1
1506	Fifteenth Floor—South	6 – 2½
1507	Fifteenth Floor—North	6 – 2½
1508	Fifteenth Floor—South	4 – 1
1509	Fifteenth Floor—North	5 – 2
1510	Fifteenth Floor—South	6 – 2½
1511	Fifteenth Floor—North	5 – 2
1512	Fifteenth Floor—South	5 – 2

Each Unit has immediate access to the Common Areas and Facilities or Limited Common Areas and Facilities adjacent to the Unit including, but not limited to, the balcony or balconies, and the access hallway. No Unit Owner shall, by deed, plat or otherwise, subdivide or in any manner cause his Unit to be separated into tracts, parts or parcels smaller than the whole Unit as shown on the Drawings, or separate his Unit from the interest in Common Areas and Facilities appurtenant thereto.

2. **Ownership of a Unit**. Except with respect to any of the Common Areas and Facilities located within the bounds of a Unit, each Unit Owner shall be entitled to the exclusive ownership and possession of his Unit, and to the ownership of an undivided interest of the Common Areas and Facilities in the percentage expressed in Exhibit E hereto.

ARTICLE VII
COMMON AREAS AND FACILITIES

1. **Description**. Except as otherwise provided in this Declaration, the Common Areas and Facilities shall consist of all parts of the Condominium Property except the Units. Without limiting the generality of the foregoing, the Common Areas and Facilities shall include the following, whether or not located within the bounds of a Unit:

(a) the foundations, columns, girders, beams, supports, supporting walls,

roofs, halls, corridors, lobbies, penthouse, lounges, those areas

– 13 –

designated by the Drawings as party and recreational rooms, elevator shafts, stairs, stairways, fire escapes, entrances, and exits of the Building;

(b)   the basement, the land on which the Building is located, yards, gardens, surface parking areas, roads, walks, underground garages, ramps and storage spaces;

(c)   all commercial space shown on the Drawings, including without limitation the space presently used and occupied by the restaurant, party rooms, beauty shop and office space;

(d)   installations of central services such as power, light, telephone, gas, hot and cold water, heating, air-conditioning, rubbish compaction and sewerage, and all pipes, ducts, wires, conduits, fan coil units, receptacles, switches, grills, thermostats and control devices which are a part of, connected to, or used in conjunction with any of the foregoing;

(e)   the elevators, tanks, pumps, motors, fans, compressors, and, in general, all apparatus and installations existing for common use;

(f)   the doors and windows in the perimeter walls of a Unit;

(g)   two apartment units which may be devoted to lodging staff members, or as otherwise determined by the Board, which apartment units are designated as unit numbers 101 and 111;

(h)   all other parts of the Condominium Property necessary or convenient to its existence, maintenance, and safety, or normally in common use, or which have been designated as Common Areas and Facilities in the Drawings; and

(i)   all balconies other than those balconies which constitute Limited Common Areas and Facilities and which are described in Article VIII hereof;

(j)   all personal property owned by BA relating to the maintenance, repair and operation of the Building, other than office furniture and fixtures located in the general office area on the ground level at the southerly end of the Building, and the appliances, appliance parts, and other personal property located in storage room "BA" in the basement of the Building;

(k) all repairs and replacements of any of the foregoing.

2. **Ownership of Common Areas and Facilities.** The Common Areas and Facilities shall be owned by the Unit Owners as tenants in common, and ownership thereof shall remain undivided. No action for partition of any part of the Common Areas and Facilities shall be maintainable, except as specifically provided in Chapter 5311, nor may any Unit Owner otherwise waive or release any rights in the Common Areas and Facilities; provided, however, that if any Unit is owned by two or more persons, including, but not limited to, Units owned as partners, as tenants in common, as tenants by the entireties or as joint tenants, nothing contained herein shall be deemed to prohibit a voluntary or judicial partition of such Unit ownership as between such persons.

3. **Use of Common Areas and Facilities.** Except with respect to Limited Common Areas and Facilities and Exclusive Use Areas, each Unit Owner may use the Common Areas and Facilities in accordance with the purposes for which they are intended, subject to the Rules, which right shall be appurtenant to and run with his Unit.

4. **Interest in Common Areas and Facilities.** The percentage of interest of each Unit in the Common Areas and Facilities has been determined by BA in accordance with the provisions of Chapter 5311 of the Ohio Revised Code and is set forth in Exhibit E hereto.

ARTICLE VIII

LIMITED COMMON AREAS AND FACILITIES AND EXCLUSIVE USE AREAS

1. **Limited Common Areas and Facilities.** Each Unit Owner is hereby granted an exclusive and irrevocable license to use and occupy such of the Limited Common Areas and Facilities as are reserved exclusively for the use of his Unit. The Limited Common Areas and Facilities shall consist of (a) the balconies and the windows and doors in the perimeter walls of a Unit, the use and occupancy of which shall in each case be limited to the adjoining Unit and (b) all of the Common Areas and Facilities as may be located within the bounds of a Unit, which are intended solely for the service of the Unit, the use and occupancy of which shall in each case be limited to such Unit. No Unit Owner shall decorate, landscape or adorn any balcony in any manner contrary to this Declaration, the Bylaws or the Rules unless he shall first obtain the written consent of the Association, nor shall any Unit Owner decorate or apply any finishing or other material to

the exterior surface of any door (other than a glass door) or any surface of any window or glass door which is not part of a Unit, except that a Unit Owner may clean the interior and exterior surfaces of any such window or glass door.

2. **Exclusive Use Areas.** Each Unit Owner is hereby granted an exclusive but revocable license to use and enjoy such Exclusive Use Areas as the Association may allocate to such owner; provided, however, that the Association may at any time and from time to time revoke such license and reassign the use of such areas in accordance with such standards as it may from time to time establish. The Association may require that maintenance of any Exclusive Use Area shall be the sole responsibility of the Unit Owner to whom any such Exclusive Use Area is allocated.

ARTICLE IX
ASSOCIATION

BA shall cause to be formed an association for the administration of the Condominium Property to be called the One Bratenahl Place Condominium Association or a name similar thereto. Each Unit Owner shall be a member of the Association, which membership shall terminate upon the sale or other disposition by such member of his Unit, at which time the successor Unit Owner shall become a member of the Association. The Association shall be governed by Bylaws in the form attached hereto as Exhibit F, which Bylaws may be amended from time to time as therein provided. The Bylaws may contain, in addition to the provisions required to be included therein by Chapter 5311 of the Ohio Revised Code, any further provisions deemed by the Association to be desirable and not inconsistent with this Declaration.

ARTICLE X
AGENT FOR SERVICE OF PROCESS

Andrew Service Corporation, a corporation organized and existing under the laws of the State of Ohio with its principal place of business in the county in which the Condominium Property is situated and whose business address is 1800 Union Commerce Building, Cleveland, Cuyahoga County, Ohio 44115 is hereby appointed as the agent to receive service of process for the Association.

ARTICLE XI

GENERAL PROVISIONS AS TO UNITS AND COMMON AREAS AND FACILITIES

1. **Easements.** (a) In the event that (i) by reason of the construction, reconstruction, settlement or shifting of the Building any part of the Common Areas and Facilities encroaches or shall hereafter encroach upon any part of any Unit or any part of any Unit encroaches or shall hereafter encroach upon any part of the Common Areas and Facilities or any other Unit or (ii) by reason of the design or construction of any Unit it shall be necessary or advantageous to a Unit Owner to use or occupy, for normal uses and purposes, any portion of the Common Areas and Facilities consisting of unoccupied space within the Building and adjoining his Unit, valid easements for the maintenance of such encroachment and for the use of such adjoining space are hereby established and shall exist for the benefit of such Unit and the Common Areas and Facilities, as the case may be, so long as all or any part of the Building containing such Unit shall remain standing; provided, however, that in no event shall a valid easement for any encroachment be created in favor of any Unit Owner or in favor of the Unit Owners as owners of the Common Areas and Facilities if such encroachment occurred due to the willful conduct of said Unit Owner or Unit Owners.

(b) Each Unit shall be subject to such easements of access as may be necessary for the inspection, maintenance, repair or replacement of any Common Areas and Facilities or the operation of the Building in which such Unit is located and shall be subject to such easements as may be necessary for the installation, inspection, maintenance, operation, repair, removal or replacement of any pipes, ducts, wires, conduits, or structural components in the interior walls of such Unit.

(c) The Condominium Property shall have the benefit of easements B-1, B-2, B-3, B-4 and B-5 as set forth in the Deed of Easements and shall be subject to easements A-1, A-2, A-3, A-4, A-5, A-6 and A-7 as described in the Deed of Easements. The Unit Owners shall, for all purposes of said Deed of Easements, be deemed to be and shall constitute the "Owner of Parcel I" as defined therein.

(d) The Association may, with the approval of (i) Unit Owners entitled to exercise a majority of the voting power of all Unit Owners present, in person or by proxy, at an annual or special meeting of members of the Association duly held for such purpose, and (ii) all mortgagees holding mortgages constituting first liens on twenty-five (25) or more Units, on behalf of the Unit Owners, grant, amend or release easements, and any obligations incident thereto, relating to the

— 17 —

Condominium Property or any part thereof, including without limiting the generality of the foregoing, easements of the type created pursuant to the Deed of Easements. Each Unit Owner by his acceptance of a deed to his Unit and each mortgagee by its acceptance of a mortgage deed to any Unit agrees from time to time to execute, acknowledge, deliver and record for and in the name of such Unit Owner or mortgagee, as the case may be, such instruments as may be necessary to effectuate the foregoing.

2.   **Use of Common Areas and Facilities.**   No person shall use the Common Areas and Facilities or any part thereof in any manner contrary to or not in accordance with this Declaration or the Rules pertaining thereto. Without limiting the generality of the foregoing, the Association or the Board shall have the right, but not the obligation, to promulgate from time to time Rules governing the use of the Common Areas and Facilities by Unit Owners and Occupants and their respective families, tenants, guests, invitees and servants, as well as to provide for the exclusive use by a Unit Owner and his guests, for specific occasions, of the lounges, recreational areas or other similar facilities. Such use may be conditioned upon, among other things, the payment by the Unit Owner or Occupant of such special assessments as may be established by the Association or the Board for the purpose of defraying the costs of such use.

3.   **Management, Maintenance, Repairs and Replacement of Common Areas and Facilities.**   Except as otherwise provided herein, or in the Bylaws or in the Rules, the management, maintenance, repair and replacement of the Common Areas and Facilities shall be the responsibility of the Association. The Association may delegate all or any portion of its authority to discharge such responsibility to one or more independent contractors or to a managing agent. Such delegation to a managing agent may be evidenced by one or more management contracts, none of which shall exceed three (3) years in duration, which shall provide for termination for cause and shall provide for the payment of reasonable compensation to said managing agent as a Common Expense. Upon the expiration of the initial term of any such management contract, the Association may renew such contract from time to time for successive periods, none of which shall exceed three (3) years in duration or enter into a new management contract for an additional period of not in excess of three (3) years, or designate a different managing agent. The managing agent, for the period ending three (3) years after the date this Declaration is filed for record, shall be BA (or any other entity designated by BA to act in such capacity) and BA (or such other entity) shall be entitled to receive reasonable compensation for its services in such capacity. The rights of the Association to designate a different managing agent as above provided shall be subject to the rights of BA (or such other

— 18 —

entity) under any contract entered into, renewed, or extended in accordance herewith.

    4. **Maintenance of Units.** (a) The Association, at its expense, shall be responsible for the maintenance, repair and replacement of those portions of the Common Areas and Facilities located within the bounds of a Unit, excluding, however, (i) the interior surfaces of the perimeter walls, floors, doors and ceilings, (ii) the surfaces of any interior walls which are part of the Common Areas and Facilities and (iii) other portions of the Common Areas and Facilities within the bounds of a Unit the maintenance, repair or replacement of which is the responsibility of a Unit Owner under any other provision of this Declaration.

    (b) The responsibility of each Unit Owner shall be as follows:

        (1) to maintain, repair and replace at his expense all portions of his Unit, and all internal installations of such Unit such as appliances and plumbing and electrical fixtures and installations located within the bounds of such Unit and not constituting a part of the Common Areas and Facilities;

        (2) to maintain, repair and replace at his expense such portions of any Exclusive Use Area licensed, granted or otherwise assigned to such Unit Owner, as the Association shall from time to time determine;

        (3) to keep clean and free of snow, ice and accumulations of water, at his expense, any balcony which constitutes part of the Limited Common Areas and Facilities reserved exclusively for the use of his Unit and to repair, at his expense, any damage to such balcony caused by his negligence, misuse or neglect;

        (4) to repair and replace at his expense any doors and windows constituting a part of the Common Areas and Facilities that may be damaged or broken by the Unit Owner or any of his Occupants, tenants, guests, invitees or servants;

        (5) to perform his responsibilities in such manner so as not unreasonably to disturb other persons residing within the Building;

        (6) not to paint or otherwise finish or decorate or change the appearance of any portion of the Building not within the bounds of the Unit, without the prior written consent of the Association;

        (7) to report promptly to the Association or its managing agent any defect or need for repairs of which he has knowledge, the responsibility for the remedying of which is with the Association;

(8)   not to make any alterations in any portions of the Building which are to be maintained by the Association or to remove any portion thereof or make any additions thereto or do anything which would or might jeopardize or impair the safety or soundness of the Building without the prior written consent of the Association; and

(9)   not to impair or obstruct any easement without the prior written consent of the Association and of any other person for whose benefit such easement exists.

(c)   Nothing contained herein shall be deemed to impose any contractual liability on the Association for the maintenance, repair or replacement of the Common Areas and Facilities or any portion thereof, but the Association's liability shall be limited to damages resulting from negligence.

5.   **Repairs to Common Areas and Facilities and Unit Owner's Acts**.   Each Unit Owner agrees to maintain, repair and replace at his expense all portions of the Common Areas and Facilities which may be damaged or destroyed by reason of his own or his Occupant's act or neglect, or by the act or neglect of any tenant, guest, invitee, or servant of such Unit Owner or Occupant.

6.   **Construction Defects**.   The obligation of the Association and of Unit Owners to repair, maintain and replace the portions of the Condominium Property for which they are respectively responsible shall not be limited, discharged or postponed by reason of the fact thay any such maintenance, repair or replacement may be necessary due to latent or patent defects in material or workmanship in the construction of the Condominium Property.

7.   **Effect of Insurance or Construction Guarantees**.   Notwithstanding the fact that the Association or any Unit Owner may be entitled to the benefit of any policies of insurance providing coverage for loss or damage for which they are respectively responsible, the existence of any such insurance coverage shall not excuse any delay by the Association or any Unit Owner in performing its or his obligations hereunder.

ARTICLE XII
COMMON EXPENSES AND ASSESSMENTS

1.   **Obligation of Unit Owners to Pay Assessments**.   The common profits of the Condominium Property shall be distributed among and the Common Expenses shall be charged to the Unit Owners according to the percentages of interest in the Common Areas and Facilities of their respective Units as set forth in Exhibit E hereto. Every Unit Owner shall pay his proportionate share of assessments for Common Expenses and any special assessments levied against him.

2. **Failure to Pay Assessments When Due**. In the event any Unit Owner fails to pay any assessment made by the Board within ten (10) days after the same shall have become due and payable, the Board may, in its discretion and in addition to any other right or remedy conferred by law or contained herein or in the Bylaws, discontinue any or all services to the Unit owned by such Unit Owner which may be included as a part of the Common Expenses. Any assessment not paid within ten (10) days after the same shall have become due and payable shall bear interest until the same shall have been paid at a rate, not in excess of eight percent (8%) per annum, as determined by the Board.

3. **Statement of Unpaid Expenses**. Any prospective grantee or mortgagee of an Ownership Interest may request in writing a written statement from the Board or managing agent of the Association setting forth the amount of unpaid assessments with respect to the Ownership Interest to be sold or encumbered, and the Board shall, within ten (10) days after receipt of such request, furnish such a statement. In the case of a sale of any Ownership Interest, no grantee shall be liable for, nor shall any Ownership Interest be subject to a lien for, any unpaid assessments which became due prior to the date of the making of such request and which are not set forth in such statement. In the case of the creation of any mortgage, any lien of the Association for unpaid assessments which became due prior to the date of the making of such request shall be subordinate to such mortgage, if such unpaid assessments are not set forth in such statement.

4. **Responsibility of Unit Owners for Unpaid Assessments**. Except as otherwise provided in paragraph 3 of this Article XII, in the case of any voluntary conveyance of any Ownership Interest (except transfer to a mortgagee having a first mortgage lien on such Unit by a Deed in lieu of foreclosure), the grantee thereof shall be jointly and severally liable with the grantor for all unpaid assessments against the latter up to the time of transfer, without prejudice to the grantee's right to recover from the grantor the amounts paid by the grantee therefor. A Unit Owner shall be liable for all assessments made while he is the owner of a Unit, and no Unit Owner shall be liable for any such assessments made after he ceases to be the owner of a Unit.

5. **Lien for Unpaid Assessments**. The Association shall have a lien upon each Ownership Interest for the payment of all assessments, whether for Common Expenses or levied as special assessments, against the Unit constituting a part of such Ownership Interest which remain unpaid for ten (10) days after the same have become due and payable in like manner and with the same effect as the lien of the Association for Common Expenses accorded by Chapter 5311.

ARTICLE XIII
SALE, LEASING OR OTHER ALIENATION

1. **Sale or Lease**.   Any Unit Owner, other than BA, who wishes to sell or lease his Ownership Interest or any interest therein to any person (or any lessee of any Ownership Interest wishing to assign or sublease such Ownership Interest) other than to his spouse, his children, his parents or his brothers or sisters, or any one or more of them, shall give written notice to the Board of the terms of any proposed sale or lease, together with his name and address, the Unit of which he is the owner and which is to be the subject matter of the proposed sale or lease, the name and address of the proposed purchaser or lessee, the amount deemed by him to constitute the fair market value of such Ownership Interest or interest therein, and the amount of any liens and encumbrances thereon, which notice shall be given not less than thirty (30) days prior to the date of the proposed sale or lease. The members of the Board, acting on behalf of consenting Unit Owners as hereinafter provided, shall at all times have the first right and option to purchase or lease such Ownership Interest or interest therein upon the same terms, which option shall expire thirty (30) days after the date of receipt by it of such notice; provided, however, that if the proposed purchase or lease shall be for a consideration which the Board does not deem to reflect the fair market value of such Ownership Interest or interest therein, the Board may elect to exercise such option in the manner, within the period, and on the terms set forth in paragraph 2 of this Article XIII. If said option is not exercised by the Board within the aforesaid option period, the Unit Owner or lessee may, upon the expiration of said option, contract to sell or lease (or sublease or assign) such Ownership Interest or other interest to the proposed purchaser or lessee named in such notice upon the terms specified therein. Anything herein to the contrary notwithstanding, no Unit shall be leased to any transient tenant and no lease of any Unit shall be for less than sixty (60) days.

2. **Inter Vivos Gift**.   Any Unit Owner, other than BA, who wishes to make an *inter vivos* gift of his Ownership Interest or any interest therein to any person or persons other than to his spouse, his children, his parents or his brothers or sisters, or any one or more of them, shall give written notice to the Board of his intent to make such gift not less than sixty (60) days prior to the date of the proposed gift. The Unit Owner shall specify in such notice his name and address, the Unit of which he is the owner and which is to be the subject matter of the proposed gift, the name and address of the intended donee, the contemplated date of said gift, the amount deemed by him to constitute the fair market value of such Ownership Interest or interest therein, and the amount of any liens and encumbrances thereon. The members of the Board, acting on behalf of consenting Unit Owners as hereinafter provided, shall at all times have the first right and option to purchase or

otherwise acquire such Ownership Interest or interest therein for cash at the fair market value thereof less the amount of any liens and encumbrances thereon. If the Board does not deem the amount specified in said notice to be the fair market value of such Ownership Interest or interest therein, the Board may, within ten (10) days after the service of such written notice by the Unit Owner, so notify the Unit Owner in writing and specify a different amount as the fair market value of said Ownership Interest or interest therein. The fair market value of the Ownership Interest or interest therein involved shall be deemed to be the amount specified by the Unit Owner, or if the Board has specified a different amount as provided herein, then the amount specified by the Board, unless either (i) the Board and the Unit Owner at any time within twenty (20) days after the service of such notice by the Unit Owner agree upon a different amount or (ii) either the Unit Owner or the Board, within said twenty (20) day period (but not thereafter) serves a written notice on the other that he or it desires that the determination of such fair market value shall be made by a board of appraisers. A determination by any such board of appraisers shall be made by the majority vote of a board of three appraisers, one of whom shall be appointed by the Board and one of whom shall be appointed by the Unit Owner, each such appointment to be made within five (5) days after the receipt by the other party of the aforesaid notice. The third member of such board of appraisers shall be appointed by the first two appraisers within five (5) days after the last of their respective appointments. Upon a determination of fair market value by said appraisers, they shall promptly give written notice thereof to the Unit Owner and the Board. The Board's option to purchase or otherwise acquire said Ownership Interest or interest therein shall expire fifteen (15) days after the date the fair market value thereof becomes fixed as aforesaid.

3. **Devise and Inheritance.** In the event any Unit Owner dies and his Ownership Interest or any interest therein passes by devise or under the laws of intestacy to any person or persons other than to his spouse, his children, his parents or his brothers or sisters, or one or more of them, the members of the Board, acting on behalf of consenting Unit Owners as hereinafter provided, shall have the first right and option (exercisable in the manner hereinafter set forth) to purchase said Ownership Interest or interest therein either from the devisee or devisees or the heir or heirs of the deceased Unit Owner or, if a power of sale is conferred by the will of any such Unit Owner upon a personal representative named therein, from such personal representative acting pursuant to said power, for cash at the fair market value thereof, less the amount of any liens and encumbrances thereon. Within sixty (60) days after the appointment of a personal representative of the deceased Unit Owner, the Board shall give notice of this option to said devisee or devisees, heir or heirs, or personal representative, as the case may be. Such notice shall specify therein an amount

deemed by the Board to constitute the fair market value of such Ownership Interest or interest therein. If the person or persons to whom such notice is given do not deem the amount specified in said notice to be the fair market value of such Ownership Interest or interest therein, such person or persons may, within fifteen (15) days after the service of such written notice, notify the Board in writing and specify a different amount as the fair market value of said Ownership Interest or interest therein. The fair market value of the Ownership Interest or interest therein involved shall be deemed to be the amount specified by the Board or if such person or persons as aforesaid has or have specified a different amount, then the amount specified by such person or persons, unless either (i) the Board and such person or persons at any time within thirty (30) days after the service of such written notice by the Board agree upon a different amount or (ii) either such person or persons or the Board, within said thirty (30) day period (but not thereafter), serves a written notice upon the other that he, they or it desire that the determination of such fair market value shall be made by a board of appraisers. A determination by any such board of appraisers shall be made by the majority vote of a board of three appraisers, one of whom shall be appointed by the Board and one of whom shall be appointed by such person or persons, each such appointment to be made within five (5) days after the receipt by the other party of the aforesaid notice. The third member of such board of appraisers shall be appointed by the first two appraisers within five (5) days after the last of their respective appointments. Upon a determination of fair market value by said appraisers, they shall promptly give written notice thereof to such person or persons and the Board. The Board's option to purchase or otherwise acquire said Ownership Interest or interest therein shall expire thirty (30) days after the date the fair market value thereof becomes fixed as aforesaid if the personal representative of the deceased Unit Owner is empowered to sell and shall expire ninety (90) days after said date if said personal representative is not empowered to sell. Nothing contained herein shall be deemed to restrict the right of the Board or its authorized representative, pursuant to authority given to the Board by the Unit Owners as hereinafter provided, to bid at any sale of the Ownership Interest or interest therein of any deceased Unit Owner which sale is held pursuant to an order or direction of the court having jurisdiction over that portion of the deceased Unit Owner's estate which contains his or her Ownership Interest or interest therein.

4. **Involuntary Sale.** (a) In the event any Ownership Interest or interest therein is sold at a judicial or execution sale, the person acquiring title through such sale shall, before taking possession of the Unit so sold, give to the Board, not less than thirty (30) days prior to the date such person intends to take possession, written notice of such intention together with his name and address, the Unit purchased, and the purchase price. The members of the Board, acting on behalf of

consenting Unit Owners as hereinafter provided, shall have the first right and option to purchase such Ownership Interest or interest therein at the same price for which it was sold at such sale; provided, however, that such option shall not apply to a purchase at such sale by any mortgagee having a first mortgage lien on such Unit (or to a transfer to such Unit mortgagee by a Deed in lieu of foreclosure). If the Board does not deem the amount so specified in said notice to be the fair market value thereof, then the Board may elect to exercise such option in the manner, within the period, and on the terms set forth in paragraph 2 of this Article XIII. Except as otherwise provided herein, if said option is not exercised by the Board within said thirty (30) days after receipt of such notice, it shall thereupon expire and said purchaser may thereafter take possession of said Unit. The Board shall be deemed to have exercised its option if it tenders to an escrow agent selected by it, within said thirty (30) day period, the required sum of money for the account of the purchaser.

(b)   In the event any Unit Owner shall default in the payment of any monies required to be paid under the provisions of any mortgage or deed of trust on or against his Ownership Interest, the Board shall have the right to cure such default by paying the amount so owing to the party entitled thereto and shall thereupon have in addition to any right of subrogation resulting from such payment, a lien therefor against such Ownership Interest. Such lien shall have the same force and effect and may be enforced in the same manner as a lien of the Association for unpaid Common Expenses.

5.   **Consummation of Purchase.**   Any option exercisable by the Board hereunder may be exercised within the respective option period by delivery by the Board of written notice of such exercise to the person or persons required to sell any Ownership Interest or interest therein to the Board in accordance with the provisions of this Article XIII. Any purchase effected pursuant to the provisions of this Article XIII shall be made by the payment of the purchase price by the Board, on behalf of the consenting Unit Owners, in return for a conveyance of the Ownership Interest or interest therein, subject to any liens and encumbrances thereon. Such conveyance shall be to the president or other chief officer of the Association as trustee for all consenting Unit Owners. Such conveyance and payment shall be made within twenty (20) days after the exercise of any option by the Board as provided in this Article XIII.

6.   **Consent of Voting Members.**   The Board shall not exercise any option to purchase any Ownership Interest or interest therein unless it shall have been authorized to do so by the affirmative vote of Unit Owners entitled to exercise not less than seventy-five percent (75%) of the voting power of all Unit Owners and whose Units are not the subject matter of such option. The

Board may bid and purchase at any sale of an Ownership Interest or interest therein which is held pursuant to an order or direction of a court upon the prior authorization of the Unit Owners as aforesaid. Such authorization shall set forth a maximum price which the Board is authorized to bid and pay for said Ownership Interest or interest therein.

7. **Release, Waiver, and Exceptions to Option.**   Any of the options contained in this Article XIII may be waived or released in writing by BA so long as it is managing agent, or by a majority of the members of the Board. In such event, the Ownership Interest or interest therein which is subject to an option set forth in this Article XIII may be sold, conveyed, leased, given, devised or passed as contemplated in that instance without regard to the requirements of the other paragraphs of this Article. In addition, none of the options contained in this Article XIII shall be applicable to any sales, leases, or subleases of any Ownership Interest with respect to which BA is the grantor, lessor or sublessor.

8. **Evidence of Termination of Option.**   A certificate executed and acknowledged by the president or secretary of BA, if it is the managing agent, or of the Association stating that the provisions of this Article XIII as set forth above have been met by a Unit Owner, or duly waived or released, and that the rights of the Board hereunder have terminated, shall be conclusive upon the Board and the Unit Owners in favor of all persons who rely thereon in good faith. Such certificate shall be furnished upon request by the Association to any person or persons who have in fact complied with the provisions of this Article or with respect to whom the provisions of this Article have been waived or released, upon payment of a reasonable charge, not to exceed ten dollars ($10.00) in any instance.

9. **Financing of Purchase under Option.**   (a)   Acquisition of any Ownership Interest or interest therein under the provisions of this Article shall be made from the reserve for contingencies and replacements and for the account of consenting Unit Owners. If said reserve is insufficient, the Association shall levy a special assessment against each consenting Unit Owner in the proportion which his percentage of interest in the Common Areas and Facilities bears to the percentage of interest in the Common Areas and Facilities of all consenting Unit Owners, which assessment shall become a lien and be enforceable as a lien for Common Expenses.

(b)   The Board in its discretion, may borrow money to finance the acquisition of any Ownership Interest or interest therein authorized by this Article; provided, however, that no financing may be secured by an encumbrance on or hypothecation of any portion of the Condominium Property other than the Ownership Interest or interest therein to be acquired.

10. **Title to Acquired Interests.** Ownership Interests or interests therein acquired pursuant to the terms of this Article shall be held of record in the name of the president or other chief officer of the Association as trustee for all consenting Unit Owners. The president or other chief officer of the Association shall exercise the voting power appurtenant to such acquired Unit in accordance with the direction of consenting Unit Owners entitled to exercise a majority of the voting power of such consenting Unit Owners. Such holding shall be for the benefit of all the Unit Owners consenting to and participating in such acquisition. Said Ownership Interests or interests therein shall be sold or leased by the Board for the benefit of such Unit Owners. All net proceeds of any such sale or leasing shall be deposited in the reserve fund and may thereafter be disbursed or credited at such time and in such manner as the Board may determine for the account of such consenting Unit Owners.

ARTICLE XIV

**PURCHASE OF UNIT OF DISSENTING
OWNER UPON REHABILITATION**

In the event that the Association decides to have the Condominium Property renewed and rehabilitated as provided in Chapter 5311, any Unit Owner who does not vote for such renewal and rehabilitation may elect to receive the fair market value of his Ownership Interest, less the amount of any liens and encumbrances thereon, in accordance with the provisions of Article XVI hereof.

ARTICLE XV

**REMOVAL OF PROPERTY FROM
PROVISIONS OF CHAPTER 5311**

Anything in Chapter 5311 to the contrary notwithstanding, the Unit Owners, by the affirmative vote of those entitled to exercise not less than seventy-five percent (75%) of the voting power of all Unit Owners, may elect to remove the Condominium Property from the provisions of Chapter 5311. Any Unit Owner who does not vote for such removal may elect to receive the fair market value of his Ownership Interest, less the amount of any liens and encumbrances thereon, in accordance with the provisions of Article XVI hereof.

– 27 –

ARTICLE XVI

PROCEEDINGS CONCERNING DISSENTING OWNERS

Any Unit Owner who is entitled to notice of a meeting called to act upon any of the matters mentioned in Articles XIV and XV hereof and who does not vote in favor of such matters shall be entitled, upon complying with the provisions of this Article, to receive the fair market value of his Ownership Interest, as of the date such vote is taken, less the amount of any liens and encumbrances thereon. In order to become entitled to such receipt, such Unit Owner shall serve a written demand therefor, within five (5) days after receiving notice of such vote, upon the president or other chief officer of the Association. The Unit Owner shall specify in said demand his name and address, the Unit of which he is the owner and with respect to which such demand is made, the amount claimed by him to be the fair market value of such Unit, and the amount of such liens and encumbrances thereon. If the Board is unwilling to pay the amount so demanded, the Board may, on behalf of the Association, within ten (10) days after the service of such written demand, so notify the Unit Owner and make a counter offer of a different amount as the fair market value of the Ownership Interest as to which demand has been made in compliance herewith. The fair market value of the Ownership Interest involved in the demand by the Unit Owner shall be deemed to be the amount demanded by him if he has complied with the provisions of this Article, or if the Association as aforesaid has made a counter offer of a different amount, then the amount specified in such counter offer, unless either (i) the Board and the Unit Owner at any time within twenty (20) days after the service of such demand agree upon a different amount or (ii) either the Unit Owner or the Association, within said twenty (20) day period (but not thereafter) serves a written notice on the other that he or it desires that the determination of the fair market value of such Unit shall be made by a board of appraisers. A determination by any such board of appraisers shall be made by the majority vote of a board of three appraisers, one of whom shall be appointed by the Board and one of whom shall be appointed by the Unit Owner, each such appointment to be made within five (5) days after the receipt by the other party of the aforesaid notice. The third member of such board of appraisers shall be appointed by the first two appraisers within five (5) days after the last of their respective appointments. The fair market value, determined as above provided, of such Ownership Interest less the amount of any liens and encumbrances thereon as above provided shall be paid to the Unit Owner in return for a conveyance of his Ownership Interest, subject to any liens and encumbrances thereon, to the president or other chief officer of the Association as trustee for all other Unit Owners. Such conveyance and payment of the consideration therefor, which shall be a Common Expense to the Unit Owners who have not elected to receive the fair market value of their Units, shall be made within ten (10) days after the fair market value of the Ownership Interest becomes fixed as aforesaid.

ARTICLE XVII

REMEDIES FOR BREACH OF COVENANTS AND RULES

1. **Abatement and Enjoinment.** If any Unit Owner (either by his own conduct or by the conduct of any Occupant of his Unit) shall violate any covenant or provision herein or in the Bylaws or the Rules, the Association shall have the right, in addition to the rights set forth in the next succeeding paragraph and those provided by law (i) to enter any Unit in which or as to which such violation or breach exists and to summarily abate and remove, at the expense of the owner of such Unit, any structure, thing or condition that may exist therein contrary to the intent and meaning of the provisions thereof or hereof, and the Association, or its agent, shall not thereby be deemed guilty in any manner of trespass or (ii) to enjoin, abate or remedy the continuance of any breach by appropriate legal proceedings, either at law or in equity.

2. **Involuntary Sale.** If any Unit Owner (either by his own conduct or by the conduct of any Occupant of his Unit) shall violate any covenant or provision herein or in the Bylaws or the Rules, and such violation shall continue for thirty (30) days after notice in writing from the Association, or shall occur repeatedly during any thirty (30) day period after written notice or request to cure such violation from the Association, the Association shall have the right, upon the giving of ten (10) days prior written notice, to terminate the rights of such Unit Owner or Occupant to continue as a Unit Owner or Occupant and to continue to occupy, use or control his Unit. Following such notice, a legal action may be filed by the Association against such Unit Owner or Occupant for a decree of mandatory injunction against such Unit Owner or Occupant or, subject to the prior consent in writing of any mortgagee having an interest in the Ownership Interest of such Unit Owner (which consent shall not be unreasonably withheld), for a decree declaring the termination of the right of such Unit Owner or Occupant to occupy, use or control the Unit owned or occupied by him and ordering that all the right, title and interest of the Unit Owner or Occupant in his Ownership Interest or interest therein shall be sold (subject to any liens and encumbrances thereon) at a judicial sale upon such notice and terms as the court shall establish, except that the court shall enjoin and restrain such Unit Owner or Occupant from re-acquiring his interest at such

judicial sale. The proceeds of any such judicial sale shall first be paid to discharge court costs, receiver's fees and all other expenses of the proceeding, and all such items shall be taxed against such Unit Owner or Occupant in said decree. Any balance of proceeds, after satisfaction of such charges and any unpaid assessments owing to the Association or any liens required to be discharged, may be paid to the Unit Owner or Occupant. Upon the confirmation of such sale, the purchaser thereat shall, subject to the rights and privileges of the Board provided in Article XIII, be entitled to a conveyance of the Ownership Interest or interest therein and to immediate possession of the Unit so conveyed, and may apply to the court for a writ for the purpose of acquiring such possession. It shall be a condition of any such sale, and the decree shall so provide, that the purchaser shall take the interest in such Ownership Interest or interest therein subject to this Declaration.

ARTICLE XVIII

INSURANCE AND RECONSTRUCTION

1. **Insurance.** The insurance which shall be carried upon the Condominium Property shall be governed by the following provisions:

(a) All insurance policies upon the Condominium Property (except as hereinafter allowed) shall be purchased by the Association for the benefit of the Association, the Unit Owners and their respective Unit mortgagees as their interests may appear. Such insurance policies shall provide (i) for the issuance of certificates of insurance with mortgagee endorsements to the holders of first mortgages on the Units, if any, (ii) that for the purposes of such insurance, improvements to Units made by Unit Owners shall not affect the valuation of the Buildings and all other improvements upon the land, (iii) that the insurer waives its rights of subrogation against BA, Unit Owners, the Association, any managing agent and their respective families, agents, tenants, guests and employees and all persons lawfully in possession or control of any part of the Condominium Property, (iv) that the insurer waives all defenses based upon co-insurance, invalidity arising by acts of an insured, or similar defenses, and (v) that coverage under such insurance policies will not be terminated, cancelled or substantially modified without ten (10) days' prior written notice to all insureds, including each Unit mortgagee. Such policies and endorsements shall be deposited with the Insurance Trustee (as hereinafter defined) who shall first acknowledge that the policies and any proceeds thereof will be held in accordance with the terms hereof. The Association agrees for the benefit of the Unit Owners and each Unit mortgagee that it shall pay the premiums for the casualty insurance hereinafter required to be carried by the Association at least thirty (30) days prior to the expiration date of any such policies. Duplicate originals of all such casualty policies, together with proof of payment of the premiums therefor, shall be delivered by the Association to each Unit mortgagee at least ten (10) days prior to the expiration of the then current policies.

(b)   Each Unit Owner may, at his own expense, obtain insurance affording coverage upon his personal property, for his personal liability and/or casualty insurance upon any improvements to his Unit made by him in which he would have an insurable interest in excess of his interest in the casualty insurance policy purchased by the Association. Any such casualty insurance· shall provide that it shall be without contribution as against the casualty insurance purchased by the Association or shall be written by the carrier of such insurance and shall contain the waiver of subrogation referred to in subparagraph (a) hereof.

(c)   The Building and all other insurable improvements upon the land and all personal property owned by the Association shall be insured in an amount equal to the maximum insurable replacement value thereof (exclusive of excavation and foundations), as determined annually by the insurance company affording such coverage. The amount of such insurance to be maintained until the first meeting of the Board following the first annual meeting of the Association shall be at least Eleven Million Dollars ($11,000,000). Such coverage shall afford protection against the following:

(1)   loss or damage by fire and other hazards covered by the standard extended coverage endorsement including coverage for the payment of Common Expenses with respect to damaged Units during the period of reconstruction thereof; and

(2)   such other risks as from time to time customarily shall be covered with respect to buildings similar in construction, location and use as the Building, including but not limited to vandalism, malicious mischief, windstorm, boiler and machinery, plate glass and water damage. The policy providing such coverage shall provide that notwithstanding any provision thereof which gives the carrier an election to restore damage in lieu of making a cash settlement therefor such option shall not be exercisable in the case of the termination of the Condominium as provided for in this Declaration or pursuant to the provisions of Chapter 5311.

(d)   The Association shall insure itself, any managing agent, the Unit Owners and their respective families, agents, tenants, guests and employees and all persons lawfully in possession or control of any part of the Condominium Property, against liability for personal injury, disease, illness or death and for injury to or destruction of property occurring upon, in or about, or arising from or relating to the Common Areas and Facilities, including without limitation, water damage, legal liability, hired automobile, non-owned automobile and off-premises employee coverage. Until the first meeting of the Board following the first annual meeting of the Association, such insurance shall afford protection to a single limit of not less than Five Million Dollars ($5,000,000) in respect to claims for personal injury or property damage in respect to any one occurrence, and to a limit of not less than Five Hundred Thousand Dollars ($500,000) in respect to water damage legal liability claims arising out of any one occurrence. Such insurance shall not insure against liability for personal injury or property damage arising out of or relating to the individual Units. All liability insurance shall contain cross-liability endorsements to cover liabilities of the Unit Owners as a group to a Unit Owner.

(e)   The Association shall also obtain and maintain, to the extent obtainable: (i) fidelity insurance covering all employees who handle Association funds; (ii) workmen's compensation insurance; and (iii) public liability insurance covering each member of the Board of Managers, the managing agent, the manager and each Unit Owner, in such limits as the Board of Managers may deem proper. The Board of Managers shall review such limits once each year.

(f)   Premiums upon insurance policies purchased by the Association shall be paid by the Association and charged as Common Expenses.

(g)   All casualty insurance policies purchased by the Association shall be for the benefit of the Association and the Unit Owners and their respective mortgagees, as their respective interests may appear. Such casualty insurance policies shall provide that all proceeds payable as a result of casualty losses shall be paid to The Union Commerce Bank, as Trustee, or to any other bank in Cleveland, Ohio with trust powers and total assets of more than Fifty Million Dollars ($50,000,000). Such Trustee or any other bank acting as such is herein referred to as the Insurance Trustee. The Insurance Trustee shall not be liable for payment of premiums, for the renewal of the policies, for the sufficiency of coverage, for the form or contents of the policies, or for the failure to collect any insurance proceeds. The sole duty of the Insurance Trustee shall be to receive such proceeds as are paid and to hold the same in trust for the purposes stated herein, and for the benefit of the Association, the Unit Owners, and their respective mortgagees.

2. **Responsibility for Reconstruction or Repair.** (a)   If any part of the Common Areas and Facilities shall be damaged by casualty, such damaged portion shall be promptly reconstructed or repaired as hereinafter provided unless such damage renders one-half or more of the Units untenantable and Unit Owners, by the vote of those entitled to exercise not less than seventy-five percent (75%) of the voting power of all Unit Owners, elect not to reconstruct or repair such damaged part. Any such election by the Unit Owners shall be made at a meeting called for such purpose within ninety (90) days after the occurrence of the casualty, or, if within such period, the insurance loss has not been finally adjusted, then within thirty (30) days after adjustment thereof. Following any such election not to reconstruct or repair, the Property shall be subject to an action for partition at the suit of any Unit Owner or lienor, as if the Property were owned in common. In the event of such a partition, the net proceeds of sale, together with the net proceeds of all insurance policies payable by virtue of such casualty loss, shall be divided among all Unit Owners in proportion to their respective interests in the Common Areas and Facilities, provided, that no payment shall be made to a Unit Owner until there has been first paid out of his share of such proceeds, all liens on his Ownership Interest, in the order of their priority.

(b)   Any reconstruction or repair made pursuant to this paragraph shall be substantially in accordance with the Drawings.

(c)   If the damage is only to those parts of one Unit for which the responsibility of maintenance and repair is that of the Unit Owners, then the Unit Owner shall be responsible for reconstruction and repair after casualty.

(d)   In all other instances, the responsibility of reconstruction and repair after casualty shall be that of the Association.

3. **Procedure for Reconstruction.** (a)   Immediately after a casualty damage to any portion of the Condominium Property for which the Association has the responsibility of maintenance and repair, the Association shall obtain reliable and detailed estimates of the cost to place the damaged property in condition as good as that before the casualty. Such costs may include professional fees and premiums for such bonds as the Board deems necessary.

(b)   If the proceeds of insurance policies are not sufficient to defray the costs of reconstruction and repair as estimated by the Association (including the aforesaid fees and premiums, if any) one or more assessments shall be made against all Unit Owners in sufficient amounts to provide funds for the payment of such costs, and such assessments shall be deposited with the Insurance Trustee.

(c) The proceeds of insurance collected on account of a casualty, and the sums deposited with the Insurance Trustee by the Association from collections of assessments against Unit Owners on account of such casualty, shall constitute a construction fund which shall be disbursed in payment of the costs of reconstruction and repair in the following manner:

(1) The portion of insurance proceeds representing damage for which the responsibility of reconstruction and repair lies with a Unit Owner shall be paid to such contractors, suppliers and personnel as do the work or supply the materials or services required for such reconstruction or repair, in such amounts and at such times as the Unit Owner may direct, or if there is a mortgagee endorsement, then to such payees as the Unit Owner and the first mortgagee jointly direct; provided, however, that nothing contained herein shall be construed so as to limit or modify the responsibility of the Unit Owner to make such reconstruction or repair;

(2) The portion of insurance proceeds representing damage for which the responsibility of reconstruction and repair lies with the Association shall be disbursed as follows:

(A) If the amount of the estimated costs of reconstruction and repair is less than the total of the annual assessments for Common Expenses made during the calendar year immediately preceding the year in which the casualty occurred, then the construction fund shall be disbursed in payment of such costs upon the order of the Association; provided however, that upon request of a mortgagee which is a beneficiary of an insurance policy, the proceeds of which are included in the construction fund, such proceeds shall be disbursed in the manner provided in the paragraph next succeeding; or

(B) If the amount of the estimated cost of reconstruction and repair is more than the total of the annual assessments for Common Expenses made during the calendar year immediately preceding the year in which the casualty occurred, then the construction fund shall be applied by the Insurance Trustee to the payment of such costs and shall be paid to or for the account of the Association from time

– 34 –

to time as the work progresses, but not more frequently than once in any calendar month. The Insurance Trustee shall make such payments upon the written request of the Association, accompanied by a certificate, dated not more than fifteen (15) days prior to such request. Such certificate shall be signed by a responsible officer of the Association and by an architect in charge of the work, who shall be selected by the Association and shall (i) state that the sum requested has either been paid by the Association or is justly due to contractors, subcontractors, materialmen, architects, or other persons who have rendered services or furnished materials in connection with the work; (ii) give a brief description of the services and materials and the several amounts so paid for by the Association pending withdrawal of insurance proceeds; (iii) state that the sum requested does not exceed the value of the services and materials described in the certificate; (iv) state that except for the amount stated in such certificate to be due as aforesaid and for work subsequently performed, there is no outstanding indebtedness known to the person signing such certificate after due inquiry, which might become the basis of a vendor's, mechanic's, materialmen's or similar lien upon such work, the Common Areas and Facilities or any Unit; and (v) state that the cost of the work remaining to be done subsequent to the date of such certificate, as estimated by the person signing such certificate, does not exceed the amount of the construction fund remaining in the hands of the Insurance Trustee after the payment of the sum so requested.

(3)   It shall be presumed that the first monies disbursed in payment of such costs of reconstruction and repair shall be from insurance proceeds. If there is a balance in any construction fund after payment of all costs of the reconstruction and repair for which the fund is established, such balance shall be distributed jointly to the Unit Owners and their mortgagees who are the beneficial owners of the funds.

(4)   The Insurance Trustee may rely upon a certificate of the Association

certifying as to whether or not the damaged property is to be reconstructed or repaired. The Association, upon request of the Insurance Trustee, shall deliver such certificate as soon as practical.

(d) Each Unit Owner shall be deemed to have delegated to the Board his right to adjust with insurance companies all losses under policies purchased by the Association except in any case where the damage is restricted to one Unit, subject to the rights of mortgagees of such Unit.

ARTICLE XIX
GENERAL PROVISIONS

1. **BA's Rights with Regard to Unsold Units.** (a) With regard to unsold Units, BA shall be entitled to exercise the voting power appurtenant to such Units, including without limitation, the power to vote the same at meetings of the Association.

(b) BA shall have the right, so long as it is the owner of any Unit, to change the size, the layout or the price of any such Unit or Units. Such changes shall not change the interest of such Unit in the Common Areas and Facilities, as set forth in Exhibit E, provided however that if such changes include the adding of a room or rooms or a portion thereof taken from one Unit to another Unit, the respective interests of such Units in the Common Areas and Facilities may be changed so long as the aggregate interest of such Units in the Common Areas and Facilities shall remain constant.

2. **Copies of Notices to Mortgage Lenders.** Upon written request to the Board, the Board shall give to the holder of any duly recorded mortgage on any Ownership Interest a copy of any and all notices permitted or required by this Declaration to be given to the Unit Owner or Owners whose Ownership Interest is subject to such mortgage.

3. **Service of Notices on the Board.** Notices required to be given to the Board or the Association may be delivered to any two members of the Board or to the president or other chief officer of the Association, either personally or by certified mail, with postage prepaid, addressed to such members or officer at his Unit.

4. **Service of Notices on Devisees and Personal Representatives.** Notices required to be given any devisee, heir or personal representative of a deceased Unit Owner may be delivered either personally or by certified mail, with postage prepaid, to such party at his or its address appearing in the records of the court wherein the estate of such deceased Unit Owner is being administered.

5. **Compliance with Covenants.** All Unit Owners and Occupants shall comply with all covenants, conditions and restrictions set forth in any deed to which they are subject or in the

Declaration, the Bylaws, the Rules or the Deed of Easements, as any of the same may be amended from time to time.

6. **Non-Waiver of Covenants.** No covenants, conditions or restrictions, obligations or provisions contained in this Declaration, the Bylaws or the Rules shall be deemed to have been abrogated or waived by reason of any failure to enforce the same, irrespective of the number of violations or breaches which may occur.

7. **Insufficiency of Insurance.** In the event the insurance effected by the Association on behalf of the Unit Owners and Occupants against liability for personal injury or property damage arising from or relating to the Common Areas and Facilities shall, for any reason, not fully cover any such liability, the amount of any deficit shall be a Common Expense to the Unit Owners. Any Unit Owner who shall have paid all or any portion of such deficiency in an amount exceeding his proportionate share thereof (based on his percentage of interest in the Common Areas and Facilities), shall have a right of contribution from the other Unit Owners according to their respective percentages of interest in the Common Areas and Facilities.

8. **Waiver of Damages.** Neither BA nor any employee, agent, successor or assign of BA shall be liable for any claim or damage whatsoever arising out of or by reason of any actions (i) performed pursuant to or in accordance with any authority granted or delegated to them or any of them by or pursuant to this Declaration (including, without limitation, the provisions of paragraph 3 of Article XI or Article XVIII hereof and paragraph 1 of this Article XX) or (ii) in BA's capacity as Sponsor, Unit Owner, Managing Agent or seller of the Condominium Property or any part thereof, whether such claim: shall be asserted by any Unit Owner, Occupant, the Board, the Association, or by any person or entity claiming by or through any of them; shall be on account of personal injury or property damage however caused; or shall arise *ex contractu* or (except in the case of willful misconduct or gross negligence) *ex delictu*. Without limiting the generality of the foregoing, the foregoing enumeration includes all claims for or arising by reason of the Condominium Property or any part thereof being or becoming out of repair or containing any patent or latent defects, or by reason of any act or neglect of any Unit Owner, Occupant, the Board or the Association, or their respective agents, employees, guests, tenants, invitees, and servants, or by reason of the ownership, use and maintenance of any other neighboring real property or any personal property located on or about the Condominium Property, or by reason of the failure to function or disrepair of any utility services, including, without limitation, heat, air conditioning, electricity, gas, water, sewage, and the like.

9. **Parking Spaces.** The underground parking garage contains parking spaces for 350 automobiles. The garage shall constitute part of the Common Areas and Facilities and shall be operated and managed by the Board. The spaces contained in the garage shall be allocated as follows: (i) one space to each Unit shown by the Drawings to contain one bedroom; (ii) two spaces to each Unit shown by the Drawings to contain two or more bedrooms; and (iii) ten spaces for use by BA, the building manager, the managing agent, restaurant personnel, limousine service vehicles or as otherwise determined by the Board. Unit Owners may arrange through the Board to lease additional spaces to or from other Unit Owners on such terms as such Unit Owners may agree but subject to the approval of the Board.

10. **Condemnation.** In the event of a taking in condemnation or by eminent domain of all or part of the Common Areas and Facilities, the award payable for such taking shall be made payable to the Board, if less than $50,000 and to the Insurance Trustee if more than $50,000. Such proceeds shall be applied by the Board or the Insurance Trustee, as the case may be, for the repair and restoration of such Common Areas and Facilities, in a manner similar to that provided in Article XVIII hereof for the repair and reconstruction of the Property with the proceeds of insurance, unless the Unit Owners entitled to exercise seventy-five percent (75%) of the voting power of all Unit Owners elect not to repair or restore such Common Areas and Facilities. Any such election shall be made in a manner similar to that provided in Article XVIII hereof. In the event of such an election, the Board or the Insurance Trustee, as the case may be, shall disburse the net proceeds of such award to the Unit Owners in proportion to their respective interests in the Common Areas and Facilities and in a manner similar to that provided in Article XVIII hereof.

11. **Headings.** The heading to each Article and to each paragraph hereof is inserted only as a matter of convenience for reference and in no way defines, limits or describes the scope or intent of this Declaration nor in any way affects this Declaration.

12. **Severability.** The invalidity of any covenant, restriction, condition, limitation or any other provision of this Declaration, or of any part of the same, shall not impair or affect in any manner the validity, enforceability or effect of any other provision of this Declaration.

13. **Perpetuities and Restraints on Alienation.** If any of the options, privileges, covenants or rights created by this Declaration shall be unlawful or void for violation of (i) any rule against perpetuities or any analogous statutory provision, (ii) any rules restricting restraints on alienation, or (iii) any other statutory or common law rules imposing time limitations, then such provision shall continue in effect for only twenty-one (21) years after the death of the last survivor of the now living descendants of Gerald R. Ford.

−38−

14. **Covenants to Run with Land.**   All easements, rights, covenants, conditions and restrictions set forth in this Declaration, both as to the benefits and burdens thereof, are appurtenances, running with the land, perpetually in full force and effect, and at all times shall inure to the benefit of and be binding on BA, its successors and assigns, and any Unit Owner, Occupant, purchaser, lessee, mortgagee or other person having at any time an interest in the Condominium Property or any portion thereof.

15. **Interpretation of Declaration.**   The provisions of this Declaration shall be liberally construed to effectuate its purpose of creating a uniform plan for the development and operation of a luxury condominium development.

ARTICLE XX

AMENDMENTS TO DECLARATION
AND ACTION WITHOUT MEETING

1. **Amendments by Unit Owners or Board.**   The provisions of Articles VI, VII, paragraph 6 of Article XIII and of this Article XX may be amended only by the affirmative vote of all Unit Owners at a meeting held for such purpose. All other provisions of this Declaration may be amended by the Unit Owners at a meeting held for such purpose by the affirmative vote of those entitled to exercise not less than seventy-five percent (75%) of the voting power of all Unit Owners. Anything in this paragraph 1 to the contrary notwithstanding: (i) none of the provisions of this Declaration relating to BA or its rights hereunder, including, without limiting the generality of the foregoing, Article XVIII, shall be amended without the written consent of BA; (ii) the following provisions shall not be amended without the written consent of all Unit mortgagees, viz., paragraphs 2 (a), (g) and (k) of Article IV, Articles VI and VII, paragraphs 1 and 3 of Article XI, Articles XII, XV, XVIII, paragraphs 2, 7, 8, 9, 11 of Article XIX and Article XX; and (iii) no amendment of this Declaration shall conflict with the provisions of Chapter 5311. Upon the adoption of any amendment, a certificate containing a copy of the resolution adopting the amendment and a statement of the manner of its adoption shall be filed with the Recorder of Cuyahoga County and thereupon this Declaration shall be amended accordingly. Such certificate shall be signed by the president or other chief officer and the secretary or an assistant secretary of the Association.

2. **Action Without Meeting.**   Any action which may be authorized or taken at a meeting of the Unit Owners or of the Board, as the case may be, may be authorized or taken without a meeting with the affirmative vote or approval of, and in a writing or writings signed by all of the Unit Owners or all of the members of the Board respectively, which writing or writings shall

be filed with or entered upon the records of the Association. Any certificate with respect to the authorization or taking of any such action which is required to be filed with the Recorder of Cuyahoga County shall recite that the authorization or taking of such action was in a writing or writings approved and signed as specified in this Article XX.

IN WITNESS WHEREOF, BA Associates Limited has signed this instrument this _____ day of _____, 1976.

Signed and acknowledged
in the presence of:

BA ASSOCIATES LIMITED

_____

By_____

                                    General Partner

_____

Witnesses as to BA Associates Limited

— 40 —

STATE OF OHIO   )
) SS:
COUNTY OF CUYAHOGA)

BEFORE ME, a Notary Public, in and for said County and State, personally appeared the above-named BA Associates Limited, an Ohio limited partnership, by Carter Bledsoe, a general partner, who acknowledged that he did sign the foregoing instrument, and that the same is the free act and deed of said BA Associates Limited and his free act and deed.

IN TESTIMONY WHEREOF, I have hereunto set my hand and official seal at Cleveland, Ohio, this   day of   , 1976.

_____
                                                Notary Public

This instrument was prepared by   G. Christopher Meyer
                                   and Sidney B. Hopps

EXHIBIT A

Situated in the Village of Bratenahl, County of Cuyahoga and State of Ohio, and known as being a part of Original One Hundred Acre Lots Nos. 355 and 356, and bounded and described as follows:

Beginning at the intersection of the center line of Lake Shore Boulevard, 80 feet in width, with the center line of Eddy Road, 60 feet in width; Course No. 1: Thence North 35° 56' 20" West along the center line of Eddy Road, a distance of 803.20 feet to a point; Course No. 2: Thence South 54° 03' 40" West, 197 feet to its intersection with a line drawn parallel to the center line of Eddy Road and distant 197 feet Southwesterly by rectangular measurement therefrom; Course No. 3: Thence South 35° 56' 20" East along said parallel line, 196.08 feet; Course No. 4: Thence South 54° 03' 40" West, 241 feet; Course No. 5: Thence North 35° 56' 20" West 37.44 feet; Course No. 6: Thence South 54° 03' 40" West, 92 feet; Course No. 7: Thence North 35° 56' 20" West, 88.56 feet; Course No. 8: Thence South 54° 03' 40" West, 100 feet; Course No. 9: Thence North 52° 38' 05" West, 348.08 feet to a point distant South 54° 03' 40" West 730 feet from a point in the center line of Eddy Road which bears North 35° 56' 20" West 1066.53 feet from its intersection with the center line of aforementioned Lake Shore Boulevard; Course No. 10: Thence North 26° 14' 00" West, 38.55 feet; Course No. 11: Thence North 27° 03' 00" West to its intersection with the Southerly low-watermark of Lake Erie; Course No. 12: Thence in a Southwesterly direction along the Southerly low-water mark of Lake Erie to its intersection with a Westerly line of land conveyed to Bratenahl Development Corporation by deed dated October 1, 1963 and recorded in Volume 10963, Page 103 of Cuyahoga County Records; Course No. 13: Thence South 37° 28' 04" East to the most Northerly corner of land in Parcel No. 1 conveyed to William H. Dornback, Sr. by deed dated February 15, 1960 and recorded in Volume 9909, Page 703 of Cuyahoga County Records; Course No. 14: Thence Southeasterly along the Northeasterly lines of land so conveyed to William H. Dornback, Sr., being also along the center line of Dugway Brook, the following courses and distances: South 24° 35' 04" East, 117.68 feet South 43° 33' 54" East, 94.07 feet; South 52° 27' 04" East 107 feet to the Northeasterly corner of Parcel No. 1 of land so conveyed to William H. Dornback, Sr., being also the Westerly line of Original One Hundred Acre Lot No. 356, as aforementioned; Course No. 15: Thence South 0° 11' 55" West along the Westerly line of said Original One Hundred Acre Lot No. 356, a distance of 456.22 feet to its intersection with the Northwesterly line of land conveyed to Alfred A. Budnick and Josephine B. Budnick by deed dated August 23, 1966 and recorded in Volume 11874, Page 591 of Cuyahoga County Records; Course No. 16: Thence North 54° 17' 10" East along the Northwesterly line of land so conveyed to Alfred A. Budnick and Josephine B. Budnick, and along the Southeasterly line of land conveyed to Bratenahl Development Corporation by deed dated August 11, 1966 and recorded in Volume 11874, Page 589 of Cuyahoga County Records, 625.46 feet to a Southwesterly line therein; Course No. 17: Thence South 35° 56' 20" East long said Southwesterly line of land so conveyed to Bratenahl Development Corporation, 601.94 feet to the center line of Lake Shore Boulevard, as aforementioned; Course No. 18: Thence North 44° 31' 40" East along the center line of Lake Shore Boulevard, 390.90 feet to the place of beginning, according to the survey by George M. Garrett and Associates, Registered Engineers and Surveyors, be the same more or less, but subject to all legal highways and waterways. Excepting from the above described premises any part thereof resulting through change in the shore line of Lake Erie and through change in the course of Dugway Brook occasioned by other than natural causes or by natural causes other than accretion.

EXHIBIT B

Situated in the Village of Bratenahl, County of Cuyahoga and State of Ohio, and known as being a part or Original 100 Acre Lots Nos. 355 and 356, and bounded and described as follows:

Beginning in the center line of Eddy Road, 60 feet in width, at a point distant North 35° 56' 20" West, as measured along said center line, a distance of 803.20 feet from its intersection with the center line of Lake Shore Boulevard, 80 feet in width; thence South 54° 03' 40" West, a distance of 197.00 feet to its intersection with a line drawn parallel to and distant 197.00 feet southwesterly by rectangular measurement therefrom and the principal place of beginning of the premises herein to be described;

Course No. 1: thence South 35° 56' 20" East, 196.08 feet;

Course No. 2: thence South 54° 03' 40" West, 241.00 feet;

Course No. 3: thence North 35° 56' 20" West, 37.44 feet;

Course No. 4: thence South 54° 03' 40" West, 92.00 feet;

Course No. 5: thence North 35° 56' 20" West, 88.56 feet;

Course No. 6: thence South 54° 03' 40" West, 100.00 feet;

Course No. 7: thence North 52° 38' 05" West, 348.08 feet to a point distant South 54° 03' 40" West 730.00 feet from a point in the center line of Eddy Road which bears North 35° 56' 20" West 1066.53 feet from its intersection with the center line of aforementioned Lake Shore Boulevard;

Course No. 8: thence North 26° 14' 00" West, 38.55 feet;

Course No. 9: thence North 27° 03' 00" West to its intersection with the southerly low-water mark of Lake Erie;

Course No. 10: thence in a northeasterly direction along the southerly low-water mark of Lake Erie to its intersection with a line drawn parallel to the center line of Eddy Road and distant 239.54 feet southwesterly by rectangular measurement therefrom;

Course No. 11: thence South 35° 56' 20" East along said parallel line to its intersection with a line drawn perpendicular southwesterly from a point in said center line of Eddy Road distant North 35° 56' 20" West, measured along said center line of Eddy Road, 1117.92 feet from its intersection with the center line of aforementioned Lake Shore Boulevard;

Course No. 12: thence North 54° 03' 40" East along said perpendicular line, 4.52 feet to its intersection with a line drawn parallel to the center line of Eddy Road and distant 235.02 feet southwesterly by rectangular measurement therefrom;

Course No. 13: thence South 35° 56' 20" East along said parallel line, 21.50 feet;

Course No. 14: thence South 54° 03' 40" West, 4.52 feet to its intersection with a line drawn parallel to the center line of Eddy Road and distant 239.54 feet southwesterly by rectangular measurement therefrom;

Course No. 15: thence South 35° 56' 20" East along said parallel line, 293.22 feet to its intersection with a line drawn perpendicular southwesterly from a point in said center line of Eddy Road distant North 35° 56' 20" West, measured along said center line of Eddy Road, 803.20 feet from its intersection with the center line of aforementioned Lake Shore Boulevard;

Course No. 16: thence North 54° 03' 40" East along said perpendicular line, 42.54 feet to the principal place of beginning, according to the survey of George M. Garrett and Associates, Registered Engineers and Surveyors, be the same more or less, but subject to all legal highways and waterways.

EXHIBIT C

Situated in the Village of Bratenahl, County of Cuyahoga and State of Ohio, and known as being a part of Original 100 Acre Lot No. 356, and bounded and described as follows:

Beginning in the center line of Eddy Road, 60 feet in width, at a point distant North 35° 56' 20" West, as measured along said center line, a distance of 803.20 feet from its intersection with the center line of Lake Shore Boulevard, 80 feet in width;

Course No. 1: thence North 35° 56' 20" West along the center line of Eddy Road to its intersection with the southerly low-water mark of Lake Erie;

Course No. 2: thence in a southwesterly direction along the southerly low-water mark of Lake Erie to its intersection with a line drawn parallel to the center line of Eddy Road and distant 239.54 feet southwesterly by rectangular measurement therefrom;

Course No. 3: thence South 35° 56' 20" East along said parallel line to its intersection with a line drawn perpendicular southwesterly from a point in said center line of Eddy Road distant North 35° 56' 20" West, as measured along said center line of Eddy Road, 1117.92 feet from its intersection with the center line of Lake Shore Boulevard, as aforementioned;

Course No. 4: thence North 54° 03' 40" East along said perpendicular line, a distance of 4.52 feet to its intersection with a line drawn parallel to the center line of Eddy Road and distant 235.02 feet southwesterly by rectangular measurement therefrom;

Course No. 5: thence South 35° 56' 20" East along said parallel line, 21.50 feet;

Course No. 6: thence South 54° 03' 40" West, a distance of 4.52 feet to its intersection with a line drawn parallel to the center line of Eddy Road and distant 239.54 feet southwesterly by rectangular measurement therefrom;

Course No. 7: thence South 35° 56' 20" East along said parallel line, 293.22 feet to its intersection with a line drawn perpendicular southwesterly from a point in said center line of Eddy Road distant North 35° 56' 20" West, as measured along said center line of Eddy Road, 803.20 feet from its intersection with the center line of aforementioned Lake Shore Boulevard;

Course No. 8: thence North 54° 03' 40" East along said perpendicular line, 239.54 feet to the place of beginning, according to the survey of George M. Garrett and Associates, Registered Engineers and Surveyors, be the same more or less, but subject to all legal highways and waterways.

EXHIBIT E

Designation Unit	Percentage of Interest
101	House
201	.004988%
301	.005031
401	.005073
501	.005116
601	.005159
701	.005201
801	.005244
901	.005287
1001	.005329
1101	.005372
1202	.005414
1301	.005457
1401	.005542
1501	.005628
102	.004818%
202	.004818
302	.004860
402	.004903
502	.004945
602	.004988
702	.005031
802	.005073
902	.005116
1002	.005159
1102	.005201
1202	.005244
1302	.005287
1402	.005372
1502	.005457
103	.006565%
203	.006565
303	.006608
403	.006651
503	.006693
603	.006736
703	.006779
803	.006821
903	.006864
1003	.006907
1103	.007034
1203	.007077
1303	.007205
1403	.007290
1503	.007375

Designation Unit	Percentage of Interest
104	.004732%
204	.004732
304	.004775
404	.004818
504	.004860
604	.004903
704	.004945
804	.004988
904	.005031
1004	.005073
1104	.005116
1204	.005159
1304	.005201
1404	.005287
1504	.005372
105	.004221%
205	.005329
305	.004263
405	.005414
505	.004349
605	.005500
705	.004434
805	.005585
905	.004519
1005	.005670
1105	.004604
1205	.005755
1305	.004690
1405	.005883
1505	.004860
106	.006310%
206	.005244
306	.006352
406	.005329
506	.006438
606	.005414
706	.006523
806	.005500
906	.006608
1006	.005585
1106	.006693
1206	.005670
1306	.006779
1406	.005798
1506	.006949

Designation Unit	Percentage of Interest
107	.006395%
207	.005287
307	.006438
407	.005372
507	.006523
607	.005457
707	.006608
807	.005542
907	.006693
1007	.005628
1107	.006779
1207	.005713
1307	.006864
1407	.005841
1507	.007034
108	.004135%
208	.005201
308	.004178
408	.005287
508	.004263
608	.005372
708	.004349
808	.005457
908	.004434
1008	.005542
1108	.004519
1208	.005628
1308	.004604
1408	.005755
1508	.004775
109	.005585 %
209	.005585
309	.005628
409	.005670
509	.005713
609	.005755
709	.005798
809	.005841
909	.005883 (see note below)
1009	.005926
1109	.005969
1209	.006011
1309	.006054
1409	.006139
1509	.006224

Designation Unit	Percentage of Interest
110	.006608%
210	.006608
310	.006651
410	.006693
510	.006736
610	.006779
710	.006821
810	.006864
910	.006907
1010	.006949
1110	.006991
1210	.007034
1310	.007077
1410	.007162
1510	.007248
111	House
211	.004945%
311	.004988
411	.005031
511	.005073
611	.005116
711	.005159
811	.005201
911	.005244(see note below)
1011	.005287
1111	.005329
1211	.005372
1311	.005414
1411	.005500
1511	.005585
112	.004775%
212	.004775
312	.004818
412	.004860
512	.004903
612	.004945
712	.004988
812	.005031
912	.005073
1012	.005116
1112	.005159
1212	.005201
1312	.005244
1412	.005329
1512	.005414

NOTE: Unit 909 presently physically consists of six rooms and two baths, and Unit 911 of four rooms and two baths. If the incumbent tenant of Unit 909 purchases Unit 909, then the percentage of interest specified for Unit 909 above shall be changed to .007060 and the percentage of interest specified for Unit 911 shall be changed to .004067.

DOCUMENT NO. II

BYLAWS

OF

ONE BRATENAHL PLACE CONDOMINIUM

BYLAWS

OF

ONE BRATENAHL PLACE CONDOMINIUM ASSOCIATION

ARTICLE I

Meetings of Association Members

Section 1. **Annual Meetings.** The annual meeting of members of the Association shall be held at such time and on such date in the month of February of each year as may be fixed by the Board of Managers and stated in the notice of the meeting, for the election of managers, the consideration of reports to be laid before such meeting and the transaction of such other business as may properly come before the meeting.

Section 2. **Special Meetings.** Special meetings of the members of the Association shall be called upon the written request of the President or, in case of the President's absence, death or disability, the Vice President authorized to exercise the authority of the President, the Board of Managers by action at a meeting, or a majority of the managers acting without a meeting, or of members entitled to exercise at least twenty-five percent (25%) of the voting power of the Association. Calls for such meetings shall specify the purposes for which such meeting is requested. No business other than that specified in the call shall be considered at any special meeting.

Section 3. **Notices of Meetings.** Unless waived, written notice of each annual or special meeting stating the time, place and the purposes thereof shall be given by personal delivery or by mail to each member not more than forty-five (45) days nor less than seven (7) days before any such meeting. If mailed, such notice shall be directed to the member at his address as the same appears upon the records of the Association. Any member, either before or after any meeting, may waive any notice required to be given by law or under the Declaration or these Bylaws.

Section 4. **Time and Place of Meetings.** Meetings of members shall be held at such time and at such place on the Condominium Property as the Board of Managers shall designate.

Section 5. **Voting Rights.** Each member shall be entitled to exercise that percentage of the total voting power of all members which is equivalent to the percentage of interest of such member's Unit in the Common Areas and Facilities of the Condominium Property. If two or more persons, whether fiduciaries, tenants in common or otherwise, own undivided interests in a Unit, such persons shall designate, by a certificate signed by all such persons and delivered to the Association, the individual entitled to exercise the voting power of such Unit on behalf of all owners. Such certificate shall be conclusive until modified by a subsequent such certificate.

Section 6. **Quorum.** The members entitled to exercise a majority of the voting power of the Association at any meeting, present in person or by proxy, shall constitute a quorum for the transaction of business to be considered at such meeting. The vote of members entitled to exercise more than fifty percent (50%) of the voting power of the members present at such meeting, in person or by proxy, shall be determinative on all matters, provided, however, that no action required by law or by the Declaration or these Bylaws to be authorized or taken by members entitled to exercise a designated proportion of the voting power may be authorized or taken by a lesser proportion. Members entitled to exercise a majority of the voting power represented at a meeting, whether or not a quorum is present, may adjourn such meeting from time to time, until a quorum shall be present.

Section 7. **Proxies.** Any member may be represented at a meeting of members or vote thereat, and exercise consents, waivers and releases, and exercise any of his other rights, by proxy or proxies appointed by a writing signed by such person.

ARTICLE II

Board of Managers

Section 1. **Qualification.** Except as otherwise provided herein, all managers shall be Unit Owners; spouses of Unit Owners; mortgagees of Units; partners or employees of partnerships owning a Unit; officers, directors or employees of corporations or associations owning a Unit; or fiduciaries, officers or employees of fiduciaries owning a Unit.

Section 2. **Number of Managers.** Until changed in accordance with the provisions of this Article II, the number of managers of the Association shall be nine (9). The number of managers may be fixed or changed at any annual meeting or at any special meeting called for that purpose by the affirmative vote of the members entitled to exercise a majority of the voting power of all members present at the meeting in person or by proxy.

Section 3. **Election of Managers.** Managers shall be elected at the annual meeting of members, but when the annual meeting is not held or managers are not elected thereat, they may be elected at a special meeting called and held for that purpose. Such election shall be by ballot whenever requested by any member; but, unless such request is made, the election may be conducted in any manner approved at such meeting.

Managers shall be elected for such terms that the terms of one-third of the Board shall expire each year. Accordingly, at the first annual or special meeting of the Association at which managers are elected, three (3) managers shall be elected for a term of three (3) years, three (3) managers for a term of two (2) years and three (3) managers for a term of one (1) year. The candidates receiving the votes of the greatest percentages of the voting power of the Association shall be elected for the longest terms. Tie votes shall be decided by drawing of lots. Such managers shall be elected in accordance with Section 4 of this Article II. At subsequent meetings of the Association at which managers are elected, and also in accordance with Section 4 of this Article II, three (3) managers shall be elected, each for a term of three (3) years.

At each meeting of members for the election of managers, each member shall be entitled to cast one vote for each manager to be elected. The persons receiving the votes of members entitled to exercise the greatest percentage of voting power shall be managers.

Section 4. **Election of Directors by BA.** Until such time as Units entitled in the aggregate to exercise fifty percent (50%) of the total voting power of the Association have been sold by BA, BA shall elect five (5) of the nine (9) managers of the Association. When Units representing more than fifty percent (50%) but equal to or less than sixty percent (60%) of the total voting power have been sold, BA shall elect four (4) of the nine (9) managers. When Units representing more than sixty percent (60%) but equal to or less than seventy percent (70%) of the total voting power have been sold, BA shall elect three (3) of the nine (9) managers. When Units representing more than seventy percent (70%) but less than one hundred percent (100%) of the voting power have been sold, BA shall elect two (2) of the nine (9) managers. If the number of managers is amended, BA shall elect that number of managers which would equal or exceed the percentage of managers provided above. Notwithstanding any other provision in these Bylaws, managers elected by BA need not fulfill the qualifications imposed by Section 1 of this Article II or any other qualification imposed on managers elected by Unit Owners other than BA and Managers elected by

BA may be removed only by BA. At the first election of Managers, BA shall elect one (1) manager for a term of three (3) years, two (2) managers for a term of two (2) years and two (2) managers for a term of one (1) year. In the event that following an annual election of directors, Units are sold by BA such that the percentage of managers which BA would be entitled to elect is less than the number of managers elected by BA then holding office, BA shall, upon written request from the majority of the managers elected by Unit Owners other than BA, cause the resignation of one or more of the managers elected by it such that the total number of managers elected by BA and then remaining in office shall equal the number of managers which BA would have been entitled to elect if an election had been held on the date of such notice. Vacancies created by such resignations shall be filled in accordance with this Article II.

Section 5. **Removal.** Except as otherwise provided herein, the Board of Managers may remove any manager and thereby create a vacancy in the Board if by order of court he has been found to be of unsound mind, or if he is adjudicated a bankrupt or if at any time he ceases to hold the required qualifications specified in Section 1 of this Article II. Except as otherwise provided herein, all the managers or any individual manager may be removed from office, without assigning any cause, by the vote of members entitled to exercise a majority of the voting power of the Association. In case of any such removal, a new manager may be elected at the same meeting for the unexpired term of each manager removed. Failure to elect a manager to fill the unexpired term of any manager removed shall be deemed to create a vacancy in the Board.

Section 6. **Vacancies.** Vacancies in the Board of Managers may be filled by a majority vote of the remaining managers until an election to fill such vacancies is held. Members shall have the right to fill any vacancy in the Board (whether or not the same has been temporarily filled by the remaining managers) at any meeting of the members called for that purpose, and any managers elected at any such meeting of members shall serve until the next annual election of managers and until their respective successors are elected and qualified.

Section 7. **Quorum.** A majority of the Board of Managers shall constitute a quorum for the transaction of business, except that a majority of the managers in office shall constitute a quorum for filling a vacancy on the Board. Whenever less than a quorum is present at the time and place appointed for any meeting of the Board, a majority of those present may adjourn the meeting from time to time, until a quorum shall be present.

Section 8. **Organizational Meetings.** Organizational meetings of the Board of Managers shall be held immediately following annual meetings of the members of the Association, or, if no annual meeting of the members is held, or if managers are not elected thereat, then immediately following any special meeting of the members at which managers are elected. Such annual meeting of managers shall be held at the same place at which such members' meeting was held.

Section 9. **Regular Meetings.** Regular meetings of the Board of Managers shall be held at such times and places within Cuyahoga County, Ohio, as the Board of Managers may, from time to time, determine by resolution or regulation. The Secretary shall give notice of each such resolution or regulation to any manager who was not present at the time the same was adopted, but no further notice of such regular meeting need be given. At such meeting, any and all business within the power of the managers may be transacted.

Section 10. **Special Meetings.** Special meetings of the Board of Managers may be called by the President or the Secretary or any two members of the Board of Managers, to be held at such times and places within Cuyahoga County, Ohio, as may be specified in the notice given pursuant to Section 11 of this Article II.

– 3 –

Section 11. **Notice of Special Meetings.** Notice of the time, place and purposes of each special meeting shall be given to each manager by the Secretary or by the person or persons calling such meeting. Such notice shall state the purpose or purposes of the meeting and may be given in any manner or method and at such time so that the manager receiving it may have reasonable opportunity to attend the meeting. Such notice shall, in all events, be deemed to have been properly and duly given if mailed at least forty-eight (48) hours prior to the meeting and directed to the residence of the managers as shown upon the Secretary's records. The giving of notice shall be deemed to have been waived by any manager who shall attend and participate in such meeting and may be waived, in writing or by telegram, by any manager either before or after such meeting.

Section 12. **Compensation.** The managers, as such, shall not receive any salary for their services, but by resolution of the board, expenses of attendance, if any, may be allowed for attendance at each regular or special meeting of the Board of Managers; provided that nothing herein contained shall be construed to preclude any manager from serving the Association in any other capacity and receiving compensation therefor.

Section 13. **Regulations.** For the government of its action, the Board of Managers may adopt such Regulations as they deem appropriate, provided that such Regulations are consistent with the Declaration and these Bylaws.

Section 14. **Powers and Duties.** Except as otherwise provided by law, the Declaration or these Bylaws, all power and authority of the Association shall be exercised by the Board of Managers. The Board of Managers shall be responsible for the maintenance, repair and replacement of the Common Areas and Facilities. In carrying out the purposes of the Condominium Property and subject to the limitations prescribed by law, the Declaration or these Bylaws, the Board of Managers, for and on behalf of the Association, may

   (a) purchase or otherwise acquire, lease as lessee, hold, use, lease as lessor, sell, exchange, transfer, and dispose of property of any description or any interest therein;

   (b) make contracts;

   (c) effect insurance;

   (d) borrow money, and issue, sell, and pledge notes, bonds, and other evidences of indebtedness of the Association;

   (e) levy assessments against Unit Owners;

   (f) employ a managing agent to perform such duties and services as the Board may authorize; and

   (g) do all things permitted by law and exercise all power and authority within the purposes stated in the Declaration or incidental thereto.

Section 15. **Committees.** The Board of Managers may by resolution provide for such standing or special committees as it deems desirable, and discontinue the same at its discretion. Each such committee shall have such powers and perform such duties, not inconsistent with law, as may be delegated to it by the Board of Managers. Each such committee shall keep full records and accounts of its proceedings and transactions. All action by any such committee shall be reported to the Board of Managers at its meeting next succeeding such action and shall be subject to control, revision, and alteration by the Board of Managers; provided that no rights of third persons shall be prejudicially affected thereby. Each such committee shall fix its own rules of procedure and shall meet as provided by such rules or by resolutions of the Board of Managers, and it shall also meet at the call of the President of the Association or of any two members of the committee. Unless otherwise provided by such rules or by such resolutions, the provisions of Section 11 of Article II relating to the notice required to be given of meetings of the Board of Managers shall also apply to meetings of each such committee. A majority of the members of a committee shall constitute a quorum. Each such committee may act in writing or by telegram or by telephone with written confirmation, without a meeting, but no such action shall be effective unless concurred in by all members of the committee. Vacancies in such committee shall be filled by the Board of Managers or as it may provide.

ARTICLE III

Officers

Section 1. **General Provisions.** The Board of Managers shall elect a President, such number of Vice Presidents as the Board may from time to time determine, a Secretary and a Treasurer. The Board of Managers may from time to time create such offices and appoint such other officers, subordinate officers and assistant officers as it may determine. The President and any Vice President who succeeds to the office of the President shall be, but the other officers need not be, chosen from among the members of the Board of Managers. Any two of such offices, other than that of President and Vice President, may be held by the same person, but no officer shall execute, acknowledge or verify any instrument in more than one capacity.

Section 2. **Term of Office.** The officers of the Association shall hold office during the pleasure of the Board of Managers, and, unless sooner removed by the Board of Managers, until the organizational meeting of the Board of Managers following the next meeting of members of the Association at which managers are elected and until their successors are chosen and qualified. The Board of Managers may remove any officer at any time, with or without cause. A vacancy in any office, however created, shall be filled by the Board of Managers.

ARTICLE IV

Duties of Officers

Section 1. **President.** The President shall be the chief executive officer of the Association and shall exercise supervision over the affairs of the Association and over its several officers, subject, however, to the control of the Board of Managers. He shall preside at all meetings of members and shall also preside at meetings of the Board of Managers. He shall have authority to sign all contracts, notes and other instruments requiring his signature; and shall have all the powers and duties prescribed by Chapter 5311 of the Ohio Revised Code and such others as the Board of Managers may from time to time assign to him.

Section 2. **Vice Presidents.** The Vice Presidents shall perform such duties as are conferred upon them by these Bylaws or as may from time to time be assigned to them by the Board of Managers or the President. At the request of the President, or in his absence or disability, the Vice President designated by the President (or in the absence of such designation, the Vice President designated by the Board of Managers) shall perform all the duties of the President, and when so acting, shall have all the power of the President. The authority of Vice Presidents to sign in the name of the Association all contracts, notes and other instruments, shall be coordinate with like authority of the President.

Section 3. **Secretary**. The Secretary shall keep minutes of all the proceedings of the members and Board of Managers and shall have authority to sign all contracts, notes, and other instruments executed by the Association requiring his signature; give notice of meetings of members and managers; keep such books as may be required by the Board of Managers; and perform such other and further duties as may from time to time be assigned to him by the Board of Managers.

Section 4. **Treasurer**. The Treasurer shall have general supervision of all finances; he shall receive and have in charge all money, bills, notes, documents and similar property belonging to the Association, and shall do with the same as may from time to time be required by the Board of Managers. He shall cause to be kept adequate and correct accounts of the business transactions of the Association, including accounts of its assets, liabilities, receipts, expenditures, profits and losses, together with such other accounts as may be required, and upon the expiration of his term of office shall turn over to his successor or to the Board of Managers all property, books, documents and money of the Association in his hands; and he shall perform such other duties as from time to time may be assigned to him by the Board of Managers.

Section 5. **Assistant and Subordinate Officers**. The Board of Managers may appoint such assistant and subordinate officers as it may deem desirable. Each such officer shall hold office during the pleasure of the Board of Managers, and perform such duties as the Board of Managers may prescribe.

The Board of Managers may, from time to time, authorize any officer to appoint and remove subordinate officers, to prescribe their authority and duties, and to fix their compensation.

Section 6. **Duties of Officers May Be Delegated**. In the absence of any officer of the Association, or for any other reason the Board of Managers may deem sufficient, the Board of Managers may delegate the powers or duties, or any of them, of such officers, to any manager or the managing agent.

ARTICLE V

Indemnification of Managing Agents, Managers, Officers and Members of Committees

Section 1. **Indemnification**. (a) The Association shall indemnify any managing agent, manager or officer or any former managing agent, manager or officer of the Association or any person who is serving or has served at the request of the Association as a director, officer, or trustee of another corporation, joint venture, trust or other enterprise against expenses, including attorneys' fees, judgments, fines, and amounts paid in settlement actually and reasonably incurred by him in connection with any threatened, pending, or completed action, suit, or proceeding, whether civil, criminal, administrative or investigative, other than an action by or in the right of the Association, to which he was, is or is threatened to be made a party by reason of the fact that he is or was such managing agent, manager, officer, or trustee, provided it is determined in the manner set forth in paragraph (c) of this section that he did not act in bad faith and that such action did not constitute willful misconduct.

(b) In the case of any threatened, pending or completed action or suit by or in the right of the Association, the Association shall indemnify each person indicated in paragraph (a) of this section against expenses, including attorneys' fees, actually and reasonably incurred in connection with the defense or settlement thereof, provided it is determined in the manner set forth in paragraph (c) of this section and that he did not act in bad faith and that such action did not constitute willful misconduct.

(c)   The determinations referred to in paragraphs (a) and (b) of the section shall be made (i) by a majority vote of a quorum consisting of managers of the Association who were not and are not parties to or threatened with any such action, suit or proceeding, or (ii) if such quorum is not obtainable or if a majority vote of a quorum of disinterested managers so directs, in a written opinion by independent legal counsel other than an attorney, or a firm having associated with it an attorney, who has been retained by or who has performed services for the Association, or any person to be indemnified, within the past five years, or (iii) by the members of the Association, or (iv) by the court of common pleas or the court in which such action, suit or proceeding was brought.

(d)   Expenses, including attorneys' fees, incurred in defending any action, suit, or proceeding referred to in paragraphs (a) and (b) of this section, may be paid by the Association in advance of the final disposition of such action, suit, or proceeding as authorized by the managers in the specific case upon receipt of an undertaking by or on behalf of the managing agent, manager, officer, or trustee to repay such amount, unless it shall ultimately be determined that he is entitled to be indemnified by the Association as authorized in this section.

(e)   The indemnification provided by this section shall not be deemed exclusive (i) of any other rights to which those seeking indemnification may be entitled under the Declaration, these Bylaws, any agreement, any insurance purchased by the Association, vote of the members of the Association or disinterested managers, or otherwise, both as to action in his official capacity and as to action in another capacity while holding such office, or of (ii) the power of the Association to indemnify any person who is or was an employee or agent of the Association or of another corporation, joint venture, trust or other enterprise which he is serving or has served at the request of the Association, to the same extent and in the same situations and subject to the same determinations as are hereinabove set forth with respect to a managing agent, manager, officer, or trustee. The indemnification provided by this section shall continue as to a person who has ceased to be a manager, officer, or trustee and shall inure to the benefit of the heirs, executors, and administrators of such a person.

(f)   Any sum paid or advanced by the Association under this Article V shall constitute a common expense, as that term is defined in the Declaration.

ARTICLE VI

Fiscal Year

The fiscal year of the Association shall end on the thirty-first day of December in each year, or on such other day as may be fixed from time to time by the Board of Managers.

ARTICLE VII

Assessments and Finances

Section 1.   **Preparation of Estimated Budget.**   On or before the 1st day of December of each year, the Board shall estimate the amount necessary to pay the common expenses during the calendar year next succeeding and such amount as the Board may deem necessary as a reserve for contingencies and replacements, and shall on or before the December 15th next succeeding notify each Unit Owner in writing of the amount of such estimate, with reasonable itemization thereof. Said estimated cash requirement shall be assessed to the Unit Owners according to the percentage of interest in the Common Areas and Facilities of their respective Units. On or before the 1st day of

– 7 –

each month of the ensuing year, each Unit Owner shall pay to the Association or as it may direct one-twelfth (1/12th) of the assessment made pursuant to this section. If the estimated cash requirement proves inadequate for any reason, including the non-payment by any Unit Owner of his assessment, the Board may at any time prepare an adjusted estimate and levy an additional assessment, which shall be assessed to the Unit Owners according to each such percentage of interest in the Common Areas and Facilities. The Board shall give written notice of any such additional assessment to all Unit Owners stating the amount thereof, the reasons therefor and the time when the same shall become effective, which shall be not less than ten (10) days after the mailing of such notice or, if the same is not mailed, the delivery thereof. Any amount collected by the Association in excess of the amount required for actual expenses and reserves in any year shall be credited promptly after the same has been determined according to the percentage of interest in the Common Areas and Facilities of their respective Units, to the monthly installments next due from Unit Owners until exhausted, and any deficiency shall be added, according to each such percentage of interest, to the installments due in the succeeding six months after the same has been determined.

Section 2. **Reserve for Contingencies and Replacements.** The Association shall establish and maintain a reserve for contingencies and replacements in such amount as the Board may deem necessary. Extraordinary expenses not originally included in the annual estimate which may become necessary during the year shall be charged first against such reserve.

Section 3. **Budget for First Year.** When the first Board elected hereunder takes office, the Board shall determine the estimated cash requirement, as hereinabove defined, for the period commencing at the beginning of the second full month after such election and ending on December 31st of the calendar year in which said election occurs. Assessments shall be levied against the Unit Owners during said period as provided in Section 1 of this Article VII.

Section 4. **Failure to Prepare Annual Budget.** The failure or delay of the Board to prepare or notify any Unit Owner of any annual or adjusted estimate shall not constitute a waiver or release in any manner of any such Unit Owner's obligation to pay his proportionate share of the common expenses as herein provided, whenever the same shall be determined, and in the absence of any annual estimate or adjusted estimate, each Unit Owner shall continue to pay a monthly assessment at the then existing monthly rate established for the previous period until the amount of the monthly assessment is changed as herein provided.

Section 5. **Books and Records of Association.** The Association shall keep full and correct books of account, and the same shall be open for inspection by any Unit Owner or any representative of a Unit Owner duly authorized in writing, at any reasonable time or times during normal business hours. Upon ten (10) days written notice to the Board and payment of a reasonable fee, any Unit Owner shall be furnished a statement of his account setting forth the amount of any unpaid assessments or other charges due and owing from such owner.

Section 6. **Annual Statements.** At or before the annual meeting of members of the Association, or the meeting held in lieu thereof, the Board shall furnish to each Unit Owner a financial statement consisting of (a) a balance sheet containing a summary of the assets and liabilities of the Association as of a date not more than four (4) months before such meeting and (b) a statement of the income and disbursements for the period commencing with the date marking the end of the period for which the last preceding statement of income and disbursements required hereunder was made and ending with the date of said balance sheet, or in the case of the first such statement, from the formation of the Association to the date of said balance sheet. The financial statement shall have appended thereto an opinion signed by the President or a Vice President and the Treasurer or an Assistant Treasurer of the Association or by a public accountant or firm of public accountants to the effect that the financial statement presents fairly the financial position of the Association and the results of its operations in conformity with generally accepted accounting principles applied on a basis consistent with that of the preceding period, or such other opinion as is in accordance with sound accounting practice.

Section 7. **Status of Funds Collected by Association.** All funds collected hereunder shall be held and expended solely for the purposes designated herein, and (except for such special assessments as may be levied against less than all of the Unit Owners, and for such adjustments as may be required to reflect delinquent or prepaid assessments) shall be deemed to be held for the use, benefit and account of all of the Unit Owners according to the percentage of interest in the Common Areas and Facilities of their respective Units.

Section 8. **Security Deposits from Certain Unit Owners.** If in the judgment of the Board of Managers, the equity interest of any Unit Owner in his Unit at any time is not sufficient to assure payment (whether by foreclosure of any lien for common expense or otherwise) of all assessments, charges or other sums which may be levied by the Association, then, whether or not such Unit Owner shall be delinquent in the payment of any such levies, the Association may require such Unit Owner to establish and maintain a security deposit in an amount which the Board deems necessary for such purposes, provided, however, that such security deposit shall in no event exceed an amount which, when added to such Unit Owner's equity in interest in his Unit, will exceed twenty-five percent (25%) of the purchase price of such Unit. In the event that any Unit Owner shall fail to pay any assessments, charges or other sums due the Association or shall otherwise violate any covenant, term or condition of the Declaration or these Bylaws, the Association shall have the right, but not the obligation, to apply such security deposit in reduction of its alleged damages resulting from such failure or violation, which right shall be in addition to all and other remedies provided for by law or in the Declaration or these Bylaws. Upon any sale by such Unit Owner of his Unit, or at such time as such Unit Owner's equity in his Unit is, in the opinion of the Board of Managers, adequate so as to dispose with the necessity of such security deposit, any unapplied balance of said security deposit remaining to the credit of said Unit Owner shall be refunded, provided that such Unit Owner shall not be in default under any of his obligations under the Declaration or these Bylaws. The Association shall have the right to maintain all security deposits held by it as aforesaid in a single bank account and shall not be required to credit interest to any Unit Owner until such time as such security deposit is refunded. Said security deposit shall at all times be subject to any lien of the Association for common expenses and all rights thereto shall inure to the benefit of the lienor.

Section 9. **Common Expenses.** The Association, for the benefit of the Unit Owners, shall pay all common expenses arising with respect to, or in connection with, the Condominium Property, including, without limitation, the following:

    (a)   The cost of water, waste removal, electricity and telephone, heat, power, and other necessary utility service for the Common Areas and Facilities;

    (b)   Premiums for insurance effected in accordance with the provisions of the Declaration;

    (c)   Premiums for workmen's and unemployment compensation coverage to the extent necessary to comply with any applicable laws;

    (d)   Fees for the services of any person, firm or corporation employed by the Association, including, without limitation, the services of a managing agent for the Condominium Property, the services of any person or persons required for the maintenance or operation of the

– 9 –

Condominium Property, and legal and/or accounting services necessary or proper in connection with the operation of the Condominium Property, the enforcement or interpretation of the Declaration or these Bylaws and for the organization and operation of the Association;

(e) The cost of landscaping, gardening, snow removal, painting, cleaning, tuckpointing, maintenance, security services, decorating, repair and replacement of the Common Areas and Facilities and furnishings and equipment for the Common Areas and Facilities;

(f) The cost of any other materials, supplies, furniture, equipment, labor, services, maintenance, repairs, structural alterations or insurance which the Association is required to secure or pay for pursuant to the terms of the Declaration or these Bylaws or by law or which may be necessary or proper for the maintenance and operation of the Condominium Property as a high-quality residential property;

(g) The cost of any alteration, maintenance or repair of any Unit which the Board of Managers deems necessary for public safety or in order to prevent damage to or destruction of any other part of the Condominium Property, provided that a special assessment shall be levied against such Unit to the extent of such cost; and

(h) The cost of water, waste removal and/or any utilities which are not separately metered or otherwise directly charged to individual Unit Owners, provided that the Association may discontinue payment therefor at any time, in which case each Unit Owner shall be responsible for direct payment of his share of such expenses as determined by the Association and provided further that the Association may levy additional special assessments against any Unit Owner to reimburse it for excessive use by such owner of any utility service the expense of which is a common expense.

Section 10. **Additions, Alterations or Improvements by Board of Managers.** Whenever in the judgment of the Board of Managers the Common Areas and Facilities shall require additions, alterations or improvements (as opposed to maintenance, repair and replacement) costing in excess of Fifteen Thousand Dollars ($15,000.00) and the making of such additions, alterations or improvements shall have been approved by Unit Owners entitled to exercise not less than a majority of the voting power of all members present in person or by proxy at an annual or special meeting of the members duly held for such purpose and all mortgagees holding mortgages constituting first liens on twenty-five (25) or more Units, the Board shall proceed with such additions, alterations or improvements and shall assess all Unit Owners for the cost thereof as a common expense. Any additions, alterations or improvements costing Fifteen Thousand Dollars ($15,000.00) or less may be made by the Board of Managers without approval of the Unit Owners, and the cost thereof shall constitute part of the common expenses.

Section 11. **Acquisition, Lease, Sale or Exchange of Real Property.** Whenever the Board of Managers determines to acquire, lease, sell, or exchange real property or any interest therein, other than any Ownership Interest or interest therein, the Board of Managers shall submit such acquisition, lease or exchange to the vote of the Unit Owners, and, upon the affirmative vote of the Unit Owners entitled to exercise not less than a majority of the voting power of all members present in person or by proxy at an annual or special meeting of the members duly held for such purpose, the Board of Managers may proceed with such acquisition, lease, sale or exchange, in the name of the Association and on behalf of all Unit Owners, and the costs and expenses incident thereto shall constitute part of the common expenses.

Section 12. **Special Services.** The Association may arrange for special services and facilities for the benefit of such Unit Owners and Occupants as may desire to pay for same, including, without limitation, the cleaning, repair and maintenance of Units and special recreational, educational or medical facilities. The cost of any such special services or facilities shall be determined by the Association and may be charged directly to participating Unit Owners or paid as a common expense, in which case a special assessment shall be levied against such participating Unit Owners to reimburse the Association therefor.

ARTICLE VIII

Rules

The Association, by the affirmative vote of the members entitled to exercise a majority of the voting power of all members present in person or by proxy at an annual or special meeting of the members duly held for such purpose, or the Board of Managers, by the vote of a majority of the authorized number of managers, may adopt and amend Rules supplementing the rules and regulations set forth in the Declaration or these Bylaws as it or they may deem advisable governing the operation and use of the Condominium Property or any portion thereof. Written notice setting forth any such Rules shall be given to all Unit Owners and Occupants prior to the effective date of such Rules, and the Condominium Property shall at all times be subject thereto.

ARTICLE IX

Right of Access

Each Unit shall be subject to the right of access for the purpose of maintenance, repair or service of any Common Areas and Facilities located within its boundaries or accessible by or through such Unit or of any portion of the Unit itself by persons so authorized by the Board of Managers. The Board of Managers may retain a pass key to any or all Units, and no locks or other devices shall be placed on the doors to any Unit to obstruct access through the use of such pass key. In the event any such access is deemed necessary by the Board of Managers or any maintenance, repair or service is to be performed at a time when the Unit Owner is absent from his Unit, the Board of Managers or the managing agent, or any representative or any other person designated by either of them, may have access to such Unit, whether the Unit Owner is present or not.

ARTICLE X

Amendments

Provisions of these Bylaws may be amended by the Unit Owners at an annual or special meeting duly held for such purpose by the affirmative vote of those entitled to exercise not less than a majority of the voting power of the members present in person or by proxy at such meeting. No such amendment shall conflict with the provisions of the Declaration or of Chapter 5311.

– 11 –

DOCUMENT NO. III

ESCROW AGREEMENT

ESCROW AGREEMENT

May 14, 1976

The Land Title Guarantee and Trust Company
1275 Ontario Street
Cleveland, Ohio 44113

Re: Master Escrow No. 36,000
Escrow Agreement with BA Associates Limited

Gentlemen:

The purpose of this letter is to set forth the terms of an escrow agreement (the "Escrow Agreement") between you and BA Associates Limited as the Sponsor-Seller of 178 apartment units at One Bratenahl Place, Bratenahl, Ohio, pursuant to the terms of a Plan to Convert to Condominium Ownership dated May 15, 1976 (the "Plan"). A copy of the Plan has been heretofore furnished to you and is incorporated herein by reference thereto.

The Plan provides for BA Associates Limited (the "Sponsor") to enter into sale agreements of apartment units (the "Units") at One Bratenahl Place, Bratenahl, Ohio, substantially in the form included in Part II of the Plan (the "Agreements"), and further provides (1) that when 25% of the Units (45 in number) have been sold, the Sponsor may declare the Plan effective, (2) that when 50% of the Units (89 in number) have been sold (if the Sponsor has not previously declared the Plan effective), it must do so, (3) that if 25% of the Units have not been sold in a period of 12 months following the date of the Plan (that is, by May 14, 1977), the Sponsor may terminate the Plan, and (4) if 25% of the Units have not been sold in a period of 18 months following the date of the Plan (that is, by November 14, 1977), the Plan shall terminate. If and when the Plan is declared effective, you are to file for record the following:

(1)   the Condominium Drawings;

(2)   the Declaration and the Bylaws attached thereto; and

(3)   deeds conveying the sold Units to the purchasers thereof,

and you are to disburse the purchase prices of the Units to the Sponsor in accordance with the terms of the Plan and Agreements. Any interest earned on funds deposited in escrow shall be paid to the respective purchasers under the Agreements provided the purchaser has not defaulted in the performance of the Agreement. Costs and expenses are to be divided between the Sponsor and the several purchasers as provided in the Plan and by the terms of the Agreements. If the Plan is not declared effective, and is terminated, you are to return to the Sponsor the items listed in clauses (1), (2) and (3) above, and to the respective purchasers, provided a purchaser has not defaulted under the terms of an Agreement, all funds deposited in escrow, together with any interest earned thereon. In the event the Plan is terminated, the Sponsor shall reimburse you for your reasonable costs and expenses incurred in administering the escrow.

The Plan also provides (see "Escrow of Deposits"), that if at the time specified for closing, a purchaser has failed to deposit in escrow with you the balance of the purchase price required by the terms of an Agreement, then if the default shall continue for 10 days after notice to you as Escrow Agent and to the purchaser of the default, any amount on deposit, together with any interest earned thereon, shall be withdrawn from the account at Union Commerce Bank and paid to the Sponsor.

As Agreements for the sale of Units are signed by the respective purchasers and the Sponsor, a signed copy thereof will be forwarded to you, together with, (a) a deed from the Sponsor to the purchaser for the Unit covered by the Agreement, (b) a check of the purchaser for earnest money in an amount equivalent to at least 10% of the purchase price specified in the Agreement, and (c) a conveyancing fee statement signed by the purchaser and specifying the purchase price of the Unit. All earnest money received by you is to be deposited in an interest bearing account at the Union Commerce Bank, Cleveland, Ohio. For ease of administration and to assure FDIC insurance coverage of the several deposits, it is agreed that with respect to each Agreement forwarded to you, a separate escrow number identified by the Master Escrow Number and a subnumber will be established, and that the funds will be deposited at Union Commerce Bank in a separate and specifically identified interest bearing account in your name as Escrow Agent. The funds and documents are to be held by you in escrow in accordance with the specific terms of the several Agreements, the Plan, this letter and your standard conditions of acceptance of escrow responsibility (the "Conditions"). To the extent that there may be any conflict or inconsistency in the terms of the foregoing, the terms of an Agreement shall be deemed to control over the terms of the Plan, this letter and the Conditions; the terms of the Plan shall be deemed to control over the terms of this letter and the Conditions, and the terms of this letter over the Conditions.

You agree that as Agreements, funds and other documents are received by you pursuant to the next preceding paragraph, you will send acknowledgments thereof to the Sponsor and the respective purchasers acknowledging the deposits and notifying of the specific escrow number and of the deposit of the funds at Union Commerce Bank.

Deposited herewith, and signed on behalf of the Sponsor, are the following:

1.   The Condominium Drawings;

2.   The Declaration with the Bylaws attached thereto.

These have been examined by you, and you have agreed and do hereby affirm that they are in a proper and appropriate form for recording in the office of the Recorder of Cuyahoga County, Ohio, at such time as the Sponsor may declare the Plan effective. You have also agreed and affirm hereby that subject to the cancellation of existing mortgage liens, and to matters which might intervene between April 30, 1976 (at 7:59 a.m.) and the recording of the Drawings, the Declaration (with Bylaws attached) and deeds for Units sold, you will be able to issue to purchasers of Units, in usual and customary form, title guarantees which will guarantee good record title to the Units purchased as of the date and times of the recording of the deeds, subject only to those matters identified and listed in Part I of the Plan under the heading "Sale of Apartment Units by Sponsor and Model Apartments."

To acknowledge your agreement to act as Escrow Agent under the terms of the Plan, the Agreements, and hereunder, please sign and return a copy of this letter.

Very truly yours,

BA ASSOCIATES LIMITED

By _____ s/ Carter Bledsoe _____
General Partner

Accepted, agreed to and approved, this 14th day of May, 1976.

THE LAND TITLE GUARANTEE
AND TRUST COMPANY

By _____ s/ Charles L. Bekeny _____
Vice President and Trust Officer

— 3 —

DOCUMENT NO. IV

FORM OF PURCHASE AGREEMENT

A G R E E M E N T

AGREEMENT dated _____, 1976 by and between _____
_____ of _____, _____, _____,
Telephone No. _____ (herein, whether one or more, called "Purchaser"), and BA
ASSOCIATES LIMITED (an Ohio Limited partnership) of One Bratenahl Place, Bratenahl,
Ohio 44108, Telephone No. 541-4040 (herein called "Seller"). Seller and Purchaser agree as
follows:

1. DEFINITIONS

For purposes of this Agreement, the terms set forth in capital letters on Exhibit "A"
hereto shall have the meanings specified therein.

2. SALE AND PURCHASE OF UNIT

At the price specified in paragraph 3 hereof, and upon the terms and conditions set forth
herein, Seller shall sell to Purchaser and Purchaser shall purchase from Seller, Unit No. _____ on the
_____ floor of the Building, together with the undivided interest in the Common Areas of
the Condominium Property appertaining to such Unit as provided in the Declaration (herein called
the "Unit").

3. PURCHASE PRICE

The purchase price of the Unit is $_____, payable by Purchaser as follows:

(a) As earnest money (herein called "Earnest Money"), the sum of $_____ by
check (subject to collection), made payable to the order of the Escrow Agent, the receipt of which
check is hereby acknowledged by Seller; and

(b) The balance of $_____ at the time and in the manner provided in
paragraph 5 hereof.

4. DEED

The Unit shall be conveyed by Seller to Purchaser by warranty deed substantially in the
form of the warranty deed set forth in Part II of the Plan (herein called the "Deed").

5. DEPOSIT IN ESCROW

Seller, as promptly as possible, but in any event within ten (10) days after the date
hereof, shall deposit with the Escrow Agent, a signed copy of this Agreement, the Purchaser's check
representing the Earnest Money, the conveyancing fee statement signed by Purchaser with this
Agreement, and the Deed. The Escrow Agent shall send an acknowledgment of its receipt of the
foregoing to Seller and Purchaser at the addresses of each specified above, and shall acknowledge
that the Earnest Money has been deposited in an interest bearing account at the Union Commerce
Bank pursuant to the terms hereof and of the Plan. Buyer hereby authorizes the Escrow Agent to
deposit the Escrow Money in an interest bearing account at Union Commerce Bank pursuant to the
terms hereof and of the Escrow Agreement.

When Seller is prepared to, or becomes obligated to, declare the Plan effective as provided
by the terms thereof, Seller shall send notice to that effect to (a) the Escrow Agent and (b) to

Purchaser at the address of Purchaser specified above. Purchaser, as promptly as possible, but in any event within ten (10) days after receipt of such notice, shall deposit the balance of the purchase price in escrow by certified or cashier's check made payable to the order of the Escrow Agent.

6. CLOSING

As provided in the Plan, if 25% of the Units are sold (45 in number), Seller may declare the Plan effective, and if 50% of the Units are sold (89 in number), Seller must declare the Plan effective. If pursuant to the foregoing, the Plan is declared effective, the Escrow Agent shall promptly file for record, (a) the Drawings, (b) the Declaration and Bylaws, and (c) the Deed conveying the Unit to Purchaser, and shall disburse (a) the purchase price to Seller, less the amount of any expenses payable by Seller hereunder, and (b) to Purchaser, the interest earned on the Earnest Money, and shall furnish to Seller and Purchaser its escrow or closing statement in duplicate, which statement shall conform with the provisions of any applicable laws and rules and regulations issued thereunder.

7. PURCHASER'S DEFAULT; REMEDIES OF SELLER

If, after notice from Seller to Purchaser under paragraph 5 hereof that Seller is prepared to, or has become obligated to declare the Plan effective, Purchaser shall fail to deposit the balance of the purchase price in escrow within the ten (10) day period referred to therein, the Escrow Agent shall immediately notify Seller of Purchaser's default in making such deposit. Thereafter, Seller may notify Purchaser and the Escrow Agent of such default by written notice to each, and if the default is not cured by Purchaser depositing the balance of the purchase price with the Escrow Agent within ten (10) days after the mailing of such written notice, the Escrow Agent shall promptly withdraw the Earnest Money from the account at Union Commerce Bank, and shall pay the amount thereof, with any interest earned thereon, to Seller. Seller, at Seller's option, may retain such amount, with the interest thereon, as liquidated damages, in which event this Agreement shall terminate, and neither Seller, Purchaser, nor the Escrow Agent shall have any further liability or obligation hereunder or under the terms of the Plan, or Seller may retain such amount for application to its damage, and proceed with an action against Purchaser for specific enforcement of this Agreement or recovery of its actual damages.

8. TERMINATION OF AGREEMENT

If, after 12 months from the date of the Plan, viz., by May 14, 1977, 25% of the Units in the Building have not been sold by Seller, Seller may terminate the Plan, and if after 18 months from the date of the Plan, viz., by November 14, 1977, 25% of such Units have not been sold, the Plan shall terminate. In the event of a termination of the Plan pursuant to the foregoing sentence, this Agreement shall terminate, the Escrow Agent shall (a) promptly withdraw the Earnest Money from the account at Union Commerce Bank, pay the amount thereof to Purchaser, with any interest earned thereon, (b) return to the Seller, the Declaration (with the Bylaws attached thereto), the Drawings and the Deed, and (c) neither Seller, Purchaser, nor the Escrow Agent shall have any further liability or obligation hereunder or under the terms of the Plan, except that Seller shall pay the Escrow Agent its reasonable costs and expenses of administering the escrow.

9. TITLE GUARANTEE

At the expense of Seller, as of the time of the filing of the Deed for record, the Escrow Agent shall issue to Purchaser, a title guarantee in the amount of the purchase price and in usual and customary form, guaranteeing Purchaser of good record title to the Unit free and clear of all liens and encumbrances other than taxes and assessments not delinquent and all other matters referred to and described in the Plan and in the Deed. If on the Closing Date, the Escrow Agent is unable to issue a title guarantee to the Purchaser as aforesaid, then the Escrow Agent shall promptly notify both Seller and Purchaser of that fact and of the nature of the lien or encumbrance which prevents the issuance of the title guarantee. Purchaser may then waive the lien or encumbrance not referred to or described in the Plan or in the Deed, but in any event Seller shall have ninety (90) days from the date of the notice from the Escrow Agent within which to cure or remove any lien or encumbrance not referred to or described in the Plan or in the Deed. If during such ninety (90) day period, Seller is able to cure or remove the lien or encumbrance not referred to in the Plan or in the Deed, or Purchaser waives the matter, the Escrow Agent shall promptly proceed with closing in accordance with the terms hereof. If at the end of the ninety (90) day period Purchaser has not waived the lien or encumbrance and Seller has not been able to cure or remove it, then this Agreement shall terminate, the Earnest Money, together with any interest earned thereon shall be withdrawn from the Union Commerce Bank and paid to Purchaser, and neither Seller, Purchaser nor the Escrow Agent shall have any further liability or obligation hereunder.

10. POSSESSION

If, as of the Closing Date, Purchaser is in possession of the Unit under a pre-existing lease or occupancy agreement, then Purchaser shall continue in possession and any prepaid rent shall be prorated by the Escrow Agent as of that date. If, as of the Closing Date, Purchaser is not in possession of the Unit, and the Unit is not then occupied by a tenant or occupant, possession will be delivered to Purchaser on such date. If as of the Closing Date, Purchaser is not in possession and the Unit is in the possession of a tenant or occupant, then Purchaser's right of possession shall be subject to the rights of the existing tenant or occupant as more particularly described on page 10 and 11 of Part I of the Plan.

11. DAMAGE OR DESTRUCTION

If, prior to the filing of the Drawings, the Declaration, the Bylaws and the Deed for record, the Building is destroyed, or is damaged to such an extent that in Seller's sole judgment, reconstruction or repair is not desirable, then by written notice from Seller to the Escrow Agent and the Purchaser given within sixty (60) days after the date of such destruction or damage, Seller may terminate this Agreement. In the event of such termination, the Escrow Agent shall promptly withdraw the Earnest Money from the account at Union Commerce Bank, shall pay the amount thereof to Purchaser, with any interest earned thereon, return the Drawings, the Declaration, the Bylaws and the Deed to Seller, and neither the Escrow Agent, Seller nor Purchaser shall have any further obligation or liability hereunder. If pursuant to the foregoing, Seller does not elect to terminate this Agreement, then the Agreement shall remain in full force and effect and shall be performed in accordance with the terms, without any reduction in the purchase price, provided, however, that Seller shall undertake expeditious reconstruction and repair of the Building, and that if the Unit itself has been damaged, if Purchaser so requests, then closing will be delayed until reconstruction and repair of the Unit has been completed.

12. BROKER'S COMMISSION

Purchaser represents to Seller, that Purchaser has not dealt with a real estate broker in connection with the transaction contemplated hereby, other than _____
_____. Any real estate commission which shall become due to the aforesaid broker upon the consummation of the transaction contemplated hereby, shall be paid by Seller upon such consummation; Purchaser shall indemnify and save Seller harmless from any loss, cost or expense as a result of any breach of the representation hereinbefore made.

— 3 —

13. PRORATION OF REAL ESTATE TAXES

If the Plan is declared effective, and the Drawings, Declaration, Bylaws and Deed are filed for record during the year 1976, then the Escrow Agent shall prorate real estate taxes for the year 1976 as of the date of the filing thereof on the basis of a calendar year and using the estimated annual real estate taxes for the Unit shown on Schedule A to the Plan. The Escrow Agent shall pay the credit for the prorated taxes to the Seller, and the Seller shall pay the real estate taxes on the Unit for the year 1976 as the same become due and payable. In the event that the real estate taxes applicable to the Unit for the year 1976 exceed the estimated real estate taxes shown on Schedule A to the Plan, Seller shall pay such taxes without any further contribution from Purchaser, but if the real estate taxes applicable to the Unit for the year 1976 are less than the estimated real estate taxes shown on Schedule A, Seller shall adjust the proration of the taxes on the basis of the actual taxes applicable to the Unit for the year 1976, and pay to Purchaser any amount due to Purchaser as a result of such adjustment. If the Plan is declared effective, and the Drawings, Declaration, Bylaws and Deed are filed for record during the year 1977, then the Escrow Agent shall prorate real estate taxes for the year 1977 as of the date of the filing thereof on the basis of a calendar year and using the amount of real estate taxes shown by the last available County Treasurer's tax duplicate. The Escrow Agent shall pay the credit for the prorated taxes to the Purchaser, and the Purchaser shall pay the real estate taxes for the year 1977 and subsequent years as the same become due and payable.

14. DIVISION OF EXPENSES

Seller shall pay (a) the cost of recording the Drawings, the Declaration and the Bylaws, (b) the State of Ohio conveyancing fee applicable to the filing of the Deed for record, (c) the cost of the title guarantee to be issued to the Purchaser, and (d) one-half of the Escrow Agent's escrow fee. Purchaser shall pay (a) the cost of recording the Deed, (b) the cost of recording any mortgage placed upon the Unit by Purchaser, and (c) one-half of the Escrow Agent's escrow fee.

15. CONDITIONS OF PURCHASE; REPRESENTATIONS AND WARRANTIES

Purchaser has examined the Unit and is purchasing the Unit in its present physical condition. Purchaser is not relying upon any warranties or representations as to the size, dimensions or other physical characteristics of the Unit, or as to financial data or available income tax deductions. Purchaser is purchasing the Unit subject to all of the terms, provisions and conditions of the Declaration, the Bylaws and the Plan and agrees to comply with and abide by all of the terms, provisions and conditions thereof.

16. ASSIGNMENT PROHIBITED

Purchaser shall not assign or permit any assignment of this Agreement, or of any interest in or right under this Agreement, voluntarily or by operation of law, without the prior written consent of Seller. If any such assignment is attempted, Seller may declare this Agreement terminated and retain the Earnest Money, together with any interest earned thereon, as liquidated damages.

17. ENTIRE AGREEMENT

This Agreement constitutes the entire agreement of the parties hereto as to the subject matter hereof, and there are no agreements, representations, warranties or promises except as set forth herein. Any amendments, modifications, supplements or changes hereto must be in writing and unless made in a writing signed by both Seller and Purchaer shall not be binding on either party.

IN WITNESS WHEREOF, Seller and Purchaser have signed this Agreement, in triplicate, as of the day and year first above written.

PURCHASER   BA ASSOCIATES LIMITED

_____   By _____

_____

– 5 –

EXHIBIT A

PLAN: Parts I and II of the Offering Plan entitled "A Plan to Convert to Condominium Ownership premises at One Bratenahl Place, Bratenahl, Ohio" dated May 1, 1976, copies of which have been furnished to Purchaser and the receipt of which Purchaser acknowledges.

BUILDING: The building known as One Bratenahl Place, Bratenahl, Ohio, and more particularly identified and described in the Plan, and in the Declaration and Drawings constituting a part of the Plan.

CONDOMINIUM PROPERTY: The Building, the parcel of land upon which the Building is situated and which is more particularly described on Exhibit "A-1" attached hereto and made a part hereof, the underground parking garage and all other improvements located on the parcel of land, all easements, rights and privileges appurtenant thereto, and articles of personal property existing for the common use of Unit owners as more particularly identified and described in the Plan.

CONDOMINIUM STATUTE: Chapter 5311 of the Ohio Revised Code relating to condominium property.

DECLARATION: The Declaration of Condominium Ownership for the One Bratenahl Place Condominium made by Seller pursuant to the Condominium Statute. A copy of the Declaration is contained in Part II of the Plan and has been furnished to the Purchaser as a part thereof. A signed copy of the Declaration is on deposit with the Escrow Agent pursuant to the terms of the Plan, and will be filed for record in the office of the Recorder of Cuyahoga County if and when the Seller declares the Plan effective pursuant to the terms thereof.

DRAWINGS: The Drawings relating to the Condominium Property which were prepared pursuant to the Condominium Statute and a copy of which are on file in the office of the Seller at the Building. A signed copy of the Drawings are on deposit with the Escrow Agent pursuant to the terms of the Plan and will be filed for record in the office of the Recorder of Cuyahoga County if and when the Seller declares the Plan effective pursuant to the terms thereof.

UNITS: The apartment units in the Building which are identified and described in the Plan, and in the Declaration and Drawings constituting a part thereof.

COMMON AREAS: All portions of the Condominium Property other than the Units.

BYLAWS: The Bylaws for the Unit Owners Association made by Seller pursuant to the Condominium Statute. A copy of the Bylaws is contained in Part II of the Plan and has been furnished to the Purchaser as a part thereof. A copy of the Bylaws is on file with the Escrow Agent and will be filed for record with the Declaration if and when the Plan is declared effective.

ESCROW AGENT: The Land Title Guarantee and Trust Company, 1275 Ontario Street, Cleveland, Ohio 44113.

ESCROW AGREEMENT: The Escrow Agreement between Seller and the Escrow Agent dated April 30, 1976, a copy of which is included in Part II of the Plan and which has been furnished to the Purchaser as a part thereof.

EXHIBIT A-1

Situated in the Village of Bratenahl, County of Cuyahoga and State of Ohio, and known as being a part of Original One Hundred Acre Lots Nos. 355 and 356, and bounded and described as follows:

Beginning at the intersection of the center line of Lake Shore Boulevard, 80 feet in width, with the center line of Eddy Road, 60 feet in width; Course No. 1: Thence North 35° 56' 20" West along the center line of Eddy Road, a distance of 803.20 feet to a point; Course No. 2: Thence South 54° 03' 40" West, 197 feet to its intersection with a line drawn parallel to the center line of Eddy Road and distant 197 feet Southwesterly by rectangular measurement therefrom; Course No. 3: Thence South 35° 56' 20" East along said parallel line, 196.08 feet; Course No. 4: Thence South 54° 03' 40" West, 241 feet; Course No. 5: Thence North 35° 56' 20" West 37.44 feet; Course No. 6: Thence South 54° 03' 40" West, 92 feet; Course No. 7: Thence North 35° 56' 20" West, 88.56 feet; Course No. 8: Thence South 54° 03' 40" West, 100 feet; Course No. 9: Thence North 52° 38' 05" West, 348.08 feet to a point distant South 54° 03' 40" West 730 feet from a point in the center line of Eddy Road which bears North 35° 56' 20" West 1066.53 feet from its intersection with the center line of aforementioned Lake Shore Boulevard; Course No. 10: Thence North 26° 14' 00" West, 38.55 feet; Course No. 11: Thence North 27° 03' 00" West to its intersection with the Southerly low-watermark of Lake Erie; Course No. 12: Thence in a Southwesterly direction along the Southerly low-water mark of Lake Erie to its intersection with a Westerly line of land conveyed to Bratenahl Development Corporation by deed dated October 1, 1963 and recorded in Volume 10963, Page 103 of Cuyahoga County Records; Course No. 13: Thence South 37° 28' 04" East to the most Northerly corner of land in Parcel No. 1 conveyed to William H. Dornback, Sr. by deed dated February 15, 1960 and recorded in Volume 9909, Page 703 of Cuyahoga County Records; Course No. 14: Thence Southeasterly along the Northeasterly lines of land so conveyed to William H. Dornback, Sr., being also along the center line of Dugway Brook, the following courses and distances: South 24° 35' 04" East, 117.68 feet South 43° 33' 54" East, 94.07 feet; South 52° 27' 04" East 107 feet to the Northeasterly corner of Parcel No. 1 of land so conveyed to William H. Dornback, Sr., being also the Westerly line of Original One Hundred Acre Lot No. 356, as aforementioned; Course No. 15: Thence South 0° 11' 55" West along the Westerly line of said Original One Hundred Acre Lot No. 356, a distance of 456.22 feet to its intersection with the Northwesterly line of land conveyed to Alfred A. Budnick and Josephine B. Budnick by deed dated August 23, 1966 and recorded in Volume 11874, Page 591 of Cuyahoga County Records; Course No. 16: Thence North 54° 17' 10" East along the Northwesterly line of land so conveyed to Alfred A. Budnick and Josephine B. Budnick, and along the Southeasterly line of land conveyed to Bratenahl Development Corporation by deed dated August 11, 1966 and recorded in Volume 11874, Page 589 of Cuyahoga County Records, 625.46 feet to a Southwesterly line therein; Course No. 17: Thence South 35° 56' 20" East long said Southwesterly line of land so conveyed to Bratenahl Development Corporation, 601.94 feet to the center line of Lake Shore Boulevard, as aforementioned; Course No. 18: Thence North 44° 31' 40" East along the center line of Lake Shore Boulevard, 390.90 feet to the place of beginning, according to the survey by George M. Garrett and Associates, Registered Engineers and Surveyors, be the same more or less, but subject to all legal highways and waterways. Excepting from the above described premises any part thereof resulting through change in the shore line of Lake Erie and through change in the course of Dugway Brook occasioned by other than natural causes or by natural causes other than accretion.

DOCUMENT NO. V

FORM OF DEED

WARRANTY DEED

KNOW ALL MEN BY THESE PRESENTS, that BA ASSOCIATES LIMITED, an Ohio limited partnership, the Grantor, claiming title under deed recorded in Volume ____, page ____ of the Deed Records of Cuyahoga County, for the consideration of Ten Dollars ($10.00) and other good and valuable considerations received to its full satisfaction of   , the Grantee, whose tax mailing address will be Suite No.   , One Bratenahl Place, Bratenahl, Ohio 44108 does hereby GIVE, GRANT, BARGAIN, SELL AND CONVEY unto the Grantee, and the Grantee's heirs and assigns, forever, the following described premises:

Situated in the Village of Bratenahl, County of Cuyahoga and State of Ohio, and known as being all of Unit No.   of the One Bratenahl Place Condominium located on the   floor, One Bratenahl Place, together with an undivided   % interest, in and to the Common Areas of One Bratenahl Place Condominium, as described in the Declaration of Condominium Ownership and Bylaws for the One Bratenahl Place Condominium recorded in Volume   , page   of the Deed Records of Cuyahoga County and as shown in the Drawings recorded in Volume   of Condominium Maps, page   to   of Cuyahoga County Records, be the same more or less, but subject to all legal highways.

Together with and subject to all the rights, duties, easements, options, conditions and restrictions contained in the Declaration, Bylaws and Drawings referred to above and incorporated herein as if set forth herein in full.

TO HAVE AND TO HOLD the above granted and bargained premises with the appurtenances thereunto belonging unto the Grantee, and Grantee's heirs and assigns, forever.

And Grantor does for itself, its successors and assigns, covenant with the Grantee and the Grantee's heirs and assigns, that at and until the delivery of these presents Grantor is well seized of a good and indefeasible estate in fee simple and has good right to bargain and sell the same in manner and form as above written, and that the same are free from all liens and encumbrances whatsoever except as set forth above, and further excepting covenants, rights, restrictions, reservations, easements, and conditions of record, zoning ordinances, if any, and taxes and assessments, general or special, not delinquent; and that Grantor will warrant and defend the premises with the appurtenances thereunto beloinging to the Grantee and Grantee's heirs and assigns, against all lawful claims and demands whatsoever, except as above set forth.

As part of the consideration for this deed and in consideration of the inclusion of like covenants in all conveyances of other Units in the One Bratenahl Place Condominium, the Grantee, by acceptance of this deed, agrees for Grantee and Grantee's heirs and assigns to and with the Grantor and its successors and assigns, for the benefit of the Grantor and of every person, firm or corporation who shall or may become the owner of or have any title derived immediately or remotely through or under the Grantor, its successors and assigns, to any Unit of said One Bratenahl Place Condominium, to be bound by all the terms and conditions of the Declaration and Bylaws and to include a covenant similar hereto in each and every subsequent conveyance or encumbrance of the above described premises.

The benefits and obligations hereunder shall inure to the benefit of and be binding upon the respective successors, heirs, executors, administrators and assigns of the respective parties.

IN WITNESS WHEREOF, BA ASSOCIATES LIMITED has caused these presents to be signed in its behalf by a duly authorized general partner this _____ day of _____, 1976.

Signed and acknowledged
in the presence of: BA ASSOCIATES LIMITED

_____   By _____
                                                                              General Partner

_____

Witnesses as to BA Associates Limited

STATE OF OHIO   )
) SS:
COUNTY OF CUYAHOGA)

BEFORE ME, a Notary Public in and for said County and State, personally appeared the above-named **BA ASSOCIATES LIMITED** by   , its General Partner, who acknowledged that he did sign the foregoing instrument on behalf of said partnership and that the same is the free act and deed of said partnership and his free act and deed personally and as a general partner thereof.

IN WITNESS WHEREOF, I have hereunto set my hand and official seal at Cleveland, Ohio this _____ day of _____, 1976.

                                                              _____
This instrument was   Notary Public
prepared by

– 2 –

DOCUMENT NO. VI

FORM OF MANAGEMENT AGREEMENT

MANAGEMENT AGREEMENT

by and between

ONE BRATENAHL PLACE CONDOMINIUM ASSOCIATION

and

BA ASSOCIATES LIMITED

Dated: _____ , 197_

TABLE OF CONTENTS

MANAGEMENT AGREEMENT

THIS AGREEMENT made as of the _____ day of _____ 197_, by and between ONE BRATENAHL PLACE CONDOMINIUM ASSOCIATION, an unincorporated association having an office at One Bratenahl Place, Bratenahl, Ohio 44108 (the "Association") and BA ASSOCIATES LIMITED, an Ohio limited partnership having an office at One Bratenahl Place, Bratenahl, Ohio 44108 ("Manager").

W I T N E S S E T H:

WHEREAS, the Association is an association comprised of the owners of apartment units, together with specific percentage interests in common areas and facilities appurtenant to such units, in a building known as One Bratenahl Place and located on a parcel of real property located in Bratenahl, Ohio, and more particularly described in Exhibit A-1 attached hereto, which property, together with the building, all improvements and appurtenances and all personal property owned by the Association is hereinafter referred to as the "Condominium"; and

WHEREAS, the Condominium has been submitted to the provisions of Chapter 5311 of the Ohio Revised Code, by virtue of the Declaration of Condominium Ownership for One Bratenahl Place Condominium (the "Declaration"), filed for record with the Recorder of Cuyahoga County, Ohio on _____, 197_, and recorded at Volume _____ Page _____ of the Deed Records of Cuyahoga County; and

WHEREAS, the Association will employ Manager as its exclusive managing agent for the Condominium on the terms and conditions hereinafter set forth, and Manager will accept such employment on such terms and conditions;

NOW, THEREFORE, in consideration of the mutual covenants and agreements herein contained, One ($1.00) Dollar by each paid to the other, receipt of which is hereby acknowledged, and other good and valuable consideration, it is agreed by the parties hereto as follows:

1.   **Term.**

The term of this Agreement (the "Term") shall commence as of the date of the filing of the Declaration for record and shall continue for a term of three (3) years thereafter, unless sooner terminated as provided herein.

2.   **Management.**

(a)   The Association hereby employs Manager, and Manager hereby accepts such employment as managing agent of the Condominium, and all portions thereof, for the Term and in accordance with the provisions hereof.

(b)   Manager, as managing agent, shall have full, complete and absolute authority for the managing of the Condominium, and, in furtherance thereof, shall perform the following services:

(i)   Cause the common areas and facilities of the Condominium to be maintained in such condition as Manager shall determine, including interior and exterior cleaning thereof, and planting and other gardening therein, and cause such repairs and alterations thereof to be made as Manager shall determine to be necessary or desirable and proper, including, but not limited to, plumbing, steam fitting, carpentry, elevator repair, decorating and other similar alterations or changes;

(ii) Cause all such acts and things to be done in and about the Condominium as shall be necessary to comply with any and all orders or violations affecting the Condominium placed thereon by any federal, state or municipal authority having jurisdiction thereover; subject, however, to the limitations with respect to the amount of expenditures involved with the making of repairs and alterations contained in subparagraph 5(c) hereof, except that Manager may cause such order or violation to be complied with irrespective of the cost thereof in the event that a failure immediately to comply with any such order or violation would or might expose the Association or Manager to criminal liability;

(iii) Enter into contracts for electricity, gas, steam, elevator, telephone, window cleaning, maid service, rubbish removal, fuel oil, coal, detective agency protection, vermin extermination and other services or such of them as shall be deemed advisable by Manager and at prices to be determined by Manager; purchase all supplies which shall be necessary properly to maintain and operate the Condominium; and make all such contracts and purchases in either the Association's or Manager's name;

(iv) Operate, or at Manager's option, enter into contracts for the operation of the parking garage in the Condominium and supervise the management thereof, such contracts to be in the name of either Manager or the Association but for the account of and on behalf of the Association;

(v) Enter into leases for the renting of the commercial space;

(vi) Check all bills received for services, work and supplies ordered in connection with maintaining and operating the Condominium and pay, subject to the provisions of subparagraph 5(c) hereof, all such bills and water charges, sewer rent, assessments, real estate taxes, and corporate taxes, if any, relevant to the Condominium as and when the same shall become due and payable;

(vii) Supervise the moving in and the moving out of unit owners and, as far as possible, arrange for dates and timing thereof so that there shall be a minimum of disturbance to the operation of the Condominium and inconvenience to the other unit owners;

(viii) Bill unit owners for common area charges; collect such charges; sue for charges which may at any time be or become due to the Association from any unit owner in respect to the Condominium; institute proceedings to recover possession of units; and employ counsel, at the Association's expense, if necessary, for any such purpose;

(ix) Consider and, where reasonable, attend to the complaints of unit owners with respect to the common areas and facilities of the Condominium;

(x) Cause to be prepared and filed the necessary forms for unemployment insurance, social security, taxes and withholding taxes and all other forms required by any federal, state or municipal authority or unions in respect of all persons employed pursuant to subparagraph 3(b) hereof;

(xi) Prepare and submit annually to the Board of Managers of the Association an operating budget setting forth the anticipated income and expenses of the Association for the ensuing year with respect to the Condominium;

(xii)   Use its best efforts to cause to be effected and maintained fire, rent, plate glass, boiler, water damage, liability, workmen's compensation, disability and such other insurance with respect to the Condominium as may be required by the Declaration or other applicable instrument or as Manager shall deem necessary or advisable. It is specifically understood and agreed that Manager, or any person or entity designated by Manager, shall have the right to obtain all insurance covering the Condominium and to receive customary fees in consideration therefor; and

(xiii)   Attend all meetings of the Association and the Board of Managers and, in general, perform any and all other functions usually and customarily performed by a managing agent of condominium apartment complexes and commercial facilities ancillary thereto.

3.   **Other Rights and Obligations.**

(a)   Manager may in its sole discretion at the cost and expense of the Association maintain offices in the Condominium for use by Manager, in the location of the office space shown on the Drawings of the Condominium, and may use such offices for the performance of its management responsibilities.

(b)   Manager shall cause to be hired, paid and supervised, all persons who, in Manager's judgment, are necessary to be employed to maintain and operate the Condominium who, in each instance, shall be the Association's and not Manager's employees; Manager shall cause to be discharged all persons who, in Manager's judgment, are unnecessary or undesirable in connection with such maintenance or operation. Manager undertakes to use due care in the selection of each person employed to maintain and operate the Condominium or any portion thereof, but Manager shall not have any responsibility whatsoever for any act or omission of any such person. The duties to hire, pay, supervise and discharge may be delegated by Manager, in whole or in part, to one or more persons in the general employ of Manager. Manager undertakes to use due care in the selection of each person in the general employ of Manager to whom such duties or any of them are delegated.

(c)   Manager shall have the right, on behalf of and at the expense of the Association, to consult with Manager's own counsel or with the Association's counsel with respect to all legal documents relating to the Condominium or the managing of any portion of the Condominium, and to submit to the appropriate governmental agency all information as may be required pursuant to the laws and regulations of any governmental department, subdivision or agency having jurisdiction over the Condominium.

(d)   The Association shall use its best efforts to include in each insurance policy obtained pursuant to subparagraph (xii) of subparagraph 2(b) above a waiver of the insured's rights of subrogation against Manager or the inclusion of Manager as an additional insured, but not a party to whom any loss shall be payable. If such waiver or agreement shall not be, or shall cease to be, obtainable without additional charge, the Association shall pay such additional charge. Notwithstanding the foregoing, Manager shall be listed as an additional insured in each policy of general liability insurance in connection with the Condominium.

4.   **Records.**

(a)   Manager shall maintain in a satisfactory manner the books of account, check book and other records for the Condominium, including but not limited to records of monies received from unit owners or from any other source and records of all disbursements made by Manager with respect to the Condominium.

(b)   Manager shall cooperate with the certified public accountant of the Association in connection with the preparation and filing of federal, state and other tax returns required by any governmental authority.

(c)   Manager and the Association shall each cooperate with the certified public accountant of the other in connection with the preparation of an annual audit each year of Manager's and the Association's books of account for the Condominium.

5.   **Banking and Payment of Expenses.**

(a)   Manager shall cause all monies received from unit owners or from any other source to be deposited in a locked box in a branch ("Branch") of Union Commerce Bank ("UCB") to be selected by Manager. Manager shall notify the Association of the name and address of the Branch at which such receipts are to be deposited. The Association agrees to open an account (the "Association's Account") at the Branch, and to instruct UCB that the deposits referred to in this subparagraph 5(a) shall be deposited in the Association's Account.

(b)   The Association shall, on or before the last business day of each calendar month, deposit in the account of the Manager ("Manager's Account") at the UCB, provided Manager shall have given the Association notice of the account name and number and the name and address of branch ("Manager's Branch") of UCB at which Manager's Account is kept, a sum of money equal to (i) anticipated expenses for the Condominium for the ensuing month as shown on the Budget including Manager's compensation, plus (ii) any sums of money for specific expenditures to be made in the ensuing month which the Board of Managers of the Condominium shall have previously approved.

(c)   Manager shall pay all employees, contractors and other persons supplying services, work and supplies ordered in connection with the maintenance and operation of the Condominium, including Manager's compensation hereinafter specified, as and when the same shall become due. Notwithstanding anything to the contrary contained herein, ordinary repairs or alterations involving an expenditure in excess of One Thousand Dollars ($1,000.00) for any one item shall be made only with the prior approval of the Board of Managers of the Association, except that emergency repairs immediately necessary for the preservation or safety of the Condominium or for the safety of unit owners or other persons or required to avoid the suspension of any necessary service at the Condominium may be made by Manager irrespective of the cost thereof without any prior approval of the Board of Managers of the Association. Any expenditure shown on the Budget, regardless of magnitude, shall be deemed to have been approved by the Board of Managers of the Association unless they shall have notified Manager within thirty (30) days of receipt of the Budget in question that the item or the entire Budget was not approved.

(d)   Any payments made by Manager under this Agreement may, at Manager's option, be made out of such funds as Manager may from time to time hold for the account of the Association, or as may be provided by the Association pursuant to subparagraph (b) hereof. Manager shall not be obligated to make any advance to or for the account of the Association with respect to the performance by Manager of any of its duties hereunder, or to pay any amount except out of funds held or provided as aforesaid, nor shall Manager be obligated to incur any liability or obligation unless the Association shall furnish Manager with the necessary funds for the discharge thereof. If Manager shall advance voluntarily for the Association's account any amount for the payment of any necessary obligation or necessary expense connected with the Condominium, the Association shall reimburse Manager on demand if the Association shall have authorized such advance by this Agreement.

(e)   Manager shall be entitled to write checks for any amount properly payable pursuant to the terms of this Agreement. It is understood and agreed that any one (1) of Willard

– 4 –

C. Barry, Jean Kehic and Myron E. Glass and any one (1) of Martin Fink, E. Moore Rodgers shall sign all checks written on Manager's Account but that a facsimile signature may be used on such checks to make any regular and proper payments from the Manager's Account. Notwithstanding the foregoing, the signatures of any one (1) shall be necessary for the transfer of funds from the Association's Account to Manager's Account.

6. Compensation.

(a) The Association shall pay Manager as compensation for services during the Term at the rate of One Thousand Dollars ($1,000.00) per month payable, in advance, on the first day of each calendar month.

(b) The Association shall pay to Manager any disbursements reasonably incurred by Manager, its employees, contractors or agents, in furtherance of the performance of Manager's obligations under this Agreement, including but not limited to legal fees, advertising costs, telephone charges and other expenses reasonably incurred by Manager in connection with Manager's duties under this Agreement.

7. Interruption of Services.

Manager shall have the right to interrupt, curtail or suspend the services required to be furnished by Manager pursuant to this Agreement when the necessity therefor arises by reason of accident, emergency, or mechical breakdown, or when required by any law of any federal, state, county or municipal authority, or for any other cause beyond the reasonable control of Manager.

8. Surety Bond.

Manager shall at all times maintain with a surety company authorized to do business in the State of Ohio a bond in the amount of   1,000,000.   Dollars ($) covering Manager against defalcation by its partners and employees and by the employees of the Association who have been hired by Manager for work in connection with the Condominium. Such bond shall be paid for by the Association at the Association's sole cost and expense.

9. Hold Harmless.

The Association agrees (i) to hold and save Manager, its officers and employees free and harmless from damages, penalties, fines, costs and expenses, including attorneys' fees, statutory or otherwise, for injuries to person and property by reason of any cause whatsoever either in or about the Condominium or elsewhere resulting from Manager carrying out the provisions of this Agreement, or acting under the directions of the Association; (ii) to reimburse Manager on demand for any monies which the latter is required to pay out for any reason whatsoever, either in connection with, or as an expense of defense of, any claim, civil or criminal action, proceeding, charge or prosecution made, instituted or maintained against Manager or against the Association and Manager, jointly or severally, resulting from Manager's carrying out the provisions of this Agreement or affecting or due to the conditions or use of the Condominium or the acts or omissions of Manager; and (iii) to defend promptly and diligently, at the Association's sole expense, any claims, action or proceeding brought against Manager or against Manager and the Association, jointly or severally, arising out of or in connection with any of the foregoing, and to hold harmless and fully indemnify Manager from any judgment, loss or settlement on account thereof, except for any claim, action or proceeding resulting from the gross negligence or willful misconduct of Manager or its employees or agents. It is expressly understood and agreed that the foregoing provisions of this paragraph shall survive the termination of this Agreement.

– 5 –

10. **Representations.**

(a)   Manager shall be entitled to rely on oral or written instructions received from the President or Vice President of the Association as to any and all acts performed under this Agreement by Manager or any members of its organization, and the same shall be deemed to be instructions from the Association.

(b)   Manager is clothed with such general authority and powers as may be necessary or advisable to carry out the spirit and intent of this Agreement. The Association authorizes Manager to perform any act or do anything necessary or desirable to carry out Manager's obligations hereunder, and everything done by Manager under the provisions hereof shall be done as agent of the Association.

(c)   The Association hereby irrevocably makes, constitutes and appoints Manager and each general partner thereof as its agent and attorney-in-fact with full power of substitution for the purpose of executing, acknowledging, and delivering such agreements and documents as Manager shall deem necessary to carry out the purposes and intent of this Agreement.

(d)   Whenever the Association's consent or approval is required under this Agreement, the Association shall not unreasonably withhold or delay its consent or approval.

11. **Termination.**

(a)   This Agreement may be terminated (i) at any time by the written agreement of Manager and the Association, (ii) at any time by the Association, for cause, and (iii) following the sale by BA Associates Limited of 75% of the units in the Condominium, upon thirty (30) days' written notice to Manager from the Board of Managers of the Association.

(b)   Upon termination of this Agreement, Manager shall retain from all monies collected by Manager pursuant to this Agreement such sums as are owed to Manager as compensation or reimbursement or otherwise, and, in the event the amount of such collected monies is insufficient to fully compensate Manager in accordance with the terms of this Agreement, the Association shall on demand pay such excess amount to Manager. Upon termination, Manager shall deliver to the Association all books and records and other instruments relating to the Condominium and the Association shall furnish Manager with reasonable security against any outstanding obligations or liabilities which Manager may have incurred hereunder. Manager shall be entitled to keep for its own records copies of all documents delivered to the Association pursuant to this paragraph.

12. **Other Businesses.**

The Association and Manager may each independently engage in such other business activities as they may, in their sole discretion, deem desirable, including activities relating to the development, ownership, sale, rental or management of other apartment complexes in the Cleveland, Ohio, metropolitan area or elsewhere, and activities relating to the real estate business in general in the Cleveland, Ohio, metropolitan area or elsewhere.

13. **No Assignment.**

Manager may not assign this Agreement without the prior written consent of the Association, provided that such consent shall not be unreasonably withheld.

14. **Notices.**

Any notice, demand or request which, under the terms of this Agreement, must or may be given or made by the parties hereto, must be in writing, and must be given or made by personal delivery or by registered or certified mail, postage prepaid, return receipt requested, to the Association at its address as given on page 1 hereof, and to Manager at its address as given on page 1 hereof. Any notice, demand or request made in accordance with this Paragraph 14 shall be deemed given on the date so delivered or mailed.

15. **Captions.**

The captions in this Agreement are inserted for convenience and reference only and shall in no way affect, define, limit or describe the scope, intent or construction of any provision hereof.

16. **Governing Law.**

This Agreement shall be governed by and construed in accordance with the laws of the State of Ohio.

17. **Entire Agreement.**

This Agreement contains the entire agreement between the parties hereto and any executory agreement hereafter made shall be ineffective to change, modify, waive, release, discharge, terminate or effect an abandonment of this Agreement, in whole or in part, unless such executory agreement is in writing and signed by the party against whom enforcement of the change, modification, waiver, release, discharge, termination or the effecting of abandonment is sought.

18. **Severability.**

Any provision of this Agreement that is non-enforceable under the laws of the State of Ohio shall be construed to be severable from the other provisions of this Agreement without affecting the enforceability of the remaining provisions.

19. **Successors.**

This Agreement and every provision hereof shall bind, apply to and run in favor of the Association and Manager and, subject to the provisions of Paragraph 13 hereof, their respective successors and assigns.

20.   **Further Assurances.**

The parties hereto shall and will at all times and from time to time hereafter and upon every reasonable request to do so, make, do, execute, deliver, cause to be made, done, executed and delivered all such further acts, deeds, assurances and things that may be required to more effectively implement and carry out the true intent and meaning of this Agreement.

IN WITNESS WHEREOF, the parties hereto have executed this Agreement the day and year first above written.

"THE ASSOCIATION"

Signed and acknowledged
in the prsence of:

ONE BRATENAHL PLACE CONDOMINIUM
    ASSOCIATION

_____   By _____

_____
Witnesses as to ONE BRATENAHL
    PLACE CONDOMINIUM ASSOCIATION

"MANAGER"

BA ASSOCIATES LIMITED

_____   By _____
                                        Carter Bledsoe, General Partner

_____
Witnesses as to BA ASSOCIATES
    LIMITED

EXHIBIT A-1

Situated in the Village of Bratenahl, County of Cuyahoga and State of Ohio, and known as being a part of Original One Hundred Acre Lots Nos. 355 and 356, and bounded and described as follows:

Beginning at the intersection of the center line of Lake Shore Boulevard, 80 feet in width, with the center line of Eddy Road, 60 feet in width; Course No. 1: Thence North 35° 56' 20" West along the center line of Eddy Road, a distance of 803.20 feet to a point; Course No. 2: Thence South 54° 03' 40" West, 197 feet to its intersection with a line drawn parallel to the center line of Eddy Road and distant 197 feet Southwesterly by rectangular measurement therefrom; Course No. 3: Thence South 35° 56' 20" East along said parallel line, 196.08 feet; Course No. 4: Thence South 54° 03' 40" West, 241 feet; Course No. 5: Thence North 35° 56' 20" West 37.44 feet; Course No. 6: Thence South 54° 03' 40" West, 92 feet; Course No. 7: Thence North 35° 56' 20" West, 88.56 feet; Course No. 8: Thence South 54° 03' 40" West, 100 feet; Course No. 9: Thence North 52° 38' 05" West, 348.08 feet to a point distant South 54° 03' 40" West 730 feet from a point in the center line of Eddy Road which bears North 35° 56' 20" West 1066.53 feet from its intersection with the center line of aforementioned Lake Shore Boulevard; Course No. 10: Thence North 26° 14' 00" West, 38.55 feet; Course No. 11: Thence North 27° 03' 00" West to its intersection with the Southerly low-watermark of Lake Erie; Course No. 12: Thence in a Southwesterly direction along the Southerly low-water mark of Lake Erie to its intersection with a Westerly line of land conveyed to Bratenahl Development Corporation by deed dated October 1, 1963 and recorded in Volume 10963, Page 103 of Cuyahoga County Records; Course No. 13: Thence South 37° 28' 04" East to the most Northerly corner of land in Parcel No. 1 conveyed to William H. Dornback, Sr. by deed dated February 15, 1960 and recorded in Volume 9909, Page 703 of Cuyahoga County Records; Course No. 14: Thence Southeasterly along the Northeasterly lines of land so conveyed to William H. Dornback, Sr., being also along the center line of Dugway Brook, the following courses and distances: South 24° 35' 04" East, 117.68 feet South 43° 33' 54" East, 94.07 feet; South 52° 27' 04" East 107 feet to the Northeasterly corner of Parcel No. 1 of land so conveyed to William H. Dornback, Sr., being also the Westerly line of Original One Hundred Acre Lot No. 356, as aforementioned; Course No. 15: Thence South 0° 11' 55" West along the Westerly line of said Original One Hundred Acre Lot No. 356, a distance of 456.22 feet to its intersection with the Northwesterly line of land conveyed to Alfred A. Budnick and Josephine B. Budnick by deed dated August 23, 1966 and recorded in Volume 11874, Page 591 of Cuyahoga County Records; Course No. 16: Thence North 54° 17' 10" East along the Northwesterly line of land so conveyed to Alfred A. Budnick and Josephine B. Budnick, and along the Southeasterly line of land conveyed to Bratenahl Development Corporation by deed dated August 11, 1966 and recorded in Volume 11874, Page 589 of Cuyahoga County Records, 625.46 feet to a Southwesterly line therein; Course No. 17: Thence South 35° 56' 20" East long said Southwesterly line of land so conveyed to Bratenahl Development Corporation, 601.94 feet to the center line of Lake Shore Boulevard, as aforementioned; Course No. 18: Thence North 44° 31' 40" East along the center line of Lake Shore Boulevard, 390.90 feet to the place of beginning, according to the survey by George M. Garrett and Associates, Registered Engineers and Surveyors, be the same more or less, but subject to all legal highways and waterways. Excepting from the above described premises any part thereof resulting through change in the shore line of Lake Erie and through change in the course of Dugway Brook occasioned by other than natural causes or by natural causes other than accretion.

APPENDIX V

STATE PROTECTION

Although few states have well-defined protection for purchasers of cooperatives and condominiums, the state agencies listed herein have a responsibility to try to answer your questions.

ALABAMA
Securities Commission
64 North Union Street
Montgomery, AL 36104
(205) 832-5733

ALASKA
Attorney General
Pouch K—State Capitol
Juneau, AK 99801
(907) 465-3600

ARIZONA
Arizona State Department of
Real Estate
1645 West Jefferson
Phoenix, AZ 85007
(602) 271-4345

ARKANSAS
Department of State
Little Rock, AR 72201
(501) 371-3000

CALIFORNIA
Department of Real Estate
714 P Street
Sacramento, CA 95814
(916) 445-6776

COLORADO
Real Estate Commission
110 State Services Building
Denver, CO 80203
(303) 839-2633

CONNECTICUT
Real Estate Commission
90 Washington Street
Hartford, CT 06115
(203) 566-5130

DELAWARE
Real Estate Commission
State House Annex
Dover, DE 19901
(302) 678-4186

FLORIDA
Secretary of State
Tallahassee, FL 32301
(904) 488-8472

GEORGIA
Real Estate Commission
166 Pryor Street, SW
Atlanta, GA 30303
(404) 656-3916

HAWAII
Department of Regulatory
Agencies
P.O. Box 3469
Honolulu, HI 96801
(808) 548-4100

IDAHO
Real Estate Commission
633 North Fourth Street
State Capitol Building
Boise, ID 83720
(208) 384-3285

ILLINOIS
Dept. of Registration and
Education
Commissioner of Real Estate
55 Jackson Street
Chicago, IL 60601
(312) 341-9810

INDIANA
Real Estate Commission
State Office Building
Indianapolis, IN 46204
(317) 633-5386 232-2980

IOWA
Real Estate Commission
Capitol Building
Des Moines, IA 50319
(515) 281-3183

KANSAS
Securities Commissioner
State Office Building
Topeka, KS 66612
(913) 296-3307

KENTUCKY
Real Estate Commission
Republic Building
Suite 610
Louisville, KY 40202
(502) 588-4462

LOUISIANA
Louisiana Department of Real
Estate
P.O. Box 44517
Baton Rouge, LA 70804
(504) 389-7755

MAINE
Department of Business
Regulations
State Office Annex
Augusta, ME 04330
(207) 289-3735

MARYLAND
Real Estate Commission
One Calvert Street—8th Floor
Baltimore, MD 21201
(301) 383-2130

MASSACHUSETTS
Dept. of Registration Real
Estate Broker
Leverett Saltonstall Building
100 Cambridge Street
Boston, MA 02202
(617) 727-3055

MICHIGAN
Corporation and Securities
Bureau
Condominium Section
6546 Mercantile Way
Lansing, MI 48926
(517) 373-8026

MINNESOTA
Real Estate Licensing Section
260 State Office Building
St. Paul, MN 55102
(612) 296-9458

MISSISSIPPI
Securities Division of Secretary
of State
New Capitol, Room 120
Jackson, MS 39216
(601) 354-6548

MISSOURI
Office of Secretary of State
Jefferson City, MO 65101
(314) 751-2331

MONTANA
Real Estate Commission
State Capitol Building
Helena, MT 59601
(406) 449-2961

NEBRASKA
Real Estate Commission
State Capitol Building
Lincoln, NE 68509
(402) 471-2004

NEVADA
Real Estate Division
Department of Commerce
201 S. Fall Street
Carson City, NV 89701
(702) 885-4280

NEW HAMPSHIRE
Real Estate Board
State House Annex
Concord, NH 03301
(603) 271-1110

NEW JERSEY
Department of Community
Affairs
363 W. State Street
Trenton, NJ 08625
(609) 292-6420

NEW MEXICO
Office of Attorney General
P.O. Box 2246
Santa Fe, NM 87501
(505) 988-8851

NEW YORK
Office of Attorney General
Two World Trade Center
New York, NY 10047
(212) 488-4141

NORTH CAROLINA
Real Estate Licensing Board
115 Hillsborough Street
P.O. Box 266
Raleigh, NC 27602
(919) 833-2771

NORTH DAKOTA
Real Estate Commission
410 Thayer Avenue
Bismarck, ND 58501
(701) 224-2749

OHIO
Division of Securities
Department of Commerce
180 East Broad Street
Columbus, OH 43215
(614) 466-3440

OKLAHOMA
Real Estate Commission
4040 Lincoln Boulevard
Oklahoma City, OK 73105
(405) 521-3387

OREGON
Department of Commerce
Real Estate Division
Commerce Building
Salem, OR 97310
(503) 378-4170

PENNSYLVANIA
Real Estate Commission
P.O. Box 2649
Harrisburg, PA 17101
(717) 787-2852

RHODE ISLAND
Department of Business
Regulation
100 North Main Street
Providence, RI 02903
(401) 277-2255

SOUTH CAROLINA
Real Estate Commission
2221 Divine Street
Columbia, SC 29205
(803) 758-3981

SOUTH DAKOTA
Real Estate Commission
P.O. Box 638
Pierre, SD 57501
(605) 224-3600

TENNESSEE
Dept. of Insurance and Division
of Securities
114 State Office Building
Nashville, TN 37219
(615) 741-2947

TEXAS
State Securities Board
Lyndon Johnson Building
Austin, TX 78711
(512) 475-4561

UTAH
Real Estate Division
330 E. Fourth South
Salt Lake City, UT 84111
(801) 533-5661

VERMONT
Real Estate Commission
Seven East State Street
Montpelier, VT 05602
(802) 828-3228

VIRGINIA
Real Estate Commission
Ninth Street Office Building
Richmond, VA 23202
(804) 786-7285

WASHINGTON
Licensing Department
Real Estate Division
P.O. Box 247
Olympia, WA 98501
(206) 753-6909

WEST VIRGINIA
Securities Commission
State Auditor's Office
Charleston, WV 25305
(304) 348-2257

WISCONSIN
Department of Regulation and
Licensing
819 N. Sixth Street
Milwaukee, WI 53203
(414) 244-4655

WYOMING
Real Estate Board
313 Capitol Building
Cheyenne, WY 82001
(307) 777-7660

INDEX